The People of
St Edmund's College

by
David J S Kay
Vice-President of The Edmundian Association

Foreword
Dr Mark Loughlin
Headmaster of St Edmund's College

Early Personalities Associated with St Edmund's College
Duncan A Gallie
College Archivist & Housemaster of Challoner

First published 2003
by The Edmundian Association

A catalogue record for this book is available from the British Library and elsewhere.

ISBN 0-9546125-0-7

Designed and Printed in Great Britain by
Aldridge Print Group

**With gratitude to Fr Pinot,
the last priest-schoolmaster
in the Douay tradition**

*The picture overleaf shows Fr Joseph
Murray teaching French; the students are
(from left to right) Denis Calnan, Donald
Smith, Jack Belton, Alan McGavin, Peter
Fletcher, Thomas Stack & William Scholl*

Contents

Foreword

S T EDMUND'S COLLEGE is the oldest Catholic school in England, founded during the English Reformation, exiled during the French Revolution and today at the forefront of curriculum development and pastoral care.

The successful education the students of St Edmund's enjoy is a powerful reflection of the College's aim, unchanged for over 400 years – since its foundation in 1568 – to foster the spiritual, intellectual, physical and emotional development of each person in the community.

This book will acquaint its readers with the achievements of a variety of Edmundians who have been associated with the development of St Edmund's College since it was established at Old Hall Green in 1793.

It is being published to commemorate the 150th anniversary of The Edmundian Association which, since 1853, has been active in bringing together former students and staff on a social basis and for the betterment of the College. Many thousands of Edmundians have belonged to the Association over its 150 years and consequently it has been able to make substantial financial donations to the College.

Former staff and pupils can boast a most interesting and varied collection of achievements. Some distinguished themselves as religious leaders, in military or public service, in sporting achievements, in publishing, or in some other notable way. Some have been self-effacing about their achievements. This book includes those who were famous or infamous, some remarkable teachers and those who have given outstanding service to the College.

Dr Mark Loughlin
November 2003

Introduction & Acknowledgements

I HAVE COMPILED THIS BOOK to commemorate the sesquicentenary of the foundation of The Edmundian Association. Originally intended to be a collection of 150 short biographies – one for each year of the Association's life – it soon became apparent that it would be hard to justify who was to be included and who had to be left out. Instead it includes details about the lives of a wide range of interesting people by documenting some of their achievements. It is by no means a definitive list of every important Edmundian, and I have no doubt that many more will be brought to my attention in the future. To be included, generally a subject must have studied, lived or worked at St Edmund's, or have had some other strong connection with the place since 1793.

In 1995 I started to compile a definitive list of all Edmundians, as no completed one had existed before. Needless to say, this is an endless task. By the year 2000 it was possible to publish the list via the internet to members of the Association. My research for *The Edmundian Directory* led me to find out about Edmundians of whom I had not heard before, as well as gaining greater knowledge about some whose names were more familiar.

People arrived at and left St Edmund's for a multitude of reasons. They came from a variety of backgrounds and went on to greater diversity after leaving. It is actually in later life that many Edmundians come to appreciate some of the benefits the College brought to them. This can be demonstrated by the success of a number of recent year group reunions, which have been thoroughly enjoyable experiences for those who attended.

In preparation for compiling this book, I asked members of The Edmundian Association in 2002 to nominate their favourite Edmundian. To add a sense of balance and perspective, I also consulted some of those who are cognisant with the history of the College. Although I did not necessarily agree with every suggestion, each nominee has been included somewhere within this book. The ten most liked Edmundians are listed in the designated chapter called Notable Staff.

The topics covered in some of the chapters of this book would make entire books in themselves, as indeed would some of the individual subjects.

The College has spawned three Cardinals, four Archbishops, dozens of bishops and hundreds of other clergy. Former Edmundians include military heroes, international sportsmen, eminent judges, diplomats and successful entrepreneurs. There are different Edmundians who are famous for saving an endangered species, designing a fashion icon, painting one of the most widely recognised trademarks in the world, and for having a Number One hit record. There was a President of the College who fired a shotgun out of his study window, a former student who became a matador, and another who ate live scorpions to seek attention. There is even an official Edmundian ghost.

Every effort has been made to trace the owners of the copyrights of all items quoted and to request permission for their use. Should anyone owning such rights not have been contacted, I offer my apologies.

I am especially grateful to John Hayes, the current editor of *The Edmundian*, for permission to quote extensively from the magazine, and also to his predecessors Gavin Dorey and Canon Peter Phillips. The magazine is rich in information and I have read each of its 224 editions! The obituaries in *The Edmundian* are normally a useful source of reference material. However, the editorial standards have varied over the years with some obituaries being full of valuable details, whilst others are scant or full of unnecessary waffle. Take for example that of Daniel Gilbert (1843-53), who helped set up the famous Providence Row shelter for the homeless in London. Of the 820 words in his obituary in 1895, 60% describe in great detail the two days leading up to his death by bronchitis, and there is only a passing reference to his charitable work.

I am grateful to Bill Gribbin, John Hayes and Alex Roberts, whose photographs I have used extensively to illustrate this book, together with anyone else whose photographs I have reproduced. I also take this opportunity to thank Dr David Black for his work in reorganising the Association's photographic archive.

I would like to thank the following people for their personal contributions (with the subject in brackets if different): Fr Scott Archer (Fr Thomas Byles), J H Bodenham of J Floris Ltd (James & Robert Floris), Rebekah Bristow (Edward Sproll), Francis Clayton, Fr Jeremy Davies (list of parish priests of Old Hall Green), Fr Ian Dickie (Canon Clement Parsons), Canon Reginald Fuller, Miguel Hamber (photograph of Canon Reginald Fuller), Jeremy Janion, Clare Johnstone Gilsig (Michael Johnstone), A C Jones (Colonel Francis Macerone), Stephen Quin (Fr Michael Garvey) & Bill Wright (Fr Denys Lucas).

The following have given their permission to draw from their publications: Allen C Drake of the El Paso, Illinois, Community History Web Page (Fulton Sheen), Etienne Dupuch of Etienne Dupuch Jr Publications, John Tracy Ellis author of the 1977 *Word Book Encyclopædia* (Fulton Sheen), Seán Hackett of the Offaly Historical & Archaelogical Society (James & Bernard Molloy), & Geoffrey MacLean (Michel Cazabon).

Information has also been gleaned from the following publications: *The Australian* (Sir Leo Curtis), Catholic Post newspaper of the Diocese of Peoria, Illinois (Fulton Sheen), National Heritage Library, Trinidad (Michel Cazabon), Providence Row Charity (Mgr Daniel Gilbert), Times Newspapers (Sir Neville Stack), *The Story of 'Nipper' and the 'His Master's Voice' picture* by Leonard Petts (Francis Barraud), *The Barraud Family* by Fr Bernard Lagrue (Francis Barraud), *Adrian Fortescue: Priest & Scholar* by Michael Davies (Dr Adrian Fortescue), *The History of St Edmund's College* by Bernard Ward, *St Edmund's College Chapel* by Bernard Ward, and every edition of *The Edmundian*.

I am extremely grateful to Duncan Gallie, the College Archivist and Custodian of the Douay Museum, for his knowledgeable input, for proof-reading, and for writing the historical foreword to this book entitled *Early Personalities Associated with St Edmund's College*. I also thank members of the committee of The Edmundian Association for their assistance with this project.

Within the book, the academic qualifications of certain individuals have been included when known and if relevant in that context. A glossary of the abbreviations used is given on page xv. For Edmundians where there is a principal entry, their full name, date of birth, years at the College, and date of death will be provided if known. Years are shown in the format XXXX-XX if in the same century, or XXXX-XXXX if their time spans two centuries. Because of pressure of space, generally only the year of first arrival and the year of final leaving are shown. Years split by a straight hyphen (-) indicate continuous presence at the College. Years split by a curly hyphen (~) indicate that the Edmundian was not present for the entire period.

I am grateful to have been given the opportunity, with this book, to record the achievements of some of the people of St Edmund's College, and I hope you will find the contents of it illuminating and entertaining.

David J S Kay
November 2003

Early personalities associated with St Edmund's College

The history of an institution like St Edmund's College is bound to produce a whole host of persons, for it is first and foremost a community of people. The College has a long and distinguished history, going back to the sixteenth century. Penal restrictions under Queen Elizabeth I forced English Catholics to educate their sons abroad in a safer climate. At Douay, in France, scholars and students had abandoned Oxford and Cambridge Universities and attached themselves to the newly founded university in that town.

Cardinal William Allen

William Allen

One of these ex-Oxford men, William Allen – later to be made a Cardinal – established a College there for these English exiles. During its first ten years, its students were mature scholars taking courses in theology in the College itself or in the university. Students who fled from the English universities had to complete their theological preparation for the priesthood. With its temporary transfer to Rheims in 1578 it received younger students needing instruction in philosophy and the grammar school courses in humanities. The Douay Diaries show us that under Allen, the College was a mixture of '*vir, juvenis, adolescens, puer, nobilis* and *pauper'*. Over the years, this community was joined by rich and poor sent over from England. Douay accommodated *convictors* who were self-funding and *alumni* who were provided for by bursaries. The lists of students contain many the names of those from many recusant families.

Professor Beales in his book *Education Under Penalty* credits William Allen's foundation with saving Catholic education from extinction.

His college was the backbone of popular education in England before Catholic emancipation. It produced missionaries, the first and the last English Martyrs, and lay teachers; it educated clerics and laymen from all social backgrounds.

The advent of the French Revolution and the declaration of war by France against England drove out the Douay collegians in 1793. Their College confiscated, they were to return home to an England now less harsh than in the first exile. The first four students accompanied by their professors arrived with the Vicar Apostolic of the London District, Bishop John Douglass, on 16 November 1793. They came to Old Hall, about thirty miles from London. They settled in the school known as the Old Hall Green Academy which had been in existence on this site since 1769, a fee-paying school for the education of Catholic laymen. This school, too, had a venerable history. It was on that day that he placed the combined foundation under the patronage of the saint whose feast day it happened to be: Saint Edmund of Abingdon, the thirteenth-century Archbishop of Canterbury who had died in exile in France in 1240. In 1795, some of these students left Old Hall and went north; this group founded Crook Hall, and the institution eventually settled at Ushaw, near Durham being known as St Cuthbert's College. In 1795 more students from Douay, and its sister college of St Omer, arrived together with the first President of Saint Edmund's, Dr Gregory Stapleton.

Gregory Stapleton

Dr Stapleton had been the last President of St Omer. The Secular College at St Omer had originally been started by the Jesuits in 1593, but in 1762 the French Government expelled the Jesuit Order and they moved to Bruges. (In 1773 upon the suppression of the Jesuits by Pope Clement XIV, a number of the staff and students took refuge at the College in Liege, and when driven from there by the French Revolution, this community took refuge in England in the mansion of Stonyhurst, in Lancashire, which had been transferred into the hands of the secular clergy.) The College was handed over to the English secular clergy of Douay, and by a decree of the French Government, the Rev Thomas Talbot, brother of Bishop James Talbot, was appointed its first President. The Secular College had but a comparatively short existence as it too was overtaken by the events associated with the French Revolution in 1793. The list of its Presidents includes Rev Alban Butler, the author of *Butler's Lives of the Saints*. However, as Bernard Ward says in his *History of St Edmund's College*, St Omer had 'few traditions of its own, and these were borrowed from Douay, of which it was an affiliation.' Perhaps its best known student was Daniel O'Connell, the Irish 'liberator'.

Richard Challoner

The school at Old Hall Green on to which the Douay foundation was grafted by Bishop Douglass could trace its roots back to a school founded sometime prior to 1660 in Hampshire. This school had spent most of its life at Twyford, near Winchester, but in 1745 fear of repercussions following the Jacobite Rebellion had prompted Bishop Richard Challoner to close it down. The Catholic aristocracy, as well as Challoner himself, were doubtless anxious to find a place to educate their sons at home rather than abroad. Challoner determined that the school would be started somewhere else, and in 1749 it moved to Standon Lordship, in Hertfordshire, a manor house owned by the Catholic Aston family, relatives of the Talbot family, many of whom had been educated at Douay and Twyford. There it stayed until 1767, when it had to move again temporarily to a smaller house in the village of Hare Street, only to move again in 1769 to Old Hall Green.

James Talbot

The Hon James Talbot, brother of the Earl of Shrewsbury and by this time Challoner's coadjutor bishop, bought the manor house of Old Hall secretly, through a friendly intermediary, the Penal Laws preventing the valid purchasing of land by Catholics. Bishop Talbot had the honour of being the last priest in England to be tried for saying Mass, this happening in the same year that the new 'Old Hall Green Academy' was established. (He was later tried again in 1771 for exercising his episcopal functions.) The first master was Rev James Willacy. The list of students includes members of all the principal Catholic families of the time. We find, for example, such names as Arundel, Bedingfield, Blount, Charlton, Clifford, Dormer, Giffard, Howard, Jerningham, Langdale, Petre, Salvin, Stapleton, Stonor and Talbot. Many of these names recur in the lists preserved from 1769 to 1782.

We could dwell on some of these, for they give us a good idea of the character of the school. The first two boys mentioned in the 1769 list, William and Charles Mawhood, were the sons of Bishop Challoner's friend Mr William Mawhood, a well-to-do army clothier. He shielded the Bishop in his Finchley house during the Gordon Riots, and found his reward in the extraordinary preservation of his town house which was attacked by the mob and suddenly abandoned by them without any obvious reason.

Both these boys became army officers and served in the American War of Independence. In 1772 two of Bishop Talbot's nephews entered the school, being the sons of his brother Charles. The younger, John Joseph, was the father of one of the most distinguished Edmundians of the nineteenth century, John, sixteenth Earl of Shrewsbury. Two more half-brothers of the earl were educated at the College later on.

Another couple of brothers who came to Old Hall in 1772 were James Everard Arundell, afterwards ninth Lord Arundell of Wardour, and Thomas Raymond Arundell. They remained at the school for six and eight years respectively. Lord Arundell's eldest son, in his turn, was one of the early students at the College. An interesting name occurs in 1772: Charles Robert Blundell, a great benefactor, not only of the College, but of the London clergy in general. He was the son of Henry Blundell Esq. of Ince-Blundell, a well-known collector of works of art. By his mother he was first cousin of the Talbots already mentioned. On the death of his father, from whom he was estranged, he was partially disinherited, and he retained only the smaller property of Ince-Blundell. On his death without children he bequeathed a large part of his property to the College, amounting in value to nearly £5,000. The last name that occurs in 1772 is that of Thomas Hugh Clifford, known later as Sir Thomas Clifford-Constable. He was grandson of the third Lord Clifford of Chudleigh, and forms an interesting link with Standon Lordship as his mother, Barbara, was one of the daughters and co-heiresses of James, the last Lord Aston and owner of that manor.

The year 1773 opens with the names of two Howards, Bernard, who became twelfth Duke of Norfolk in 1815, and Henry, his younger brother. Bernard's son, Henry who succeeded him as Duke, was also an Edmundian, and was the first English Catholic returned to Parliament after the Emancipation Act. In the same year we find the names of Robert Petre, afterwards tenth Lord Petre, and his brother George. In the succeeding years among less well-known names we find Sir Richard Bedingfeld. His descendant, Mr Henry Bedingfeld, the present York Herald, in correspondence concerning the matriculation of our coat of arms in 1993, recalled his ancestors' connection with the College when it was Old Hall Academy.

In 1778 we find a name long associated with the history of the College: Jerningham. George William Jerningham was the lineal descendant of the Venerable William Howard, Viscount Stafford, who was to be a candidate for beatification. Viscount Stafford had lost his honours in 1680. This George Jerningham succeeded in obtaining a reversal of the attainder in 1824, and as a consequence the extinct Barony of Stafford was revived in his favour, he becoming the second Baron Stafford after a lapse of nearly a century and a half. In 1779 came three brothers, Walter, Edward and George Blount, Walter became the seventh baronet, and Edward later on sat in the Reform Parliament of 1832, thus being one of the earliest Catholic Members of Parliament. In the same year we find Stonors and Barretts; also Bishop Stapleton's (the first president of the newly-constituted Saint Edmund's College in 1795) younger brother, John, who became in later years father of the Rev Joseph Stapleton, an Edmundian who was Prefect (at that time the equivalent of Headmaster) between 1810 and 1816. The last Jerningham to be educated at the College was Sir Henry Jerningham, who died without an heir in 1935.

He presented the magnificent 18th century 'Costessey Monstrance' which is still to be seen in our College Museum.

From these names it will be seen that Bishop Talbot's Old Hall Green Academy enjoyed the confidence of the leading Catholics of those days and held a position which it did not lose when in 1793 and during the succeeding years it developed into St Edmund's College. Many of these boys had sons and nephews at the College in the first decade of the nineteenth century. But the bond uniting them to the College became gradually weakened as time went on, partly owing to mismanagement of the College. However, before considering this change in character, the Vicar Apostolic responsible for bringing together the Douay refugees and the Old Hall Green Academy should be considered.

John Douglass

Bishop John Douglass, although born in England, came from Jacobite and Catholic parentage. At the age of 13 he was sent across the sea to Douay College, where he showed brilliance as a student. After ordination he spent some time at the English College in Valladolid, before returning to England in 1773. In 1790 he was appointed coadjutor with right of succession to Bishop Talbot, and he was consecrated at Lulworth Castle, the home of the Weld family. He presided over the logistics of settling the problems produced by the dispersal of the Colleges abroad with the advent of the French Revolution. As we have seen, it was he who chose to place the new foundation under the patronage of St Edmund. It is noteworthy that of all the schools claiming descent from foundations originally started abroad, our College alone is known by its patronal name – unlike Ushaw, Oscott, Stonyhurst, Downside or Ampleforth. In his diary, Douglass identified the aim and scope of the College which was "for the purpose of promoting the good of religion and society by forming Catholic youth, particularly of the London District, for the duties of sacred ministry, or of the civil life, according to each one's vocation". The Douay regimen would be followed, "with such alterations and improvements as the change of circumstances requires." The other great work of his life, apart from the establishment of the College as the 'new Douay', was also related to the expulsion of the Church from France. Hundreds of French priests and nuns were given refuge in England. Douglass organised their welfare and found financial support for them. These French exiles proved to be very helpful in the expansion and development of the Catholic Church in England after the Relief Act of 1778. Douglass died in 1812, and his mortal remains were returned to the College in 1908.

Bishop John Douglass

William Poynter

Dr William Poynter was the second President of St Edmund's after Bishop Stapleton. We need to spend a little time on him, because it was during his time as President and Vicar Apostolic that the fortunes of the College went into a decline. He was Prefect of Studies at Douay during its last days, and with some of the students who did not manage to escape in 1793, was imprisoned at Doullens. It is said that under these circumstances he gave a splendid example to all of everything that was best in the Douay tradition. He was President of the College and at the same time Vicar Apostolic of the London District. He was consecrated a bishop in the College's Chapel in 1803, 200 years ago this year, and his consecration was the first time for many years that full ceremonial of the Roman Pontifical was carried out, with all the necessary co-consecrating bishops.

During his frequent absences on episcopal duties, matters at the College deteriorated, culminating in the Great Affair of 1809. Accounts reveal relatively trivial beginnings which would not have been so damaging had there not already been an unsettled and discontented atmosphere at the College. While Dr Poynter was away administering the Sacrament of Confirmation in Hampshire, and therefore absent from his functions as President of the College, the Vice-President, Francis Tuite, refused a 'play day' or whole holiday. One of the students of in the Class of Syntax had received an order to be thrashed by the Prefect, but such a punishment had hitherto been inflicted only on small boys, and never on a senior boy. Finally, another student was discovered to have consumed a bottle of wine with his friends, and again was ordered to be thrashed. This final event proved to be the last straw. Rebellion erupted and thirty students left the College, walked to Waltham Cross and lodged in the inn. When Constables were sent to find them, the party divided and some of them had the idea of making for Scotland. The boys were eventually persuaded by intermediaries to return to the College. When Bishop Poynter returned, he took a very strong view of the case refusing to accept certain compromise conditions which had been offered to induce students to return. He saw each of the students individually and told them that their conduct was inexcusable and that they would have to be punished. He expelled the three ringleaders, and eight others left of their own accord.

The College became quiet and orderly, but there was still a good deal of discontent below the surface. "We are at length outwardly tranquillized," wrote one of the church students, "though inwardly disgust and disaffection are still very prevalent, nor do I think it will ever be otherwise... " In fact this statement serves to remind us of the uneasy coexistence of lay and church students in a college which had as a principle aim the education of future priests. Even Bishop Poynter himself had recognised that the church students were often laughed out of their vocations by the younger gentlemen of the world. An Edmundian priest who received all his education at the College during this period wrote, "Now at that time, things were not well regulated for students destined for the Church. We were all mixed together with future Lords, Earls, and Dukes, and other lay students, who, at the end of each vacation, used to return full of London news and London pleasures, and I got more harm than good from such conversation." For their part, the lay students no doubt felt that the supervision was much stricter than that which obtained in most Anglican public schools at that time. Lay student numbers declined after the Great Affair, and so therefore did the patronage of many of those families whose names had been present on College lists going right back to Douay. Formerly, they had outnumbered church boys by seven to one; by 1818 they were forty to forty, and at length Poynter determined to make the College purely ecclesiastical. However, the lay establishment continued in a preparatory department, and in fact the College never lost the lay element.

At this point we may consider some of the personalities in the student body educated at Old Hall during the first twenty-five years of the nineteenth century. The Rev **Mark Tierney**, who had been a student at the College, was one of the most distinguished of scholarly ecclesiastics St Edmund's produced during the nineteenth century. It was he who edited *Dodd's Church History of England*. At the time Thomas Griffiths became President, he was procurator, but he resigned after a year to go on what was still referred to as the 'mission'. He died in 1862, and was one of the first Canons of Southwark Diocese. Perhaps the most celebrated layman at this period was John Talbot, great-nephew of Bishop James Talbot, and afterwards the well-known, saintly and charitable sixteenth Earl of Shrewsbury who did so much for Catholicism in the Midlands, and for Catholic architecture through his patronage of Pugin. He had been a student for a year or two at Stonyhurst, but he came for his higher studies to St Edmund's. He gained distinction in his work and carried off the prize medal in the Class of Rhetoric. Another eminent layman was Arthur Clifford, grandson of the last Lord Aston. We may also mention Henry Howard, afterwards thirteenth Duke of Norfolk, Valentine Brown (Lord Castlerose, afterwards the second Earl Kenmare), Charles Petre, son of the tenth Lord Petre, Thomas Stonor, third Lord Camoys and James Everard, tenth Lord Arundell of Wardour.

Thomas Griffiths

As we have seen, the fortunes of the College waned somewhat during the presidency of Bishop Poynter. However under the presidency of Dr Thomas Griffiths, the College received a new vigour, life and direction. Thomas Griffiths was the first President of the College to have been wholly educated within its walls. He was only 27 when Bishop Poynter appointed him President and he remained in this post for 16 years. It was he who put the College back to a flourishing state after the decline had set in following the 'Great Affair'. As the internal state of the College improved, both financially and otherwise, confidence was gradually restored, and the increased number of students bore witness to its regeneration. After he resigned the Presidency to succeed Bishop Bramston as Vicar Apostolic of the London District, he continued to be a frequent visitor to the College and continued to the end of his life to take an active interest in its affairs.

One of the students to arrive in September 1827 was one **William Henry Bower**. He was a student from then until 1836, and after a prosperous life as a sheep farmer in Australia, he returned to the College in 1872 upon the death of his wife. He lived at the College until his death in 1905. I first heard about 'the Old Man', as he became known, on the day I came for interview in the summer of 1976. At dinner that evening, I sat next to Canon Clement Parsons who was living in retirement at the College. He had arrived in 1903 as a small boy, and told me that he had spent many an hour conversing with William Bower in the three years before the latter's death. Thus was 150 years of College history spanned for me in half an hour! William Bower left an account of College life during Dr Griffiths' presidency, from which I shall take a few extracts. After he had arrived at the College, "A servant met us and led us up to the President's room. There I was introduced to Dr Griffiths, whose kind greeting 'I am to be your father now' made an impression which still lasts... his hair was cut quite short and powdered white... he wore spectacles and had on a University gown, and when he showed us around the house, wore a mortar-board cap. . ..I was a student at St Edmund's on and off for ten years... we always had a high place among the Catholic Colleges, acknowledged as the first and chief successor of old Douay... Mr Ambrose Phillips de Lisle also spent a considerable time at the College soon after his conversion."

Ambrose Phillips de Lisle and another well-known convert from Cambridge, Kenelm Digby, used to get up very early of a Sunday morning to ride the 25 miles from Cambridge to Old Hall in order to be present for the community High Mass. De Lisle and Digby were non-matrculated students at the University – Catholics were not at that time permitted to proceed to degrees in either Oxford or Cambridge – and at that time Old Hall was the nearest Catholic church to Cambridge. Ambrose's son, **Everard Phillips de Lisle**, attended St Edmund's between 1847 and 1849. His subsequent army career took him to India where he died during the siege of Delhi in 1857, being awarded a posthumous VC.

Another distinguished Old Edmundian who was at the College in the years after Dr Griffiths' presidency was **Henry James Stonor**, a member of that recusant family whose name I have recalled earlier in this essay. Having spent a year at Oscott, he arrived at St Edmund's in 1832. He left the College in 1837, and, as his mother's father was the well known lawyer Charles Butler, the first Catholic KC since the Emancipation Act of 1829, it was perhaps natural that he should himself proceed to the bar. He eventually ended up a County Court Judge, and it was said that some of his judgements were of such quality that they came to be quoted as leading cases, as if he were a High Court Judge. He left the College an oil painting of his illustrious relative, the Douay professor Alban Butler, author of the famous *Butler's Lives of the Saints,* and he maintained his interest and benefactions to the College for over a quarter of a century, dying in 1906.

James Laird Patterson

In 1869, Archbishop Manning removed the theological students from St Edmund's and placed them in the new St Thomas's Seminary, at Hammersmith, in the buildings now used by the Sacred Heart Convent School. A new President was appointed in the person of Mgr James Laird Patterson, one of the Oxford converts. He introduced a new spirit into the College, one which was not altogether welcomed by many of its longer inhabitants. Mgr Patterson was a 'Romanist', and this went somewhat against the 'old Catholic' inclinations of the old place. The spirit of the College was Gothic and fanatically Gothic; it was also conservative and opposed to any change. In 1853 the fine chapel in the Gothic style designed by the great architect Pugin had been opened. Now this chapel was 'Romanised', even to the extent of some gothic-style vestments being cut down to the approved Roman shape. Birettas, hitherto unseen in the College, were introduced. One priest recalled when writing Mgr Patterson's obituary in the College magazine that the first question put to him was whether he was a Goth or a Roman. When he replied that he was a Roman, imagining that they meant by the term a Catholic, he was taken to task by some of the students, and warned that though he might curry favour with the superiors, he would make himself an object of suspicion with his fellow students by joining the unpopular party! However, this same priest also recalled that it was Patterson's genial and lovable character that disarmed opposition and won the hearts of staff and students alike. The ten years of Patterson's presidency were years when many feared that the character of the College would be changed out of all recognition because of the removal of divines, and it took all the strength of this gentle and genial character to hold the place. together. It was he who turned a small villa in the grounds, originally built by Pugin for fellow Oxford convert William George Ward, into St Hugh's Preparatory School, so that the junior boys in the College could be catered for separately.

Bernard Ward

No survey would be complete without mention of Monsignor Bernard Ward. He was the son of William George Ward, 'Ideal' Ward. When W.G. Ward converted to Catholicism in 1844, he was deprived of his degrees and his living by the University of Oxford. He and his family were taken in by the President, Dr Cox, and in spite of some murmurings, he, a married layman and recent convert, was appointed professor of dogmatic theology in the seminary. (Some of these murmurings subsided after Pope Pius 9th awarded Ward a Papal doctorate.) Young Bernard thus grew up in St Edmund's and got to know it thoroughly.

He eventually became the fifteenth President in the Centenary year of 1893, and, until his appointment as first Bishop of Brentwood in 1916, he presided over the College, bringing "to fruition the ideal for St Edmund's that Douglass had set out for it one hundred years previously" A decline had set in after Mgr Patterson's presidency, to such an extent that Archbishop Vaughan gave Ward one year to either make the place or close it. He was only appointed Pro-President at first. Ward's first move was to use the centenary of the refugees' arrival at Old Hall to galvanise the College spirit and set it on its new route. Incredibly enough it would seem that but for Ward's strong historical sense, this event might also have been overlooked. This was but the start of a great catalogue of achievement. He wrote the College history, founded the modern printed version of *The Edmundian* magazine, oversaw the return of the theological students to the College, introduced cricket as a College game, built west and north wings, added a shrine chapel to the main College chapel and brought heating, hot water and telephones to the College.

The number of lay and church students grew to the highest ever, and he provided them with excellent and conscientious staff, most notably with his priest Vice-President, Dr **Edwin Burton** and Prefect of Studies, the layman Dr **Alfred Herbert**. The first meeting of the Conference of Catholic Colleges was held at the College during his presidency. His achievements as a historian were acknowledged when he was made a Fellow of the Royal Historical Society in 1909, and by his election to the Old Brotherhood of the Secular Clergy.

It was Mgr Bernard Ward who may be said to have laid the foundations for the St Edmund's of the twentieth century. Since his time there have been several momentous changes. The seminary left the buildings he had had erected in 1975, and moved to London, as it had in 1869. A house system was introduced by Cardinal Bourne in 1922, the first three houses being named after the Vicars Apostolic who played such a great part in the history of the College. The school is now exclusively for lay students and is now coeducational, and is at its largest numbers ever, with over 600 pupils aged between 3 and 18. There have, therefore, been several deeply significant changes since his presidency. But we may hope that he would recognise that the essential spirit of the College lives on. As Edmundians we must always keep before us the fundamental aims of promoting 'the good of religion and society by forming Catholic youth' in the circumstances we find ourselves. Under God, we shall remain to the Edmundian spirit. And what is that? In the words of one of our most notable Old Edmundians, Cardinal Francis Bourne: "The Edmundian spirit, if it be true and worth the name, must be none other that the spirit of St Edmund himself. We have no right to call ourselves 'Edmundians' unless we be honestly striving to imitate the love of God and Church, the generosity, the unselfishness, the patient energy, the love of learning, the steadfastness, and the humility which are ever associated with our Patron's name."

Avita pro Fide – For the Faith of Our Fathers

Dr Alfred Herbert

Duncan A Gallie
November 2003

Glossary of Abbreviations

Below is an alphabetical list of the abbreviations – mostly academic and professional qualifications and awards – which are used in this book, together with their meanings.

ACIB	Associate, Chartered Institute of Bankers
ACIS	Associate, Institute of Chartered Secretaries and Administrators
AdvDipRE	Advanced Diploma in Religious Education
AE	Air Efficiency Award
AFC	Air Force Cross
AIB	Associate, Institute of Bankers
AIL	Associate, Institute of Linguists
ARCS	Associate, Royal College of Science
Asst	Assistant
BA	Bachelor of Arts
BBC	British Broadcasting Corporation
BChir	Bachelor of Surgery
BD	Bachelor of Divinity
BEd	Bachelor of Education
BEM	British Empire Medal
BS	Bachelor of Surgery
BSc	Bachelor of Science
BSc(Econ)	Bachelor of Science in Economics
Bt	Baronet
Capt	Captain
CB	Companion, Order of the Bath
CBE	Commander, Order of the British Empire
CChem	Chartered Chemist
Cdr	Commander
CertEd	Certificate in Education
CH	Companion of Honour
CMG	Companion, Order of St Michael & St George
Cpl	Corporal
CVO	Commander, Royal Victorian Order
DCM	Distinguished Conduct Medal
DD	Doctor of Divinity
DFC	Distinguished Flying Cross
DHE	Diploma of Higher Education
DipArch	Diploma in Architecture
DipCG	Diploma in Corporate Governance
DipEd	Diploma in Education
DL	Deputy Lieutenant
DPhil	Doctor of Philosophy
Dr	Doctor
DRCOG	Diploma of Royal College of Obstetricians and Gynaecologists
DSC	Distinguished Service Cross
DSO	Distinguished Service Order
DTheol	Doctor of Theology
FBIM	Fellow, British Institute of Management
FCA	Fellow, Institute of Chartered Accountants
FCIOB	Fellow, Chartered Institute of Building
FCIPD	Fellow, Chartered Institute of Personnel & Development

FCJ	Faithful Companion of Jesus
FCMI	Fellow, Chartered Insitute of Management
FFB	Fellow, Faculty of Building
FHCIMA	Fellow, Hotel Catering and Institutional Management Association
FRAS	Fellow, Royal Astronomical Society
FRCO	Fellow, Royal College of Organists
FRCR	Fellow, Royal College of Radiologists
FRGS	Fellow, Royal Geographical Society
FRHistS	Fellow, Royal Historical Society
FRIC	Fellow, Royal Institute of Chemistry
FRSA	Fellow, Royal Society of Arts
FSA	Fellow, Society of Arts
FZS	Fellow, Zoological Society
GCMG	Knight Grand Cross, Order of St Michael & St George
HM	His/Her Majesty's
HMS	His/Her Majesty's Ship
HonARIBA	Honorary Associate, Royal Institute of British Architects
IC	Institute of Charity (Rosminians)
KCB	Knight Commander, Order of the Bath
KCHS	Knight Commander, Order of the Holy Sepulchre
KCSG	Knight Commander, Order of St Michael & St George
KGCHS	Knight Grand Commander, Order of the Holy Sepulchre
KHS	Knight, Order of the Holy Sepulchre
KM	Knight of Malta
KSG	Knight, Order of St Gregory the Great
LHS	Lady, Order of the Holy Sepulchre
LLB	Bachelor of Laws
LLD	Doctor of Laws
LRCP	Licentiate, Royal College of Physicians, London
LSS	Licentiate in Sacred Scripture
Lt	Lieutenant
LTCL	Licentiate, Trinity College of Music, London
MA	Master of Arts
MBAE	Member, British Association of Electrolysis
MBE	Member, Order of the British Empire
MC	Military Cross
MCh	Master of Surgery
MChir	Master of Surgery
MD	Doctor of Medicine
Mgr	Monsignor
MIMgt	Member, Institute of Management
MInstP	Member, Institute of Physics

MLitt	Master of Letters		RAChD	Royal Army Chaplains Department
MM	Military Medal		RAF	Royal Air Force
MP	Member of Parliament		RD	Reserve Declaration
MPhil	Master of Philosophy		RE	Royal Engineers
MRCP	Member, Royal College of Physicians, London		Rev	The Reverend
MRCS	Member, Royal College of Surgeons of England		RIBA	Member, Royal Institute of British Architects
			RN	Royal Navy
MRSC	Member, Royal Society of Chemistry		Rt Rev	The Right Reverend
MSc	Master of Science			
MusB	Bachelor of Music		Sgt	Sergeant
			SHCJ	Sister of the Holy Child Jesus
NPQH	National Professional Qualification for Headteachers		SJ	Society of Jesus (Jesuits)
			Sqn-Ldr	Squadron Leader
			St	Saint
OBE	Officer, Order of the British Empire		STL	Sacrae Theologiae Lector (Reader of Sacred Theology)
OCD	Order of Discalced Carmelites			
OE	Old Edmundian		Sub-Lt	Sub-Lieutenant
OFM	Order of Friars Minor (Franciscans)			
OM	Order of Merit		TD	Territorial Declaration
OSB	Order of St Benedict (Benedictines)		TITC	Trained Infants Teaching Certificate
OSM	Order of St Michael (Michaelines)			
PC	Privy Councillor		VA	Vicar Apostolic
PhD	Doctor of Philosophy		VG	Vicar General
PhL	Licentiate in Philosophy		VRD	Royal Naval Volunteer Reserve Officers' Decoration
Pte	Private			
			V Rev	The Very Reverend
QC	Queen's Counsel			

Significant dates

1568	English College at Douay founded		**1953**	**Centenary of The Edmundian Association**
1685	Silkstead opened			
1692	Moved to Twyford			Junior House disbanded
1745	Twyford suspended		1960	Junior House reopened
1753	Standon Lordship opened		1970	Poynter House opened
1762	Secular College at St Omer opened		1972	Griffiths House opened
1767	Hare Street opened		1975	Allen Hall moved to Chelsea
1769	Old Hall Green Academy opened			Stapleton & Margaret Pole Houses opened
1793	St Edmund's College founded at Old Hall Green		1984	Griffiths House disbanded
			1990	Margaret Pole House disbanded
1795	St Edmund's College formally constituted			Pole House opened
			1993	Junior House disbanded
1853	**The Edmundian Association founded**		1996	St Hugh's Nursery & Infant Department opened
				Stapleton House disbanded
1869	Theology students left		1997	Garvey's opened in main building as girls' boarding area
1874	St Hugh's Preparatory School opened			
1904	Theology students returned		2000	St Gregory's opened as junior boys' boarding area
1905	Divines' Wing opened			
1922	House system introduced – Challoner, Douglass & Talbot Houses			
	Divines' Wing renamed Allen Hall		**2003**	**Sesquicentenary of The Edmundian Association**
1945	Junior House opened			

chapter 1

Facts & figures

There is a short article in The Edmundian of December 1895 which states

> *"The numerous Flynns are perplexing. Known as Flynn 1, Flynn 2, Flynn 3 & Flynn 4, each being unrelated to the other three. They are not equally studious."*

In those days it must have been very difficult to maintain accurate records of pupils, and as the College grew, the task of doing so must have become more daunting.

The concept of an Edmundian "directory" was first alluded to in *The Edmundian* in December 1920. However, it was 19 years later that Desmond Measures (1925~40) compiled a list of the names of some 7,000 students, having extracted information from Canon Burton's lists, Prefects of Studies Books, Class Lists and other sources. He never completed the task, but until 1946 the records were updated by Hal King, the Headmaster.

In 1995 the author undertook to bring the list up to date as a project for The Edmundian Association to mark the Millennium. Using modern computer technology, *The Edmundian Directory* of students and academic staff was first published in 2000 on the Association's website, and is currently available there to members of the Association. This chapter covers some little known statistics which came to light during its compilation.

Student numbers

Since 1793 there have been 12,227 students at St Edmunds, of these 10,264 were boys, 1167 were girls, and 796 were adults solely in the seminary. There have been 830 academic staff, 256 of whom had also been students at the College.

The year in which the highest number of students entered the school was this year, in which there have been 214 new students at the time of writing. The year in which the lowest number entered was 1832, when there were just nine new students.

The highest number of leavers in one year was 160 students in 2002. The lowest was six in 1795.

William Bower, greatest span of years

Joan King, longest continuous resident of the College

Greatest total span of years between arrival and departure

78 William Bower (1827~1905)
77 Canon Clement Parsons (1903~80)
60 Mrs Joan King (1943-present)
59 Fr Michael Pinot de Moira (1944~present)
    Herbert Willett (1915-74)
57 Charlie Smith (1946-present)
55 Canon Thomas Doyle (1812~67)
53 Hal "Rex" King (1930-83)
49 Canon Edward Mahoney (1905~54)
    Fr Edmund Tunstall (1845~94)
48 Bishop Bernard Ward (1868~1916)
    Francis Jaynes (1913-60)
        Fr Bernard Lagrue (1946~93)
46 Mgr George Smith (1906~52)
45 Dr Alfred Herbert (1874~1919)
44 Fr Michael Garvey (1940~84)
42 Canon Denis Britt-Compton (1926~68)
    Ernest Berry (1919-59)
    Mgr Reginald Butcher (1924~64)
    Dr William Weathers (1828~68)
39 John Vaughan-Shaw (1964-present)
    Archbishop Edward Myers (1893~1932)

Actual number of years at the College

60 Mrs Joan King (1943-present)
    Herbert Willett (1915-74)
57 Fr Michael Pinot de Moira (1944~present)
    Charlie Smith (1946-present)
53 Hal "Rex" King (1930-83)
46 Canon Edward Mahoney (1905~54)
45 Francis Jaynes (1913-60)
43 Fr Bernard Lagrue (1946~93)
42 William Bower (1827~1905)
40 Ernest Berry (1919-59)
    Fr Michael Garvey (1940~84)
    Mgr George Smith (1956~52)
    Dr William Weathers (1828~68)
39 John Vaughan-Shaw (1964-present)
38 Henry Smith (1932-70)
36 Mrs Angela Chapman (1960-96)
    Hugh Strode (1950-86)
35 Miss Sally Sullivan (1885-1920)
34 Bishop Bernard Ward (1868~1916)
33 Dr David Black (1970-2003)
    Kenneth Hall (1970-present)
    Archbishop Edward Myers (1893~1932)

Dr Alan Wigfield was the College doctor for 38 years between 1927 and 1965.

Most common surname

82	Smith
60	Murphy
46	White
44	Brown
41	Jones
36	O'Brien
34	O'Connor
33	McCarthy
	Thompson
32	King
	Ryan

Most popular male student forename

834	John
405	James
346	William
311	Michael
304	Thomas
299	Joseph
265	Francis
263	Charles
251	Edward
225	Peter

Most popular male staff forename

93	John
39	William
26	James
23	Charles
21	Joseph
19	Richard
	Thomas
18	Peter
17	Edward
15	Michael

Most popular female student forename

28	Sarah
27	Charlotte
19	Catherine
17	Rebecca
16	Sophie
15	Elizabeth
14	Helen
	Lucy
	Maria
13	Caroline
	Emma
	Olivia

Most popular female staff forename

15	Margaret
13	Mary
12	Ann/Anne
8	Elizabeth
	Patricia
7	Carol/Carole
6	Catherine
	Helen
	Jennifer
5	Joan

Largest span between names

The largest span of years between the same surname was one of 203 years from John Bradshaw (1794-1801) until Edward Bradshaw (1990-97). The largest span between forenames is 210 years between Thomas Cook (1793-96) and four students called Thomas currently at the College.

Longest surname

The longest overall surname belonged to Francisco Martinez-Torregrosa Vera-Meseguer (1994-95) which has 30 letters excluding the space and hyphens. The longest single word surname belonged to Peter Haythornthwaite (1865-69) with 15 letters.

Longest full name

Adalbert Gaston Henri Leopold Bernard de Forceville (1907-08) had 45 letters and 6 spaces in his name.

Shortest surname

There have been 36 students with the two-letter surname Ho, Hu, Im, Ip, Ko, Li, Lo, Lu, Ng, Ni or Yu.

Shortest full name

These belong to Jia Hu (2001-present) & Fei Li (1999-99).

Oldest Edmundians to die

William Bickford (1918-23) is believed to have died in 2002 at the age of 95; Sir Leo Curtis (1915-18) died in 2001, aged 94 years 38 days.

Current oldest known living former students
(year of birth in italics)
Dr Reginald Fuller (1926~49) *(1908)*
Basil Jackson (1924-27) *(1909)*
Felix Britt-Compton (1927-33) *(1914)*
Squadron Leader Jocelyn Millard (1928-31) *(1915)*
Paul Roche (1934-43) *(1916)*
Francis Clayton (1934-38) *(1918)*
Peter Fletcher (1930-37) *(1919)*
Tony Hewson (1935-44) *(1920)*
Gaston Marbaix (1930-37) *(1920)*
Brian Boshell (1931-37) *(1920)*
Canon Peter Phillips (1940~67) *(1922)*
Mgr David Norris (1936~53) *(1922)*

Shortest time at the College
Edward Sproll (1938-38) was at the College for one hour (see below). The name of Afam Enwonwu (1975-75) remains a legend for a certain generation of students in Junior House: for a considerable time his name appeared on class lists, he had a common room locker and a bed, but he does not appear to have stayed for long.

Edward Sproll
Edward James Peter Sproll; born 14 March 1922; Douglass 1938-38; died 22 April 1965

He has the unusual distinction of being the Edmundian who stayed the shortest amount of time at the College. A convert to Catholicism, it is understood he was sent to St Edmund's for a good education and, his parents hoped, vocation to the priesthood. Neither was to happen. The records show that he did not stay more than an hour, leaving on a bicycle after seeing his housemaster, Fr John McKenzie. What was discussed between them is not known, however it is now believed that the bicycle was in fact a prized possession and, as he was not allowed to keep a bicycle at the school at that time, he decided not to stay. After his brief spell at St Edmund's, Edward Sproll took up an apprenticeship with the BBC at Brookman's Park as an engineering technician, interrupted by service in the RAF during the Second World War, and later as a television copywriter for several advertising agencies. He married in 1946 and had four children, but later tragically took his own life.

Edward Sproll

chapter 2

Presidents & governors

Presidents

The post of President originates from the College's time in Douay, and was formally constituted at St Edmund's in 1795. There have been 24 Presidents since then, with an average length of completed service of just under nine years. The longest serving were Monsignor Bernard Ward (23 years), Bishop Christopher Butler (18 years), Monsignor William Weathers (17 years) and Bishop Thomas Griffiths (16 years). The shortest serving was Dr John Bew who served for just six months.

At the centenary in 1893 it was proposed that a series of portraits of the Presidents should be painted for the College. With funds provided by The Edmundian Association, the series was originally completed in 1901 with the further Presidents' portraits being added since. The paintings were intended for the Refectory, and they now hang in the Ambulacrum in chronological order of their terms of office.

In 1793 Fr John Potier was appointed temporary president. Educated at Douay, Fr Potier came to Old Hall Green Academy in 1785 as assistant master and became chief master in 1792. He remained in charge until 1795, when the first President was appointed, and then carried on as parish priest until 1810, when he moved to Puckeridge to work as a private tutor. In 1813 he went to Shefford, Bedfordshire, taking his pupils with him, and died there in 1826. He is buried in Standon Churchyard, a corner of which was allocated to Catholics. No portrait of him is known to exist.

1st President 1795-1801: Rt Rev Gregory Stapleton DD
Gregory Stapleton; born 1748; staff 1795-1801; died 23 May 1802

Dr Gregory Stapleton

Dr Stapleton was the last President of the secular college at St Omer. He took control of St Edmund's College on 15 August 1795 and had Dr William Poynter as his Vice-President.

During his time, various buildings on the site were used to accommodate the College. The Hermitage was used as a preparatory school, Old Hall contained accommodation for professors and dormitories, The Ship housed the divinity students, and classes were held in "The School in the Garden". These latter two buildings no longer exist.

Stapleton supervised the plans and the work for the main College building which was completed in 1799 at a total cost of £12,000. He was not allowed to enjoy the fruits of his labours for very long, because after about a month of moving into the new building he was called upon to make an important journey to Rome on Church business and subsequently was appointed Vicar Apostolic of the Midland District. He never returned to the College and died the following year.

2nd President 1801-1813: Rt Rev William Poynter DD
William Poynter; born 20 May 1762; staff 1795-1813; died 10 April 1827

Dr William Poynter

Formerly a professor at Douay, Dr Poynter worked closely with Dr Stapleton as a co-founder of the College, and took over from him in 1801. The chief building work which took place during his presidency was the addition of the north and south extensions to the main building which now contain the Religious Education classrooms and the Library respectively.

As has already been described in detail in an earlier part of this book, Poynter's duties as co-adjutor to Bishop Douglass took him away from the College and the number of lay students declined. Upon the death of Douglass, Poynter became Vicar Apostolic of the London District and for a while he endeavoured to continue as President, but the two roles were incompatible and he retired from the presidency at Midsummer 1813.

Fr Joseph Kimbell

3rd President 1813-1817: Rev Joseph Kimbell
Joseph Kimbell; date of birth unknown; staff 1795-1817; died 5 December 1835

Dr Poynter's successor was the Fr Joseph Kimbell, who had earlier been Prefect. The traditions established during the previous years continued without much alteration. The building of the new parish church was commenced (it was completed in 1818); the building is now the squash courts.

Conscious that the College was not prospering under his control, Kimbell offered his resignation in 1816, though this was not accepted, and Dr Poynter persuaded him to stay. Staff changes followed, including the appointment of Fr Thomas Griffiths as Vice-President.

By the end of the year it was apparent that the College was not becoming more successful, and when Kimbell tendered his resignation again it was accepted; he left on 11 February 1817.

4th President 1817-1817: Rev John Bew DD
John Bew; date of birth unknown; staff 1817-17; died 25 October 1829

Dr John Bew

When Fr Kimbell left, no immediate arrangements could be made to fill his place, and it was some five months later that the unexpected appointment of Dr Bew was made. He was the founder of the college at Oscott and was working in Brighton when he was called upon to be President of St Edmund's. The main change he implemented was the separation of church and lay students, who had previously studied together.

Dr Bew was only in office from July until the end of December 1817. He resigned because he was unable to cope with the pressures the role entailed, and returned to his former parish in Brighton.

5th President 1818-1834: Rt Rev Thomas Griffiths DD

Thomas Griffiths; born 2 June 1791; student 1805-15; staff 1816-34; died 19 August 1847

Dr Thomas Griffiths

When Thomas Griffiths was appointed, the decision had been made for St Edmund's to be mainly an ecclesiastical college. About twenty to thirty of the older lay boys were dismissed from the school and the remaining lay students were moved from the main building into the Old Hall.

Griffiths was the youngest President on appointment, being promoted to the post just 13 years after first arriving as a student at the age of 14. The presidency of Dr Griffiths was a period of complete regeneration of St Edmund's. As confidence in the place was gradually restored, the number of students once again increased, and the place flourished.

He left when he became Vicar Apostolic of the London District. It was while he was in London that he commissioned the architect Augustus Welby Pugin to design the present College Chapel, as well as raising the funds to make the building of it possible.

6th President 1834-1837: Rev Richard Newell DD

Richard Newell; born 30 November 1797; student 1811-20; staff 1820-37; date of death unknown

Pope Pius VI

Dr Richard Newell

Little of note occurred during the time of Dr Newell, a former Prefect, who served for just three and a half years.

The official portrait of Dr Newell is a composite and is not authentic, as no original picture of him existed. He is said to have borne a remarkable resemblance to Pope Pius VI, so his portrait in the Ambulacrum is really a likeness of that Pope, with Dr Newell's hairstyle!

7th President 1838-1840: Rev John Rolfe

John Rolfe; date of birth unknown; student 1807-11 & staff 1817-18 & 1838-40; died 28 June 1851

Fr John Rolfe

During his short term of office, Fr John Rolfe, who was formerly working at Moorfields in London, did much to improve the College grounds. Land which had been acquired a few years beforehand, under the Standon Enclosure Act, was planted with trees and shrubs, and the hedges between the fields were removed. Fr Rolfe oversaw the opening up of the park in front of the main buildings and the addition of the road now known as Chestnut Drive.

8th President 1840-1851: Very Rev Edward Cox DD

Edward Cox; born 12 March 1806; student 1822-28; staff 1838-51; died 9 November 1856

When Fr Rolfe left in 1840, Dr Cox succeeded him as President and held the post until 1851. It was in this period that the present College Chapel was built, and although it was not opened until two years after he had left, the main burden of its erection fell on Dr Cox's shoulders.

As a President he was conservative and few changes were made in his time. Dr Cox later became Vicar General of the newly formed Southwark Diocese, and went to live in Southampton, where he spent the remaining five years of his relatively short life.

Dr Edward Cox

9th President 1851-1868: Rt Rev William Weathers DD

William Weathers; born 12 November 1814; student 1828-38; staff 1838-68; died 4 March 1895

During the 40 years that Dr Weathers was at St Edmund's, he held almost every office. He started teaching in 1835 whilst still a divinity student. He was Prefect of Discipline, Prefect of Studies, Procurator, Vice-President and finally President.

At the beginning of his presidency, the new College Chapel was finished, and the New Wing as it was called was also built at this time. (This is the wing which now accommodates the Refectory.)

In 1869 Dr Weathers was appointed Rector of the new national seminary in Hammersmith, a job he remained in until the seminary closed in 1892. He was appointed Bishop of Amycla in 1872.

His portrait in the Ambulacrum originally depicted him without the spectacles he normally wore; they were added later by popular request.

Dr William Weathers

10th President 1868-1870: Very Rev Frederick Rymer DD

Frederick Rymer; born 31 January 1825; student 1835-48; staff 1848~70; died 9 November 1910

Like his predecessor, Dr Rymer taught in the College whilst still a student: his first appointment was to teach algebra to a class in which the students were nearly all older than himself.

He was Vice-President from 1861 and took over the presidency in 1868 when Dr Weathers was summoned to Rome to assist with preparations for the Vatican Council.

In the summer of 1869 the College celebrated the centenary of its arrival in Old Hall Green. That same year the theological students moved to the new seminary at Hammersmith. However, owing to a divergence of views on many points between himself and Cardinal Manning, Dr Rymer ceased to be President in 1870.

Dr Frederick Rymer

11th President 1870-1880: Rt Rev Mgr James Laird Patterson MA
James Laird Patterson; born 16 November 1822; staff 1870-80; died 1 December 1902

The first President not to have studied or taught at St Edmund's, Mgr Patterson oversaw the College at a time of many great improvements. Attempts were made to modernise both the spirit and the fabric of the College, and it was feared that the character of the place would be changed out of all recognition. The terraces were constructed, the kitchen wing was built, the Ambulacrum and the Refectory were decorated, and most importantly St Hugh's Preparatory School was established. The Fourth Provincial Council of Westminster was held at the College in 1873.

Mgr Patterson resigned in 1880 due to failing health and shortly afterwards was consecrated Bishop of Emmaus. He was later appointed rector of St Mary's, Chelsea.

Mgr James Laird Patterson

12th President 1880-1882: Very Rev Canon George Akers MA
George Akers; date of birth unknown; staff 1877-82; died 14 August 1899

Canon Akers was an Oxford Movement convert who came to St Edmund's after establishing a parish in Homerton, east London. This involved the building of a church and the establishment of schools. He left the College, after a brief and uneventful term of office, to set up a further new parish in Hampton Wick, Middlesex, repeating the work he had done in Homerton. He later moved back to work in the the East End where he remained for the rest of his life.

Canon George Akers

13th President 1882-1887: Rt Rev Mgr Patrick Fenton
Patrick Fenton; born 19 August 1837; student 1855-66; staff 1882-87; died 2 August 1918

After studying for the priesthood at St Edmund's, Mgr Fenton worked in numerous parishes before his appointment as President. He was chaplain to the Hospital of St John & St Elizabeth, and was the first Conventual Chaplain of the Sovereign Military Order of Malta since the Reformation.

He resigned when it was decided to transfer church students to other schools, and he returned to parish work.

Mgr Patrick Fenton

14th President 1887-1893: Rt Rev Mgr Canon John Crook
John Edward Crook; born 25 April 1838; student 1849-58; staff 1887-93; died 1 March 1909

Mgr Crook studied at St Edmund's and in Rome, and was ordained to the priesthood in 1862. He worked in three parishes in London. The last of these was St Mary's, Chelsea, where he had been for 17 years when Cardinal Manning asked him to be President of the College. His term of office was relatively uneventful. He suffered ill health and, upon leaving, accepted the post of chaplain to Lord Petre at Thorndon, where he spent the remaining years of his life.

Mgr John Crook

15th President 1893-1916: Rt Rev Mgr Bernard Ward

Bernard Nicholas Ward; born 4 February 1857; student 1868-75; staff 1882-85 & 1890-1916; died 21 January 1920

Bishop Bernard Ward

Serving as President for longer than any other person, Bernard Ward was born at Old Hall House, now St Hugh's, and his childhood was spent there. He was the son of the Oxford convert Dr William George Ward.

He was a pupil at St Edmund's, and returned again in 1882 as General Prefect, a job which he continued until 1884. He was ordained shortly after returning to the College and remained a professor until 1885, when he left to found a new parish in Willesden and to teach at Oscott. He returned again in 1890, and this time remained for 26 years. After three years as Vice-President he was appointed President, albeit at first in an "acting" capacity, as the continuation of the school at that time was very much in the balance. However, due to his enthusiasm and generosity, the College under his management overcame its difficulties and the students grew to a record number.

During his presidency, the College celebrated its centenary celebrations in 1893, *The Edmundian* magazine was founded, the swimming pool was built (paid for personally by Bernard Ward), St Edmund's became affiliated to Cambridge University, buildings were extended, the Exhibition Room (now the Rhetoric study area) was built, the Divines' Wing was built (and then rebuilt after a fire), and there were many other improvements.

Bernard Ward published a number of books, the most notable of which were the *History of St Edmund's College* (1893), *St Edmund's College Chapel* (1903), *The Menology of St Edmund's College* (1909), *The Dawn of the Catholic Revival in England, 1781-1803* (1909), *The Eve of Catholic Emancipation, 1803-1829* (1911) and *The Sequel to Catholic Emancipation, 1829-1850* (1915).

His brothers Granville Ward (1868-73) and Wilfrid Ward (1869-73) were great benefactors of the College. Bernard Ward was appointed the first Bishop of Brentwood in 1917.

16th President 1916-1918: Very Rev Canon Edwin Burton DD FRHistS

Edwin Hubert Burton; born 12 August 1870; student 1883-85; staff 1898-1918; died 13 December 1925

The relatively short period of office served by Canon Burton belies the fact that he contributed a great deal to the College. He received schooling at St Edmund's, Oscott and Ushaw, and qualified as a solicitor before deciding on the priesthood.

He was Vice-President for 14 years. He made numerous donations towards the cost of stained glass windows in the Chapel. He reorganised the College Museum. Of the many books he wrote, one of his best is considered to be the *Life and Times of Bishop Challoner*. Ill health forced Canon Burton to resign from the College, though he was later well enough to set up a new parish in London. At the time of his death he was chaplain to a convent in Harrow.

Canon Edwin Burton

17th President 1919-1932: Most Rev Edward Myers MA
Edward Myers; born 8 September 1875; student 1893-97; staff 1903-32; died 13 September 1956

As a deacon, Edward Myers had been Prefect of Discipline and he continued to hold this office after his ordination. He had at his disposal an instrument of correction known as the "paddycock", which was a piece of heavy leather attached to a stick. It was said that no Prefect ever wielded this with more deadly accuracy or with more telling effect!

Fr Myers later became Professor of Dogmatic Theology and Patrology, a position he held for the next ten years. On one occasion, when Mgr Ward, the President, and Canon Burton, the Vice-President, were stricken simultaneously with grave illness, Fr Myers at a minute's notice was called upon to assume the duties of them both.

Fr Myers became President at a moment when, apparently, the affairs of the College were at their lowest ebb. He ruled until 1932, and it was during these years that St Edmund's emerged from that period of uncertainty into prosperity.

Archbishop Edward Myers

He oversaw the implementation of the House system, which were conceived by Cardinal Francis Bourne, and a vast building programme which included the construction of the Galilee Chapel, the School Block, and the Douay Hall.

On leaving the College, Edward Myers was appointed as Auxiliary Bishop of Westminster, and became coadjutor to Cardinal Griffin in 1951, though he did not live to succeed him.

18th President 1932-1946: Rt Rev Mgr Canon Francis Bickford VG MC
Francis Philip Bickford; born 12 January 1889; St Hugh's, College & Allen Hall 1899-1913; staff 1932-46; died 6 December 1968

Ordained at the College in 1913, Francis Bickford went on to be come a military chaplain during the First World War. He served with the 47th Lancer Division and was mentioned in despatches. He was awarded the Military Cross. After the War, he worked as an assistant priest in various parishes, and became rector at a house for late vocations in Edmonton in 1928.

After he was appointed President of St Edmund's, he set about various essential building works, such as redecorating the Chapel and resurfacing the front drive to cope with modern traffic. St Hugh's was extended.

The added responsibilities of being appointed Vicar General, together with the stress of running the College during the Second World War, took a toll on Mgr Bickford's health. He stood down and became rector of Edmonton and later, in 1958, chaplain at Tyburn Convent.

Mgr Francis Bickford

19th President 1946-1952: Rt Rev Mgr Canon John Bagshawe

John Bernard Bagshawe; born 1902: Allen Hall 1925-29; staff 1946-52; died 25 May 1971

Mgr John Bagshawe

Having spent a short time in the banking profession, Mgr Bagshawe was a late vocation to the priesthood, the early years of which he spent in the Education Department and then with the Finance Board. After a short spell as parish priest of Borehamwood he returned to Archbishop's House as Financial Secretary: a difficult task, as many churches had been damaged during the air raids and the work of getting money, building permits, materials, and so on.

He was appointed President at one of the most difficult periods in the history of the College. He was faced with the difficulties following on the post War years. He oversaw the reconstruction of St Edmund's, involving major tasks like the opening of a new infirmary, laying out more playing fields, the erection of a new wash-block, painting and redecoration of the College interior, the resuscitation of The Edmundian Association, and securing recognition of efficiency by the Ministry of Education.

When he left St Edmund's he was set the task of rebuilding the parish church of our Lady of Victories, Kensington. It was a ruin when he took over, having been bombed during the Second World War.

In his leisure time Mgr Bagshawe enjoyed game shooting, and on one occasion discharged the barrels of his shotgun – at a rabbit – from the open window of the President's Room at the front of the College!

20th President 1952-1964: Rt Rev Mgr Reginald Butcher MA

Reginald Albert Claver Butcher; born 9 September 1905; Allen Hall 1924-28; staff 1933~64; died 22 November 1975

Mgr Reginald Butcher

Reginald Butcher came into Allen Hall from Downside in 1924, and was ordained priest at the age of just 22. After five years gaining a History degree in Cambridge, he returned to the College in 1933 as an assistant master, and was appointed Housemaster of Challoner in 1937, leaving in 1942.

He spent much of the next ten years at the Cardinal Vaughan School, latterly as Headmaster, and elsewhere, before returning to St Edmund's as President in 1952.

One of the first things he did was to appoint Hal King as his Bursar. Methodically they set about tackling the remaining backlog of repairs and modernisation left by the Second World War. After making a complete survey of the condition of the College, the buildings were re-roofed, re-wired and re-plumbed. Day-boys were introduced, the sports facilities were extended, and much was done to improve the living accommodation of staff. The Godfrey Wing was built at St Hugh's.

Mgr Butcher retired shortly after suffering a stroke in 1963.

21st President 1964-1968: Rt Rev Mgr Canon Maurice Kelleher

Maurice J Kelleher; born 22 December 1912; Allen Hall 1930-36; staff 1964-68; died 13 February 1994

Maurice Kelleher was educated at St Aloysius College, Highgate, before he came to St Edmund's. After his ordination in 1936, he was assistant priest in three parishes, was appointed parish priest of St Margaret's-on-Thames in 1955, and moved to Our Lady of Willesden four years later.

In 1964, he was appointed President of St Edmund's. The four years of his presidency were crucial in the life of the Church and seminary because the decrees of the Second Vatican Council had a profound influence on professors and students, which made great demands upon the President.

Mgr Kelleher's time at St Edmund's took its toll and he was grateful to return to work in a parish. In 1968 he became parish priest of Our Lady of Victories, Kensington, where he remained until his retirement in 1983. In his later years he undertook responsibility for the welfare of sick and retired priests and was on the committee of the Catholic Children's Society.

Mgr Maurice Kelleher

22nd President 1968-1986: Rt Rev Christopher Butler OSB VG MA LLD

Basil Christopher Butler; born 1902; in residence 1967-85; died 20 September 1986

Bishop Christopher Butler

Educated at Reading School and St John's College, Oxford, where he distinguished himself by taking a triple First, Christopher Butler decided to enter the Anglican priesthood and received the diaconate before entering the Catholic Church in 1928. He went to Downside to teach and joined the novitiate there, being ordained priest in 1933. He was Headmaster of Downside from 1940 to 1946. In the latter year he was elected Abbot of the community, an office he was to hold until he was made Auxiliary Bishop in the Westminster Diocese in 1966.

When the newly consecrated Bishop Butler arrived at St Edmund's in 1967, the College already had a President, but he took over when Mgr Kelleher left the following year. His appointment coincided with the appointment of a new Rector of the seminary and a new Headmaster of the school. The Governing Body was established under Butler's chairmanship in 1969, and he remained Chairman until 1985.

The finances were not in a good condition in 1968, and Bishop Butler was called upon to give the experience of his time as Abbot of Downside, and to use his persuasive influence with Cardinal Heenan to obtain a much needed injection of capital into the College. When the time came, in 1975, for Allen Hall to move to Chelsea, it was made clear that no further subsidies were to be expected from Westminster. However, the school expanded into the vacated part of the building and flourished.

Bishop Butler was the last President who was permanently resident at St Edmund's and the only one to be Chairman of Governors.

23rd President 1986-1999: His Eminence Basil Cardinal Hume OSB OM MA STL

George Basil Hume; born 2 March 1923; died 17 June 1999

George Basil Hume was a Benedictine monk who, prior to his ordination as ninth Archbishop of Westminster, had been Abbot of Ampleforth for thirteen years.

He was installed as Archbishop on 25 March 1976 and was created Cardinal-priest of San Silvestro in Capite by Pope Paul VI on 24 May 1976.

The Cardinal was President of the Bishops' Conference of England and Wales from 1979. He was President of the Council of European Bishops' Conferences from 1978 to 1987. He was also joint President of Churches Together in England from 1990.

In 1999 the Queen conferred on the Cardinal the Order of Merit.

Cardinal Basil Hume

24th President 2000-present: His Eminence Cormac Cardinal Murphy-O'Connor STL PhL

Cormac Murphy-O'Connor; born 24 August 1932

Training for the priesthood at the Venerable English College in Rome, Cormac Murphy-O'Connor took his degrees at the Gregorian University, Rome. He was ordained priest in Rome on 28th October 1956.

Returning to England, he served in parishes in the Diocese of Portsmouth, and in 1966 he became private secretary and chaplain to the Bishop of Portsmouth, Derek Worlock. After a brief spell as a parish priest, he was appointed Rector of the Venerable English College in 1971, giving him the responsibility for the training of students for the priesthood.

On 21 December 1977, Cormac Murphy-O'Connor was ordained Bishop of the diocese of Arundel & Brighton. He was installed as 10th Archbishop of Westminster on 22 March 2000. In 2000 he was elected President of the Bishops' Conference of England and Wales.

Cardinal Cormac Murphy-O'Connor

He was created a cardinal by Pope John Paul II in February 2001, and was presented with the titular church of Santa Maria sopra Minerva. In January 2002, at the invitation of Her Majesty Queen Elizabeth II, Cardinal Murphy-O'Connor was the first member of the Catholic hierarchy since 1680 to deliver a sermon to an English monarch.

Vice-Presidents

From 1793 to 1795 Dr William Coombes (1795-1808) acted as "second in authority and respect" and was the superior of the Divines. The office of Vice-President was introduced on the formal constitution of St Edmund's in 1795. The post was disbanded in 1926 when the position of Headmaster was created.

Heads of St Hugh's were also referred to as Vice-Presidents; they are listed in the Houses chapter.

1795-1801	– Rev William Poynter DD (1795-1813)	1855-1861	– Rev Herbert Vaughan DD (1855-61)
1801-1808	– Rev William H Coombes DD (1795-1808)	1861-1868	– Rev Frederick Rymer DD (1835~70)
1808-1810	– Rev Francis Tuite (1795-1810)	1868-1870	– Rev Isaac Goddard (1854~70)
1810-1813	– Rev Joseph Kimbell (1795-1819)	1870-1877	– Rev John Rouse DD (1855~77)
1813-1816	– Rev Robert Varley (1795-1816)	1877-1880	– Rev George Akers MA (1877-82)
1816-1818	– Rev Thomas Griffiths (1805~34)	1880-1882	– Rev William J Smullen (1866~82)
1819-1824	– Rev John White (1807~24)	1882-1887	– Rev William A Lloyd (1858~87)
1824-1834	– Rev Richard Newell DD (1811~37)	1887-1889	– Rev William Traies MA (1887-89)
1834-1836	– Rev Bernard Jarrett (1818~36)	1890-1893	– Rev Bernard Ward (1868-1916)
1836-1838	– Rev John Maguire DD (1827-38)	1893-1895	– Rev Edmond Nolan (1876~96)
1838-1840	– Rev Edward Cox DD (1822~51)	1895-1901	– Rev Charles T Kuypers (1882~1901)
1840-1843	– Rev George Rolfe (1818~43)	1902-1916	– Rev Edwin H Burton DD (1905~18)
1843-1851	– Rev William Weathers DD (1843-69)	1916-1918	– Rev Edward Myers MA (1893~1932)
1851-1855	– Rev John Crookall DD (1834~55)	1919-1926	– Rev John G Vance MA PhD (1905~26)

Governing Body

The Governing Body, which first met on 5 May 1969, is responsible for the general conduct of the College as an independent Roman Catholic school. The chairman is elected by the Archbishop of Westminster, and at any one time there are not more than twelve elected governors, each initially serving for three years, and they may be re-elected for further periods, though normally not exceeding eight years in total. The Governors are responsible for the appointment of the Headmaster and the Bursar.

Chairmen
1968-1985 – Rt Rev Bishop B Christopher Butler OSB VG MA LLD (1967-86)
1985-1994 – John M Gillham MC KCSG KCHS FCIOB
1995-1999 – George P Lehrian LLB FHCIMA (1941-49)
2000-present– J Ivor O'Mahony BSc(Econ) FCA (1945-53) *Acting Chairman from 1999*

Deputy Chairmen
1987-1988 – Charles E Carey MA (1946-55)
1989-1993 – Bruce Elsmore MA PhD FRAS
1993-1994 – George P Lehrian LLB FHCIMA (1941-49)
1995-1999 – J Ivor O'Mahony BSc(Econ) FCA (1945-53)
1999-2003 – H Michael Burgess BSc (1945-51)
2003-present – Jeremy M Gillham BA (1963-69)

Governors

1969-1985 – Rt Rev Bishop B Christopher Butler
OSB VG MA LLD (1967-86)

1969-1970 – Rt Hon Earl of Longford

1969-1976 – Sir Alan C Burns GCMG (1900-03)

1969-1976 – Very Rev Canon Garrett D Sweeney MA

1969-1978 – Very Rev Canon Clement Rochford
(1919~43)

1969-1971 – Sir John Newsom CBE HonARIBA

1969-1984 – Kevin G T McDonnell BSc(Econ) PhD
(1939-45)

1969-1981 – Michael R W Ward (1941-47)

1969-1971 – F Bramston Austin *owner of Standon
Lordship*

1971-1976 – Sir Peter A G Rawlinson PC QC MP

1971-1983 – Professor John (Jack) J Scarisbrick

1974-1994 – John M Gillham MC KCSG KCHS
FCIOB

1976-1987 – Thomas D P Emblem (1931-33)

1976-1985 – Rt Rev Bishop David E Konstant MA
(1943-54)

1976-1985 – Rev John Coventry SJ

1978-1984 – Rt Rev Mgr Canon Terence D Keenan
(1916-27)

1980-1986 – Mrs Jean M Hewson BA

1981-1982 – Sister Helen Costigan FCJ

1982-1990 – Charles E Carey MA (1946-55)

1982-1990 – Sister Mary Shepherd FCJ BA

1984-1992 – David Black RD BA MLitt MSc

1984-1989 – Very Rev Mgr Canon Frederick A Miles
MA (1939~67)

1984-1992 – Very Rev Canon Peter B Phillips MA
(1940~67)

1985-1990 – Mrs Pauline Matthias BA DipEd

1985-1993 – Kenneth R Allen BSc ARCS (1951-56)

1986-1994 – Christopher R Hutchison MA MB
BChir MRCP (1956-63)

1986-1999 – George P Lehrian LLB (1941-49)

1986-1989 – John G Collier MA LLB

1986-1994 – Bruce Elsmore MA PhD FRAS

1988-1990 – Peter G Collett

1990-1998 – John D Crowley QC (1949-56)

1990-1996 – Rev Daniel C Higgins MA MusB FRCO
(1950~75)

1990-1995 – Mrs Marcia H Jaques BA(Econ) LHS

1991-2001 – Mrs Margaret Edmondson BA DipEd
DipCG

1991-1999 – Mrs Mary M Edwards LHS

1991-1994 – Peter G Morgan LLB MinstP (1956-63)

1991-1999 – Anthony F W Powell DL

1992-2000 – Very Rev Canon Brian A Frost
STL (1936-44)

1992-present – J Ivor O'Mahony BSc(Econ) FCA
(1945-53)

1993-2001 – Very Rev Canon Desmond C Sheehan
KHS (1946-58)

1994-2002 – John Tudor MB MA MRCS LRCP
DRCOG FRCR

1995-2003 – H Michael Burgess BSc (1945-51)

1995-2003 – Terence H McLaughlin PhD MA

1996-1998 – Mrs Finola M Berger LLB

1997-2000 – John Fry KCHS FCA (1946-47)

1998-present – Mrs Patricia Newton (née
Bessey) BSc DipArch FFB RIBA
MBAE LHS

1998-present – Jeremy M Gillham BA (1963-59)

1999-present – John L Lipscomb KSG KCHS MA
MSc

2000-present – Very Rev Provost Michael J Brockie
JCL (1954-67)

2000-present – David B A Hirst KSG KGCHS FCA

2000-present – Stephen Szemerenyi BA

2002-present – Mrs Jessica Bushell MA

2002-2003 – Rt Rev Mgr Phelim C Rowland VG
RAChD (1969-74)

2002-present – Mrs Mary (Moira) Lynch BSc ARCS
NPQH

2003-present – Patrick J Mitton BSc MSc

2003-present – Very Rev Canon Michael J Roberts
MA (1958~88)

2003-present – Michael J Hutchison FCA (1956-65)

2003-present – Sister Jean Sinclair SHCJ BSc

chapter 3

Headmasters & senior staff

Prefects of Studies

The office of Prefect of Studies came from Douay and, as its name suggests, it was held by the professor who organised the boys' studies. Dr William Poynter (1795-1813), the last to have held the office at Douay, was the first to do so at St Edmund's. When he became President, he was succeeded by Dr William Coombes (1795-1808). The title appears to have been abandoned after 1808, and no records exist until 1859. It was Fr William Lloyd (1858~87) who, in the 1880s, raised the academic standard to public school level in preparing students for the London University examinations. Dr Joseph Tynan (1890~1918) was also referred to as the "Headmaster". The title Prefect of Studies was discontinued in 1924. There were 16 recorded Prefects of Studies, with an average length of known completed service of just over five years, the longest serving of these, with 14 years, was Mgr Bernard Ward (1868~1916).

1795-1801	Rev William Poynter DD (1795-1813)	1877-1880	Rev George Akers MA (1877-82)
1801-1808	Rev William H Coombes DD (1795-1808)	1880-1882	Rev Charles Hogan (1861~82)
1808-1844	*No records exist for this period*	1882-1887	Rev William A Lloyd (1858~87)
Circa 1859	Rev Joseph Styles (1844~59)	1887-1890	Rev William Traies MA (1887-89)
1859-1860	Rev George Bampfield (1859-60)	1890-1904	Mgr Bernard Ward (1868~1916)
1860-1861	Very Rev Canon Thomas Doyle (1812~67)	1904-1917	Alfred Herbert MA PhD (1874~1919)
1861-1868	Rev Frederick Rymer DD MA (1835~69)	1917-1918	Rev Joseph Tynan DD PhD BA (1890~1918)
1868-1871	Rev George C Carter (1857-71)		
1871-1877	Rev John Rouse DD (1855-64)	1919-1924	Rev Thomas E Flynn MA PhD (1917-24)

General Prefects

The role of General Prefect, which was commonly abbreviated to Prefect, was introduced in 1795. Not to be confused with the current system of prefects, who are senior students, the General Prefect was a professor responsible for discipline. Indeed in its latter years, the jobholder was referred to as the Prefect of Discipline. There was a traditional term of office of three years, though this was rarely adhered to. The role ended when the House system was set up in 1922. In total there were 52 different General Prefects (four served twice), with an average length of service of about two and a half years. The longest serving of was Fr Joseph Stapleton (1800-16), who undertook the role for six years.

1795-1798	Rev John Law (1795-1800)	1825-1826	Rev Edward Ewart (1825-36)
1798-1800	Rev Francis Tuite (1795-1810)	1826-1827	Rev John Welch (1818-27)
1800-1802	Rev J C Richard D'Ancel (1795-1802)	1827-1828	Rev William Woods (1820-28)
1802-1803	Rev Francis Tuite (1795-1810)	1828-1830	Rev Charles Threlfall (1818~38)
	& Rev Walter Blount (1798-1804)	1830-1833	Rev William Hunt (1819~33)
1803-1806	Rev Joseph Kimbell (1795-1819)	1833-1834	Rev Bernard Jarrett (1818~36)
1806-1810	Rev Robert Varley (1795-1816)	1834-1836	Rev Edward Hearne (1822-36)
1810-1816	Rev Joseph Stapleton (1800-16)	1836-1839	Rev John Tilt (1824~39)
1816-1819	Rev John White (1807~24)	1839-1840	Rev John E Telford (1827-40)
1819-1820	Rev Joseph Sidden (1813-21)	1840-1843	Rev William Weathers DD (1843-69)
1820-1822	Rev Richard Newell DD (1811~37)	1843-1848	Rev Henry Telford (1827~56)
1822-1825	Rev James Holdstock (1820-25)	1848-1851	Rev Frederick Rymer DD (1835~70)

The last General Prefect and his assistants: (standing) Edward Dix, Terence Keenan, Leslie Biggie, Reginald Crook & Freddy Berringer; (seated) Jospeh McEntee (Head Prefect), Fr Robert McCliment & Stephen Rigby

1851-1851	–	Rev Michael Canty (1845-53)
1851-1856	–	Rev Henry O'Callaghan (1843-61)
1856-1861	–	Rev Thomas McDonnell (1842~61)
1861-1865	–	Rev Charles E Bell (1852~65)
1865-1866	–	Rev James R Browne (1862-67)
1866-1868	–	Rev William A Lloyd (1858~87)
1869-1869	–	Rev Edward Redmond DD (1856-69)
1869-1872	–	Rev John Brenan (1861-74)
1872-1873	–	Rev William A Lloyd (1858~87)
1873-1874	–	Rev John Brenan (1861-74)
1874-1876	–	Rev Peter Kernan (1857~76)
1876-1877	–	Rev William Herbert (1866~77)
1877-1879	–	Rev William J Smullen (1866~82)
1879-1881	–	Rev John O'Meara (1879-81)
1881-1882	–	Rev Edward Ryan (1867~82)
1882-1884	–	Rev Bernard N Ward (1868~1916)
1884-1884	–	Rev John Boase (1868~85)

1884-1884	–	Rev John Watson (1884-84)
1884-1885	–	Rev Bernard N Ward (1868~1916)
1886-1891	–	Rev William J Davies (1879~93)
1891-1894	–	Rev Frederick Hopper (1874~94)
1894-1898	–	Rev John J Wren (1884~98)
1898-1902	–	Rev James M Driscoll DD BA (1883~1902)

Also known as Prefect of Discipline from this time

1902-1905	–	Rev Edward Myers MA (1893~32)
1905-1907	–	Rev Thomas L Williams MA (1904-10)
1907-1912	–	Rev Austin A J Askew (1894~1917)
1912-1916	–	Rev Francis D Healy MA (1892~1929)
1916-1917	–	Rev Austin A J Askew (1894~1917)
1917-1917	–	Rev William J Heffernan (1903~24)
1918-1918	–	Rev Augustine Brogden (1914-18)
1918-1919	–	Rev George D Smith DD (1906~60)
1919-1922	–	Rev Robert J McCliment BA OBE (1907~22)

Headmasters

The separate post of Headmaster was created in 1926, and there have been eight Headmasters since 1926, with each completing an average of just under eleven years. The longest serving was Fr Denis Britt-Compton (19 years) and the shortest Fr Francis Healy (3 years).

1926-1929: Rev Francis Healy MA
Francis Dolores Healy; born 17 September 1882; student 1892~1908; staff 1908~29; died 11 June 1933

"Tim" Healy came to St Edmund's as a Church boy. He went to Cambridge where he took his degree in Classics. On his return to the College in the summer of 1908 he was ordained priest and was immediately appointed to the staff. For several years he taught mostly French, though he seems to have taken classes in nearly every subject in the school.

In 1912 he was made Prefect of Discipline, and he became Housemaster of St Hugh's in 1920. He became the first Headmaster on the creation of the post in 1926. He then had to run two posts at the same time, for in 1927 he took over the housemastership of Douglass. He was for years Secretary of the Edmundian Association.

Fr Francis Healy

Tim Healy left the College in 1929 for health reasons and became Rector of St Mary Moorfields in London. He died at the early age of 51 and is buried in the crypt under the College chapel.

1929-1936: Dr Albert Purdie PhD MA OBE
Albert Bertrand Purdie; born 27 August 1888; student 1900-13; staff 1922-36; died 30 May 1976

Not long after Albert Purdie's ordination in 1914 came the outbreak of war. He volunteered as a military chaplain, latterly as Senior Catholic Chaplain of the British forces at Salonika and Constantinople, being mentioned in dispatches and awarded the OBE for courage and bravery. On his return he entered Christ's College, Cambridge, where he obtained an Honours degree in Classics and a diploma in Classical Archaeology.

In 1922 Fr Purdie was appointed to the teaching staff of the College, became the first housemaster of Challoner, and later Headmaster in 1929. His dual role affected his health and, after some sick leave, he took a sabbatical year at Fribourg University, becoming a Doctor of Philosophy. He returned to the College in 1936, but later in the same year he resigned under medical advice.

Dr Albert Purdie

From 1938 until 1949 he ran Royston parish, and when war broke out in 1939 he once more became a military chaplain this time appointed to serve an RAF camp stationed on the Bedfordshire border close at hand. He retired at age 60 to Goring-on-Sea.

1936-1940: Rev Thomas Sherlock BSc
Thomas Patrick Sherlock; born c.1900; Allen Hall 1923-27; staff 1927-40; died 26 May 1945

After taking a degree in Chemistry at London University, Thomas Sherlock taught for two years at Stonyhurst before entering the seminary at Allen Hall. During his last year, he was appointed to do some teaching in the school, and remained on the staff after his ordination in 1927, his subjects being mathematics and chemistry. He became acting headmaster during Dr Purdie's absence in 1932-33, following which he became housemaster of Challoner in 1933, until he succeeded Dr Purdie in 1936.

During Thomas Sherlock's time as headmaster, the school curriculum was expanded, photographic and musical societies were founded, public examinations were taken at an earlier age, and more time was allocated to physical training. He resigned at the end of 1940 because of ill health. The subsequent strain of work in a parish in Fulham proved too much, and instead he went to Oxford to do research into the history of chemistry.

Fr Thomas Sherlock

1941-1949: J Haldane Walton-King TD KSG MA
John Haldane Walton-King; born 1907; staff 1930-76; died 13 May 1983

Known affectionately as "Rex", Hal King read History and Economics at Cambridge, and after getting his degree he began to teach in a crammers establishment near Oxford. He came to St Edmund's in 1930 to coach rugby and teach mathematics. He was one of only two or three laymen on the staff, and the only one who was not a Catholic. After only a few years he was received into the Church.

He wrote a book *Rugby Football for the Learner-player*, which became recommended as a standard text-book on the subject. He took over the Officers' Training Corps (the forerunner of the CCF) and ran this with efficiency for over 20 years. He took particular pride in the Corps of Drums, which won the band competition at the annual summer camp at Tidworth within five years of its founding. He was also an Editor of *The Edmundian* magazine.

Hal King

In December 1940, Cardinal Hinsley asked Rex King to succeed Fr Sherlock. He was faced with a difficult task: as a new convert, he was placed over a staff which consisted mainly of priests; and with no experience of housemastering, he had to direct three experienced priest housemasters, one at least of whom had probably expected to succeed Fr Sherlock.

Under his direction the numbers in the school increased and it was well run. It must have been a shock for him in 1949 when Cardinal Griffin requested that he stand down as Headmaster as he wanted a priest in that post. He accepted the demotion he had received through no fault of his own, and worked as assistant master under Fr Britt-Compton. The situation changed when Mgr Butcher was appointed President in 1952 and promptly asked Rex King to become Bursar.

More is written about him later in this book on page 119.

1949-1968: Very Rev Canon Denis Britt-Compton MA

Denis Charles Henry Britt-Compton; born 9 October 1912; Douglass & Allen Hall 1926~39; staff 1947-68; died 10 May 2002

"Britt", as he was universally known, was ordained priest in 1939, went to Downing College, Cambridge, to read Geography, and on the strength of a good degree was invited to remain in the Department of Geography and Geology as a Demonstrator, supervising students and organising field trips. He was appointed Vice-Rector of St Edmund's House. In 1947 he was recalled by the Diocese to the school teaching staff at St Edmund's and appointed Headmaster by Cardinal Griffin in 1949.

Britt was to succeed a highly respected lay Headmaster, Rex King, who had led the school through the difficult years of the Second World War. Moreover he was faced with the inevitable wartime neglect to the College buildings and services and the continuing shortage of supplies.

In fact, the school had recently suffered the indignity of failing a government inspection with the threat of a repeat and final inspection in the near future. He was credited with ensuring St Edmund's survival and continuation as a school with the necessary, official recognition as 'Efficient' by the Ministry of Education. He was also responsible for swelling the numbers in the school with the entry of day boys.

Canon Denis Britt-Compton

His interests and enthusiasms were permanently demonstrated by the meteorological 'beehive' in the College grounds and the pond that he dug behind the school block teeming with newts and frogs.

He resigned in 1968 when he was diagnosed as suffering from cancer. Yet he survived for a further 34 years, becoming the parish priest of St John Fisher's, Chorleywood, and then some years later – despite being severely injured as a passenger in a car crash – he served as chaplain at St Mary's, Shaftesbury.

1968-1984: Rev Michael Garvey MA

Michael Gustav Garvey; born 16 February 1925; Douglass & Allen Hall 1940-49; staff 1953-84; died 24 May 2002

First educated at St Ignatius' College, Stamford Hill, Michael Garvey transferred to St Edmund's in 1940, having already decided to become a priest. He became House Captain, Head Prefect and captain of the First XV. Proceeding to the seminary, Allen Hall, in 1943, he eventually became Senior Divine. After ordination to the priesthood in 1949 and study at Cambridge, Fr Garvey returned to St Edmund's, via teaching practice at Downside, as a member of the staff.

Having been Assistant Headmaster since 1964, four years later, to his dismay, he was appointed Headmaster. Only a year earlier, Michael Garvey had asked Cardinal Heenan for permission to leave the College, as he longed for a more pastoral ministry with the physically disabled.

Shortly after his appointment as Headmaster, Michael Garvey was elected to the Headmasters' Conference. He broadened the curriculum by including biology, installed a language laboratory and

Fr Michael Garvey

up-to-date craft department and increased music teaching. In anticipation of the removal of the seminary to Chelsea, the school grew, three new boys' Houses were opened in the Senior School, Junior House expanded, girls were admitted into the sixth form and overall numbers almost doubled.

Two major appeals, in 1978 and 1980, resulted in the creation of the music school, the Douay Hall becoming a theatre, the "covered playground" (now the Butler Hall) being built, and urgent preservation work being carried out on the Chapel.

He led many pilgrimages for the handicapped to Lourdes. He became an expert on the Pugin Chapel.

On retiring from the College, Michael Garvey embarked on a long-cherished plan to spend six months in a village of leprosy sufferers in India, but this had to be curtailed by ill health. After a brief period as parish priest of Rickmansworth, he became chaplain to the Carmelite nuns at Ware.

More is written about Fr Garvey later in this book on page 118.

1984-2002: Donald McEwen KCHS MA FRSA
Donald James John McEwen; born 11 December 1943; staff 1984-2002

Donald McEwen was the second lay headmaster of St Edmund's, and was formerly a housemaster at the Oratory School, Woodcote.

His period in office saw possibly the greatest number of changes at the College. New subjects were added to the curriculum, and the College had to embrace new examinations such as GCSEs and GNVQs.

With the closing of Poles Convent in the mid-1980s, St Edmund's became co-educational throughout. A thriving International Summer School was established at the College. St Hugh's was extended with a new Nursery & Infant Department. The number of students rose to a record number of 623.

At the end of his term of office, a new extension in the North quadrangle was built and named the McEwen Wing.

Donald McEwen

2002-present: Mark Loughlin PhD

The current Headmaster is a graduate of the University of Edinburgh and is a former international hockey player.

Dr Loughlin came to St Edmund's from Charterhouse, Godalming, where he had been a housemaster and head of history. His duties there included overseeing the needs of the Catholic students at the school.

He has six daughters, five of whom are currently students in the College.

He runs the College at a time when it has the highest ever number of students and staff.

Dr Mark Loughlin

Other Senior Staff

Assistant Headmasters

1958-1960	–	Rev Laurence Allan MA (1936~60)
1960-1964	–	Rev Harold E Winstone MA (1937~71)
1964-1968	–	Rev Michael G Garvey MA (1940~84)
1968-1980	–	Rev Bernard V Lagrue MA MSc FRAS (1946~93)
1980-1985	–	Cecil P A Friedlander BSc PhD ARCS (1968-85)

Deputy Headmasters & Headmistresses

1980-1986	–	Rev Bernard V Lagrue MA MSc FRAS (1946~93)
1986-1994	–	David J K Walters MA (1986-97)
1994-2001	–	David R Black BSc MPhil PhD CChem MRSC LTCL (1970-2003)
1994-present	–	Mrs Janet Neal BA (1989-present)
2001-present	–	Christopher P Long BA (2001-present)

David Walters
Deputy Headmaster 1986-1994
& Registrar 1994-1995

Dr David Black
Deputy Headmaster 1994-2001

Heads of the Centre for Advanced Studies (CFAS)

1993-1995   –   Stephen W Blake BA (1971-95)
1995-1999   –   Mrs Marie P O'Shea BA (1989-present)
1999-2003   –   James E Sheridan BSc MA (1999-2003)

Head of Boarding

2003-present –   Duncan A Gallie KM BEd
                 (1976-present)

Registrars

1992-1994   –   Graham A C P Sawyer BA AIL
                 (1992-94)
1994-1995   –   David J K Walters MA (1986-97)
1995-present –   Ross Parsons MA (1995-present)

Stephen Blake
Housemaster of Stapleton
1975-1991
Head of CFAS 1993-1995

The President & Staff 1896

Procurators & Bursars

Role of Procurator was created in 1795, the job involved managing the College finances and estate. The first person to fill the role at St Edmund's was Fr Francis Tuite (1795-1810), who had been the last Procurator at St Omer. The first reference to a "Bursar" was in 1908, when for a while the job was split into inside and outside roles, the latter being responsible for the management of the estate. From time to time there have also been Assistant Bursars. There have been a total of 45 different Procurators or Bursars (excluding outdoor Bursars and Assistants), two served twice and one three times, each completing an average of just over four and a half years service. The longest serving was Hal King (1930-76) who did the job for 24 years.

Michael McEvoy
Bursar 1993-1997

1795-1798	Rev Francis Tuite (1795-1810)
1798-1800	Rev John Law (1795-1800)
1800-1810	Rev Francis Tuite (1795-1810)
1810-1815	Rev Richard Horrabin (1801-15)
1815-1817	Rev Joseph Daniel (1808-17)
1817-1818	Rev John Rolfe (1807~40)
1818-1819	Rev Mark A Tierney (1810-19)
1819-1824	Rev Thomas Griffiths DD (1805~34)
1824-1830	Rev John Clarke (1817~30)
1830-1832	Rev Charles Threlfall (1818~38)
1832-1839	Rev James Whelan (1816~39)
1839-1843	Rev George Rolfe (1818~43)
1843-1851	Rev William Weathers DD (1843-69)
1851-1852	Henry Reilly (1851-52)
1852-1856	Rev Henry Telford (1827~56)
1856-1861	Rev Edmund Tunstall (1845~94)
1861-1878	Rev William McAuliffe (1852~78)
1878-1879	Rev Edmund Tunstall (1845~94)
1879-1880	Rev Joseph Palmer (1879-80)
1880-1883	Thomas Inwood (1869~83)
1883-1885	Rev Edward St John (1883-85)
1886-1887	Rev Arthur Byrne (1886-87)
1888-1891	Rev Charles Turner (1881-91)
1891-1893	Rev William J Davies (1879~93)
1893-1894	Rev Edmund Tunstall (1845~94)
1894-1898	Rev Cyril A Shepherd (1876~98)
1898-1901	Rev Charles T Kuypers (1882~1901)
1901-1902	Rev Francis W Gilbert (1890-1902)
1902-1903	Rev Augustine O'Leary (1890~1903)
1903-1906	James A Dobson (1884~1913)
1906-1908	Rev Joseph L Whitfield (1891~1906)

At this point the use of the word "Bursar" is introduced; the following were referred to as the "inside Bursar"

1908-1909	Rev William J Foley (1898-1909)
1909-1911	Raymund Bourne (1909-19)
1911-1912	James A Dobson (1884~1913)
1912-1915	Rev Peter J Brady (1900-15)
1915-1915	Philip Mosdell-Smith (1902~15)
1915-1915	Rev Edwin H Burton DD (1905~18)
1915-1916	Rev John G McGrath (1906~16)
1916-1919	Raymund Bourne (1908-19)

Between 1908 and 1919, Raymund Bourne acted as "outside Bursar"

1919-c.1922	Rev Wilfred Harrington (1912~c.1922)
c.1922-1926	Mortimer Harvey (c.1922-26)
1926-1937	Rev Clement Rochford (1919~43)

Known solely as "Bursar" from 1937 onwards

1937-1949	Rev F Leo Straub FCA (1932-49)
1949-1952	Rev John (Jack) Halvey (1933~52)
1952-1976	J Haldane Walton-King TD KSG MA (1930-76)
1976-1984	Capt Joseph J Phillips RN (1976-84)
1984-1992	Brigadier Charles Hince CBE FBIM (1984-92)
1993-1997	Michael N McEvoy MIMgt(1993-97)
1998-present	Graham T Black ACIS ACIB (1998-present)

Pope John Paul II congratulating Fr Leo Straub (1937-49), former Bursar, outside St Peter's in Rome, on the sixtieth anniversary of his ordination to the priesthood in 1997 (Photo © L'Osservatore Romano)

chapter 4

The Houses

It was Mgr Patterson who decided, when Dr Ward left, to use Old Hall House (as it was then called) as a preparatory school, and to make it as homely as possible to make the break between home and school life as smooth as it could be. In the autumn of 1874 boys in the lowest two years were transferred from the College into the new school, which was placed under the patronage of St Hugh. St Hugh's Preparatory School was opened by Mgr Patterson on 17 November 1874 – St Hugh's Day.

It was not until September 1922 that the next Houses were established. The House system, which was fundamentally a Catholic concept, was introduced to make the education of the College more effective, and to offer the advantages of the public school with, according to the prospectus of the time, "its insistence on manliness, initiative, character and responsibility". At the same time the Divines' Wing was renamed Allen Hall.

Each of the first Houses was self-contained in that they had their own dormitories, common rooms and dining rooms. Douglass was exclusively for those who were being groomed later to enter the priesthood (known as church boys). Challoner & Talbot Houses were intended "for those who are to aim afterwards at the services, professions, or the higher walks of commercial and industrial life". Each House is under the control of a Housemaster or Housemistress, and has a senior pupil appointed each year as House Captain. Allen Hall was under the control of a Rector, who until 1968 was also President of the College, with a Senior Divine being the equivalent of house captain.

From 1945, Douglass was no longer exclusively for church boys. Junior House was opened the same year to accommodate eleven and twelve year olds; it was disbanded in 1953 but later reopened in 1960.

As the school grew in the early 1970s, further Houses were established: Poynter House in 1970 and Griffiths House in 1972. Some of the senior girls from the school at Poles Convent (located at what is now a hotel known as Hanbury Manor) came to St Edmund's once a week to take part in General Studies classes, and from September 1974, five girls became full-time Rhetoric students at the College.

The students for the priesthood in Allen Hall moved away in 1975 when a new Allen Hall was established in Beaufort Street, Chelsea. This enabled the school to take over the space they occupied, and at that time Stapleton was established, together with a dedicated girls' House called Margaret Pole.

Subsequent organisational changes saw the disbanding of Griffiths in 1984, with the students distributed around the other Houses. Margaret Pole closed in 1990 and a new House called Pole was set up. From that year, all Houses accommodated girls and boys, but with Challoner and Poynter being exclusively for boarders, and Douglass, Pole, Stapleton and Talbot for day pupils. Junior House was disbanded in 1993, and Stapleton in 1996. Because of a reduction in the number of boarders, day pupils entered Challoner and Poynter from 2002.

The pages which follow provide, where applicable, lists of all the Housemasters and Housemistresses. For the senior school, House Captains recorded since 1954 are also listed. Before that time, the Houses each had several House Prefects, and official records are incomplete and unreliable. Information has been gleaned from *The Edmundian* magazine and other sources. House Captains will normally have served from September until July the following year (apart from Allen Hall) unless indicated otherwise.

Allen Hall

Years: 1922-1975 (the divinity students returned to the College in 1904; the Divines' Wing was completed in 1905 and was renamed Allen Hall in 1922)
Patron: Cardinal William Allen, founder of the English College at Douay in 1568
Approximate number of students since 1904: 1,100
House colours: none

Divinity Students 1904

Rectors
Rather than having their own Housemaster, the students in Allen Hall came under the control of the President of the College. Between 1968 and 1975, Mgr James O'Brien (1948~75) was Rector of Allen Hall.

Senior Divines
The senior divines were generally appointed from June to June the following year unless stated otherwise

1905-1906	– Austin A J Askew (1894~17) *from Sep*
1906-1907	– Edward O'Sullivan (1903-07)
1907-1908	– Francis Rusher (1895~08) *to Jul*
1908-1910	– Kenneth F L Wigg (1898-1910) *to Feb*
1910-1911	– G Lionel Smith (1903-11) *to Jul*
1911-1913	– Francis P Bickford (1899~46)
1913-1914	– Lancelot E Long (1906~21)
1914-1916	– Joseph J Warren (1905~24) *to Jul*
1916-1917	– Thomas F Bishop (1905-17) *to Apr*
1917-1917	– Patrick O'Donnell (1909-17) *to Dec*
1917-1918	– John E Howell (1908-18) *to May*
1918-1919	– Hugh P McCourt (1909~22)

1919-1922 – *not recorded*	1946-1947 – George Swanton (1941-47)
1922-1923 – Frederick W Dixon (1909~23)	1947-1948 – William Anthony (1944-48)
1923-1924 – Henry D Bryant (1922-24)	1948-1949 – Michael G Garvey (1940~84)
1924-1925 – James E Hathway (1915-15)	1949-1950 – Frederick A Miles (1939~67)
1925-1926 – John C Murphy (1914~32)	1950-1951 – Selwyn Horne (1945-51)
1926-1927 – Terence D Keenan (1916-27)	1951-1952 – John Keep (1946~64)
1927-1928 – Harold J Carter (1922-28)	1952-1953 – Herbert K Mullaney (1948-53)
1928-1929 – Reginald Crook (1917-29)	1953-1954 – Ernest T Bassett (1948-54)
1929-1930 – *not recorded*	1954-1955 – John Gibbons (1949-55)
1930-1931 – John F Marriott (1921-31)	1955-1956 – Thomas Power (1950-56)
1931-1932 – L Malachy Feeny (1927-32)	1956-1957 – Peter D O'Reilly (1951-57)
1932-1934 – Cuthbert Collingwood (1929-34) *2 years*	1957-1958 – D Bruce Kent (1952-58)
1934-1935 – Eric G Chadwick (1929-35)	1958-1959 – Clifford P Beecroft (1953-59)
1935-1936 – Samuel J Steer (1925-36)	1959-1960 – Patrick J Heekin (1954-60)
1936-1937 – Sidney F Dommersen (1931-37)	1960-1961 – William Lynagh (1955-61)
1937-1938 – Joseph MacCabe (1932-38)	1961-1962 – Austin Hart (1956-62)
1938-1939 – Francis Lang (1934-39)	1962-1963 – John Shea (1957-63)
1939-1940 – Denys C Lucas (1934~64)	1963-1964 – Francis Hegarty (1958-64)
1940-1941 – Wilfrid Stibbs (1935-41)	1964-1965 – Brendan Soane (1959-65)
1941-1942 – John J Clayton (1936-42)	1965-1966 – John D Younger (1960-66)
1942-1943 – Thomas Kilcoyne (1937-42)	1966-1967 – John Budden (1961-67)
1943-1944 – Joseph Law (1938-44)	1967-1968 – John Taylor (1962-68)
1944-1945 – Wilfred Soggee (1939-45)	1968-1969 – Vincent Crewe (1963-69)
1945-1946 – Francis Thomson (1940-46)	1969-1975 – *not recorded*

The last students of Allen Hall in 1975

Challoner

Years: 1922 to present
Patron: Bishop Richard Challoner,
founder of the school at Standon Lordship in 1749
Approximate number of students since 1922: 1,200
House colours: blue and silver

Challoner House 1994

Housemasters

1922-1932	– Rev Albert B Purdie PhD MA OBE (1900~36)
1932-1933	– Rev Howard Joyce (1916~33) Acting housemaster
1933-1937	– Rev Thomas P Sherlock BSc (1923-40)
1937-1942	– Rev Reginald A C Butcher (1924~42)
1942-1945	– Rev Nicholas J Kelly DHE (1924~61)
1945-1947	– Rev Timothy D Healy MA (1942-47)
1955-1960	– Rev Benedict F Westbrook MA (1927~65)
1960-1967	– Rev Frederick A Miles MA (1939~67)
1968-1971	– Paul F J Ketterer BA (1945~71)
1971-1980	– John E Murphy BSc (1969-80)
1980-1985	– Dr Cecil P A Friedlander BSc PhD ARCS FZS (1968-85)
1985-1988	– R Michael Lewis BEd (1979-present)
1988-present	– Duncan A Gallie KM BEd (1976-present)

House Captains

1954-1956	– Patrick R Sheridan (1946-56)
1956-1957	– Malcolm A Stewart (1946-63)
1957-1958	– John D (Sam) Langham Service (1947-58)
1958-1959	– Adrian R Morris (1952-59)
1959-1960	– John J Deacon (1956-60)
1960-1961	– John C M Hughes (1956-61)
1961-1962	– Derek C Lance (1957-62)
1962-1963	– Christopher J B (Kit) Slade (1953-63)
1963-1964	– Jeremy P A G Janion (1957-64)
1964-1964	– Peter A Rowe (1959-64) *to Dec*
1965-1965	– Peter A Knight (1954-65) *from Jan*
1965-1966	– Ronald A Middleton (1958-66)
1966-1966	– David J Pearson (1961-66) *to Dec*
1967-1968	– Terence P Keane (1963-68) *from Jan*
1968-1968	– Michael J Stone (1962-68) *to Dec*
1969-1969	– Peter H M Lightfoot (1959-69) *from Jan*

1969-1970	– Martin G Fairweather (1963-70) *to Feb*	1991-1992	– Roger A James (1985-92)
1970-1970	– John M Hannah (1965-70) *from Feb*		Pek Shang (Celine) Tang (1990-92)
1970-1971	– A Keith Dickinson (1961-71)	1992-1993	– Nuno M C Alves (1987-93)
1971-1971	– Richard M Ballard (1967-71) *to Dec*		Tara C Cowan (1986-93)
1972-1972	– Sergio A M Solari (1969-72) *from Jan*	1993-1994	– George M Saleh (1987-93)
1972-1973	– Simon H O'Neill (1966-73) *to Dec*	1994-1995	– Wendy L Casey (1986-95)
1974-1975	– Peter G Stone (1970-75) *from Jan*		Simon P A Lampard (1986-95)
1975-1976	– Gerard M Delaney (1971-76)	1995-1996	– Deborah M Fitz-Gibbon (1987-96)
1976-1978	– Timothy A P Weatherstone (1970-78)		Peter C D Young (1989-96)
1978-1979	– Fergal J O'Brien (1972-79)	1996-1997	– Andrew J Lampard (1987-97)
1979-1980	– Jonathan L Grace (1971-80)	1997-1998	– Thomas A Koe (1990-98)
1980-1981	– Peter J Clayson (1971-81)		Natalie M Saleh (1991-98)
1981-1982	– Michael D Holland (1975-82)	1998-1999	– Edmund K Fultang (1997-99)
1982-1983	– Victor M M Tarruela de Oriol (1977-83)	1999-2000	– Claire M Kyndt (1998-2000)
1983-1984	– Nicholas A Steele (1979-84)		Jonathan C Meyer (1991-2000)
1984-1985	– Francis J Gunn (1978-85)		Carl Toma (1996-2000)
1985-1986	– Augustine U F Imevbore (1984-86)		Claude Toma (1996-2000)
1986-1987	– Andrea Rigamonti (1984-87)	2000-2001	– Dumebi A Okwechime (1993-2001)
1987-1988	– Joseph K Kahama (1984-88)	2001-2002	– Robert T Kennedy (1995-2002)
1988-1989	– A Anthony Elegbede-Fernandez (1981-89)	2002-2003	– David Gerty (1995-2003)
1989-1990	– Jeffrey Fenech (1984-90)	2003-2004	– Sergey Kornev (1999-present)
1990-1991	– Marielle L B G Kasmiris (1985-91)		Maria J Sheridan (1999-present)
	James P O'Brien (1984-91)		

Mr Duncan Gallie
The current Housemaster

Alex Roberts (1954-61)
with his former Housemaster Canon
Frederick Miles

Dumebi Okwechime
House Captain 2000-2001

Douglass

Years: 1922 to present
Patron: Bishop John Douglass, who oversaw the construction of the main College building from 1795
Approximate number of students since 1922: 1,340
House colours: cardinal & black

Douglass House 1992

Housemasters & Housemistresses

1922-1922 – Rev Edward Myers MA (1893~1932)
           Temporary Housemaster
1922-1924 – Rev Joseph J Warren MA (1905~24)
1924-1927 – John M T Barton DD LSS FSA FRSA
           (1915-36)
1927-1929 – Rev Francis D Healy MA (1892~1929)
1929-1941 – Rev John P McKenzie (1921~41)
1941-1949 – Rev William A Purdy STL(1939-49)
1949-1953 – Rev Peter P Geraerts MA (1929~53)
1953-1960 – Rev Harold E Winstone MA (1937~71)
1960-1967 – Rev Peter B Phillips MA (1940~67)
1968-1990 – John Vaughan-Shaw BA (1964-present)
1990-1994 – Mrs Janet Neal BA (1989-present)
1994-2001 – Mrs M Carol M Lewis MSc FZS
           (1976-2003)
2001-present – Andrew L Moss (1986-present)

Dr William Purdy
Housemaster 1941-1949

House Captains

1954-1955	–	Charles E Carey (1946-55)
1955-1955	–	John D Crowley (1949-56) *to Dec*
1956-1956	–	C John McHaffie (1953-59) *from Jan*
1956-1958	–	Patrick Carey (1948-64) *2 years*
1958-1959	–	Ronald J Gladman (1954-59)
1959-1960	–	Andrew D Toomey (1950-60)
1960-1961	–	Michael A P O'Mahony (1955-61)
1961-1964	–	Christopher J Ryan (1953-64) *3 years*
1964-1964	–	F Timothy Harrison (1956-64) *to Dec*
1965-1965	–	John M Murphy (1958-65) *from Jan*
1965-1965	–	Spencer J Hamill (1956-65) *to Dec*
1966-1966	–	Paul C McGinn (1960-72) *from Jan to Dec*
1967-1967	–	Aidan F M Heathcote (1960-67) *from Jan*
1967-1969	–	John C Sidery (1962-69) *to Dec*
1970-1970	–	Mirko P Kurtanjek (1965-70) *from Jan*
1970-1971	–	John M C Bryant (1962-71) *to Dec*
1972-1972	–	Christopher D Gardiner (1965-72) *from Jan*
1972-1973	–	Johnson H T Lee (1969-73)
1973-1974	–	Jeral S d'Souza (1969-74)
1974-1975	–	Charles J Hardcastle (1971-75)
1975-1976	–	David H Thomas (1968-76)
1976-1977	–	Edmund R F Hewson (1970-77) *to Dec*
1978-1978	–	Colin C Mayor (1971-78) *from Jan*
1978-1979	–	Mark C Burnell (1970-79)
1979-1980	–	David L Hughes (1974-80)
1980-1981	–	Peter G M Stacey (1971-81)
1981-1982	–	Michael C Hughes (1974-82)
1982-1983	–	Habib K Sayegh (1976-83)
1983-1984	–	Mark H Copping (1974-84)
1984-1985	–	Ying-Kiun (Vincent) Pang (1979-85)
1985-1986	–	Mark J Lee (1979-86)
1986-1987	–	Robert J Boos (1982-87)

1987-1988	–	Daniel J Webster (1981-88)
1988-1989	–	Odafe Sideso (1982-89)
1989-1990	–	Ediri Sideso (1982-90)
1990-1991	–	Jacqueline P McIntyre (1987-91)
		Bankole A Odunuga (1984-91)
1991-1992	–	Simon J Logue (1983-92)
		Sara V K N Toruň (1986-92)
1992-1993	–	Sarah J Pedder (1986-93)
1993-1994	–	Mark J Estwick (1987-94)
		Jennifer A Hardy (1987-94)
1994-1995	–	Vanessa M Banz (1991-95)
		Simon M Thompson (1988-95)
1995-1996	–	Ryan F J Fernandes (1989-96)
		Purdey-Emma Silvester (1989-96)
1996-1997	–	Jane E Moor (1990-97)
		Mark E Vaughan-Shaw (1989-97)
1997-1998	–	Charlotte Dewson (1989-98)
		Joanna L Pinkney (1988-98)
1998-1999	–	Alastair T D'Oyley (1988-99)
		Claire L Kasza (1988-99)
1999-2000	–	Elizabeth A Hamilton-Hastings (1993-2000)
		Andrew P Murphy (1998-2000)
2000-2001	–	Victoria E Foster (1994-2001)
		Peter G Vaughan-Shaw (1993-2001)
2001-2002	–	Natalie M Kersey (1991-2002)
		Thomas O M Marks (1995-2002)
2002-2003	–	Vita Geraldi (1996-2003)
		Zubeen J Khan (2001-03)
2003-2004	–	Zara Barouch (1997-present)
		Matthew J Elliott (1995-present)
		Aimee H Foster (1997-present)
		Nicasio R Geraldi (1997-present)
		Kathryn J (Katie) Merrick (1997-present)

Purdey-Emma Silvester House Captain 1995-1996

Simon Thompson House Captain 1994-1995

Natalie Kersey House Captain 2001-2002

Griffiths

Years: 1972-1984
Patron: Bishop Thomas Griffiths, President of the College responsible for building
the present Chapel
Approximate number of students: 190
House colours: brown & silver

Griffiths House 1978

Mr Philip Ward
Assistant Housemaster
1974-1980

Housemaster
1972-1984 – William T Gribbin BA (1968-91)

House Captains
1972-1973 – Gilbert J Ellacombe (1965-73)
1973-1974 – Francis C J Dick (1970-74)
1974-1975 – Staffan A Kordina (1972-75)
1975-1976 – Thomas C Hart (1971-76)
1976-1977 – Christopher A Sanders (1972-77)
1977-1978 – Brett J Sanders (1972-78)
1978-1979 – Michael J C Martin (1972-79)
1979-1980 – M J Ailbe McCormack (1974-80)
1980-1981 – Samuel F N Mpyisi (1976-81)
1981-1982 – David J Watkins (1975-82)
1982-1982 – R Simon Duggan (1978-82) *to Nov*
1982-1983 – Andrew R Webb (1976-83) *from Nov*
1983-1984 – Séan J Murphy (1976-84)

Junior House

Years: 1945-1953 & 1960-1993
Approximate number of students: 1,400 (not all students in the earlier years are
accurately shown in the school records)
House colour: dark green

Junior House 1961

Junior House 1982

Housemasters

1945-1951 – Rev Nicholas J Kelly DHE (1924~61)
1951-1953 – Rev Laurence Allan MA (1936~60)
1960-1964 – Rev Michael G Garvey MA (1940~84)
1964-1969 – Rev Daniel C Higgins MA MusB FRCO
(1950~75)

1969-1971 – Rev Michael J Roberts (1958~88)
1971-1993 – Rev Michael P A Pinot de Moira
(1944~present)

Margaret Pole

Years: 1975-1990
Patron: Blessed Margaret Pole who was the patron of Poles Convent
Approximate number of students: 260

The first girls: (L to R) Marianne Orchard, Corinna Wood, Mary-Anne Wright-Jones, Anne Mullineaux & Catherine Thick

Mrs Dorothy Bassett Housemistress 1987-1990

Blessed Margaret Pole

Born Margaret Plantaganet on 14 August 1471, she was the daughter of the Duke of Clarence, and niece of Edward IV & Richard III. She married Sir Richard Pole in 1491 and had five children, one of whom became Reginald Cardinal Pole. Henry VIII made her Countess of Salisbury and governess to Princess Mary. When she opposed the king's plans to marry Ann Boleyn, she was driven from court. When Cardinal Pole, wrote against Henry VIII's presumptions to spiritual supremacy, the king decided to crush the family. Two of Margaret's sons were executed in 1538 for the crime of being the brothers of the Cardinal. The elderly Margaret Pole was arrested soon afterwards, falsely charged with plotting revolution, and in 1539 sent to the Tower of London where she spent her remaining two years. In 1541 she was summarily executed by beheading. She was beatified by Pope Leo XIII in 1886.

Housemistresses

1975-1976 – Mrs Deirdre J Skinner TITC (1975-76)	1981-1982 – Deborah M Ford (1980-82)
1976-1976 – Mrs Joan Freyne (1976-86)	1982-1983 – Catherine A M Mellors (1981-83)
1976-1987 – Mrs Jean M Irwin (1976-86)	1983-1984 – Cynthia F Catalino (1982-84)
1987-1990 – Mrs Dorothy A B Bassett BSc (1980-94)	1984-1985 – Alison J McGrory (1983-85)
	1985-1986 – Ailsa T C Fitzwilliam (1984-86)

House Captains

1975-1976 – not recorded	1986-1987 – Karla A M Boyce (1985-87)
1979-1980 – Carol A Kneebone (1977-80)	1987-1988 – Kirsten J Andrews (1986-88)
1980-1981 – Yuen Man (Ivy) Chan (1979-81)	1988-1989 – Sharon M Lennon (1985-89)
	1989-1990 – Emma J Wilson (1986-90)

Pole

Years: 1990 to present
Patron: Blessed Margaret Pole
Approximate number of students since 1990: 300
House colours: dark blue & silver

Pole House 1999

Housemaster & Housemistress

1990-1995 – Kevin J Corrigan BA MA (1985-95)
1995-present – Mrs Jacquelyn A Ball CertEd
(1987-present)

House Captains

1990-1991 – Joanne E Langham (1989-91)
Peter J Warmerdam (1981-91)
1991-1992 – Katharyn S Bailey (1986-92)
Matthew S Cunningham (1985-92)
1992-1993 – Jane R Gibson (1986-93)
Anthony D Kirkham (1987-93)
1993-1994 – Matthew O Davies (1988-94)
Sarah U Warnock (1987-94)
1994-1995 – Geraldine M Downer (1991-95)
James E Martin (1985-95)
1995-1996 – Michael T McGovern (1989-96)
1996-1997 – Rachel A Ives (1990-97)
Patrick M McCreesh (1990-97)
1997-1998 – Peter W Jarvis (1994-98)
Kristin M Lopez-Vito (1991-98)
Mark J Williamson (1991-98)
1998-1999 – Sam C Collins (1997-99)
Stuart J C Reid (1992-99)
Helen L Stafford (1992-99)

Alanna Easton
House Captain 2001-2002

1999-2000 – Juliet H Chipperfield (1993-2000)
Patrick J Cullinan (1993-2000)
2000-2001 – Caroline M L Affleck (1994-2001)
Siavash Khateri (1999-2001)
2001-2002 – Robert L Dodds (1991-2002)
Alanna C Easton (1995-2002)
2002-2003 – David O Flynne (1995-2003)
Claire E Thornton (1992-2003)
2003-2004 – James A Affleck (1997-present)
Astrid C O'Reilly (1997-present)

Poynter

Years: 1970 to present
Patron: Bishop William Poynter, who was the second President of the College
Approximate number of students since 1970: 720
House colours: dark green & silver

Poynter House 1982

Housemasters

1970-1990 – Brendan A Cannon BA (1964-93)
1990-1994 – Kenneth M Hall MA (1970-present)
1994-present –　Colin M Jenkinson BEd
　　　　　　　　(1980-present)

House Captains

1970-1970 – Eamonn S Vincent (1964-70) *to Dec*
1971-1971 – David J Smith (1965-71) *from Jan*
1971-1972 – Mark J Tilbury (1969-72)
1972-1974 – Martin B Smits (1967-74) *2 years*
1974-1975 – W Paul Williams (1968-75)
1975-1976 – Simon C Fuller (1966-77)
1976-1977 – Roy P D Darkin (1967-77)
1977-1978 – Christopher St J C Jackson (1971-78)
1978-1979 – Brian A Luxton (1974-79)
1979-1980 – Stephen P Marsden (1975-80)
1980-1981 – Michael K Hodges (1971-81)
1981-1982 – Stephen J McGrory (1977-82)

1982-1983 – Stephen P Pennicott (1972-83)
1983-1984 – Ashley J Cooper (1977-84)
1984-1985 – Gavin N Turney (1978-85)
1985-1986 – James T Frenzel (1979-86)
1986-1987 – Aidan P Casey (1982-87)
1987-1988 – Martin J S Da Costa (1981-88)
1988-1989 – Martin A S Cavana (1980-89)
1989-1990 – Luke J W McEvoy (1981~90)
1990-1991 – Ondine Sinfield (1986-91)
　　　　　　　John C Williams (1985-91)
1991-1991 – U Venessa Nwokoye (1990-91) *to Dec*
1991-1992 – William T Pargeter (1986-92)
1992-1992 – Jenny U Nwosu (1990-92) *from Jan*
1992-1993 – Colm M P Clarke (1986-93)
　　　　　　　Clare L Edwards (1991-93)
1993-1994 – James P G Balaam (1986-94)
　　　　　　　Annabel S Gillham (1986-94)
1994-1995 – Nicholas C McMenemy (1988-95)
　　　　　　　Caroline J Smith (1990-95)

1995-1996	– Marcus J Hayakawa (1991-96)	1999-2000	– Simon J Constant (1992-2000)
1996-1997	– Thomas D Ball (1990-97)		Martha J Gribbin (1993-2000)
	Sarah A Clark (1993-97)		Antonia I (Tina) Mortensen (1990-2000)
	Felicity R Lillywhite (1990-97)		David A Storring (1990-2000)
	Paul A Whatnell (1990-97)	2000-2001	– Bozhidara Ianeva (1994-2000)
1997-1998	– Martin L Docherty (1992-98)		Stephen R P Watson (1996-2001)
	Fern K Edwards (1991-98)	2001-2002	– Christopher J Georganas (2000-02)
1998-1999	– K Moses Igho (1996-99)	2002-2003	– Stefan Bratu (1999-2003)
	Anna F Lillywhite (1992-99)		J Toby Gribbin (1996-2003)
	Jack T I Tilley-Gyado (1997-99)	2003-present	– Tolani A Ladejo (2000-present)
			Dimitar S Stoyanov (2000-present)

Mr Brendan Cannon
Housemaster 1970-1990

Mr Kenneth Hall
Housemaster 1990-1994

Felicity Lillywhite
House Captain 1996-1997

St Hugh's

Years: 1874 to present
Patron: St Hugh of Lincoln, upon whose patronal feast day – 17 November – St Hugh's was formally opened
Approximate number of students since 1874: 2,600
House colours: red & silver

St Hugh's 1990

Patrick Foort
Headmaster 1964-1974

Heads of St Hugh's

Between 1874 and 1920, the Headmasters of St Hugh's were also known as Vice-Presidents

1874-1878	– John A Evans (1874-78)
1878-1879	– Rev James Connolly (1878-79)
1880-1884	– Rev Fenwick Skrimshire (1869~84)
1884-1884	– Rev Edward St John (1883-85)
1884-1888	– Rev Frederick Hopper (1874~94)
1888-1891	– Rev Victor Soenens DD (1868~92)
1891-1893	– Rev Charles T Kuypers (1882~1901)
1893-1897	– Rev Cyril A Shepherd (1876~1900)
1897-1899	– Henry M Cross MA (1897~1904)
1899-1900	– Rev Cyril A Shepherd (1876~1900)
1900-1903	– Rev G Nicolas Sullivan (1886~1903)
1903-1918	– Rev Ernest J Nolan (1877~1918)
1918-1920	– Francis R Stanes (1914-20)

Between 1920 and 2002, St Hugh's was led by a Housemaster or Housemistress, with one exception shown below

1920-1927	– Rev Francis D Healy MA (1892~1929)
1927-1928	– Rev Edward G H Armitage (1920~28)
1928-1933	– Rev John C (Jack) McGrath (1914~1933)
1933-1940	– Rev Leonard A Clark (1917~40)
1940-1949	– Rev Joseph Murray (1922~49)

Mrs Dorothy Elliott
Housemistress 1996-2002

1949-1964	– Rev Denys C Lucas (1934-64)
1964-1974	– Patrick I M Foort MA (1959-74)
	Headmaster
1974-1981	– Anthony H Hollington-Sawyer BA (1970~81)
1981-1988	– Peter G M Nicholson BEd (1974-88)
1988-1989	– Richard P Poole CertEd (1988-89)
1989-1996	– Robert M Maidment BA CertEd (1969~99)
1996-2002	– Mrs Dorothy M Elliott BSc (1989-2002)

From 2002 St Hugh's is led by a Headmistress

2002-present	– Mrs Jacqueline Hart MSc BEd AdvDipRE (2002-present)

Stapleton

Years: 1975-1996
Patron: Bishop Gregory Stapleton, who was the first President of St Edmund's College
Approximate number of students: 370
House colours: purple & crimson

Miss Penelope Dixon
Housemistress 1991-1996

Stapleton House 1991

Housemaster & Housemistress
1975-1991 – Stephen W Blake BA (1971-95)
1991-1996 – Penelope Dixon BA (1991-96)

House Captains
1975-1976 – *not recorded*
1976-1977 – Michael J Smith (1969-77)
1977-1977 – Douglas G H Ansley (1968-77) *to Dec*
1978-1978 – John C Hollerton (1976-78) *from Jan*
1978-1979 – Graham B Farrer (1970-79)
1979-1980 – Peter J Frost (1975-80)
1980-1981 – Vincent P Quinn (1975-81)
1981-1982 – Mark J Sweeney (1975-82)
1982-1983 – Richard A Vass (1973-83)
1983-1984 – Laith F Bazzoui (1980-84)
1984-1985 – Theodore O P Olaiya (1978-85)
1985-1986 – A Olutayo Oyekoya (1979-86)
1986-1987 – Alexandre H M Uyt den Bogaard
(1982-87)
1987-1988 – Michael R Routh (1981-88)
1988-1989 – P Abayomi Oyekoya (1979-89)
1989-1990 – Carlos A Alvarez (1985-90)
1990-1991 – Helen Y Murton (1986-91)
Robert J Pound (1986-91)

Annette Emms & Clive-Andrew Graham
House Captains 1995-1996

1991-1992 – Matthew J Campbell (1987-92)
Rebecca L Twort (1986-92)
1992-1993 – Roger G Elliott (1986-93)
Aislinn S Ryan (1991-93)
1993-1994 – Mark E Davis (1987-94)
1994-1995 – Ciara M A O'Shea (1989-95)
1995-1996 – Annette G Emms (1990-96)
Clive-Andrew J Graham (1989-96)

Talbot

Years: 1922 to present
Patron: Bishop James Talbot, who transferred the school to Old Hall in 1769
Approximate number of students since foundation: 1,150
House colours: red & silver

Talbot House 1935

Mr John Piper
Housemaster 1975-1994

Housemasters & Housemistress

1922-1925	–	Laurence E Eyres MA (1921-25)
1926-1926	–	Gerald E Headlam MA (1924-26)
1927-1933	–	Rev Leonard A Clark (1917~40)
1933-1937	–	Rev James Stevenson (1923~37)
1937-1942	–	Rev Joseph A Scholles BA (1921~42)
1942-1949	–	Rev Wilfrid Purney (1931-49)
1949-1953	–	Rev David J Norris (1936~53)
1953-1958	–	Rev Laurence Allan MA (1936~60)
1958-1964	–	Rev Oliver B Kelly MA (1942~60)
1964-1966	–	Rev C Austin Garvey (1945~66)
1966-1969	–	Rev Bernard V Lagrue MA MSc FRAS (1946~93)
1969-1975	–	Rev Daniel C Higgins MA MusB FRCO (1950~95)
1975-1994	–	John F Piper BA (1969-2000)
1994-2001	–	Mrs Patricia H Pond BSc (1991-2001)
2001-2002	–	Dominic P Wadsworth BEd (1998-2002)
2002-present	–	Adrian D Petty BA FRSA (2001-present)

House Captains

1954-1955 – Paul C Geraerts (1944-55)	1984-1985 – Ka-Lai (Joe) Chan (1979-85)
1955-1956 – Joseph J Artesani-Lyons (1952-56)	1985-1986 – Inigo Aranguren Lozano (1983-86)
1956-1957 – Christopher N Reed (1947-57)	1986-1987 – Simon P Geoghegan (1980-87)
1957-1959 – David A R Peel (1951-59)	1987-1988 – Majid N Shenouda (1982-88)
1959-1961 – S Guy A Scammell (1950-61)	1988-1989 – A George Nwokedi (1982-89)
1961-1962 – Antony L White (1957-62)	1989-1990 – George O Fernandes (1985-90)
1962-1963 – Christopher R Hutchison (1956-63) *to Dec*	1990-1991 – Massimo Lavagno (1986-91)
1964-1964 – Christopher J Gillham (1958-64) *from Jan*	1991-1992 – Helen E Piper (1987-92)
	David J Turpin (1988-92)
1964-1965 – Michael J Hutchison (1956-65)	1992-1993 – Susannah M Judd (1986-93)
1965-1965 – Adrian B Gillham (1960-65) *to Dec*	Nathan R S Long (1986-93)
1966-1966 – Anthony M Lidgate (1963-66) *Jan to Dec*	1993-1994 – Ian G Clifford (1987-94)
1967-1967 – Michael R White (1961-67) *Jan to Dec*	1994-1995 – David J Beatty (1985-95)
	Emily L Turpin (1988-95)
1968-1968 – Edward J Rooney (1963-68) *from Jan*	1995-1996 – Andrew McAleer (1989-96)
1968-1969 – David A Rozalla (1959-69)	Laura-Jane H Michelson (1989-96)
1969-1969 – Jeremy M Gillham (1963-69) *to Dec*	1996-1997 – Fleur-Louise Asser (1990-97)
1970-1970 – Andrew P Thick (1961-70) *Jan to Dec*	James D Gardiner (1990-97)
1971-1972 – Barrie F Duncan (1963-72) *from Jan*	James R O Mackay (1990-97)
1972-1972 – Henry J S Whitney (1966-72) *to Dec*	1997-1998 – Stephen A Judd (1989-98)
1973-1973 – Simon J Gillham (1966-73) *Jan to Dec*	Camilla M Sinnott (1991-98)
1974-1974 – Ian F Lovat (1968-75) *from Jan*	1998-1999 – Prisca D Hefti (1996-99)
1974-1975 – Fabio M Perselli (1971-75)	Alexander-Josef Konrath (1992-99)
1975-1977 – John A Luke (1969-77) *2 years, to Dec*	Gemma L Sandford (1992-99)
1978-1979 – C William (Liam) Shevlane (1971-79) *from Jan*	1999-2000 – George M Beckley (1993-2000)
	Rita Sedani (1993-2000)
1979-1980 – Christopher P Miller (1972-80)	2000-2001 – Carla L Murray (1991-2000)
1980-1981 – Brian A Mulholland (1971-81)	2001-2002 – Stephen Agyei-Boateng (1995-2002)
1981-1982 – Francis A Nwokedi (1975-82)	2002-2003 – David J Howie (2001-03)
1982-1983 – Gerhard H A Wallbank (1976-83)	Sophie R Wilson (1994-2003)
1983-1984 – Graham K Weston (1976-84)	2003-2004 – Kelly A Jordan (2002-present)
	Alan H Miller (1997-present)

Grand House Challenge

The Grand Challenge Cup was first awarded in 1926 and was given to the House excelling overall in a range of sports. Winners are as follows:

Challoner: 1926-27, 1933, 1939-40, 1944, 1946, 1951 *(shared with Douglass)*, 1952-53, 1958-59, 1961-63, 1966, 1971-78
Douglass: 1928-32, 1934-35, 1941-43, 1945, 1947, 1951 *(shared with Challoner)*, 1954-56, 1960, 1968-70, 1993-94, 1998, 2001 *(shared with Pole)*
Pole: 1999, 2001 *(shared with Douglass)*
Poynter: 1980-82, 1985-88, 1991, 1995-97
Stapleton: 1983-84, 1989-90
Talbot: 1936-38, 1948-50, 1957, 1964-65, 1967, 1979, 1992, 2000, 2002-03

Overall Challoner has won 24 times (once shared with Douglass), Douglass 24 times (once shared with Challoner and once with Pole); Talbot 14 times, Poynter 11 times, Stapleton 4 times, and Pole twice (once shared with Douglass).

chapter 5

Church & religion

The precise number of Edmundians who were ordained as priests is not known, although records suggest that it is in excess of 1200. Some went on to hold senior positions within the Church, most served for the rest of their lives in parishes and on overseas missions, and a few entered the teaching profession, at St Edmund's and elsewhere.

Clerical Edmundians are mentioned in many parts of this book because of different achievements. This chapter mentions a few who are not touched upon elsewhere, lists those who became bishops, and also those who were priests of the parish of Old Hall Green in which the College lies.

Dr Reginald Fuller in the south door of the Douay Hall in the late 1930s

Canon Reginald Fuller DD LSS PhD: Scripture scholar

Reginald C Fuller; born 1908; Allen Hall 1926-31 & staff 1936-49

Currently the oldest known living Edmundian, Reggie Fuller has been a priest for 72 years and is an internationally renowned Scripture scholar.

After his ordination in 1931, he completed his studies in Rome in 1936 and returned to the College to teach. The Second World War started when he was aged 31, and he volunteered to be an Army Chaplain, but was not allowed to leave St Edmund's as there was no one else available there to teach Scripture.

From his window on the second floor of Allen Hall he had a clear view of the War, this being a feature of the elevated position of the College buildings. He remembers seeing the smoke rising from the bombing of the London Docks, the destruction of Dunkirk (with curtains of smoke rising 50,000 feet), and D-Day. He recollects a sky full of aircraft from east to west. Once a bomber crashed within sight of the College, and he rushed over the fields to lend what assistance he could and for some time cradled in his arms a severely injured airman until he died.

On a lighter note, he enjoyed playing rugby for the College against teams from nearby RAF airfields. His team-mates included such luminaries as Derek Worlock (later Archbishop of Liverpool) and Francis Thomson (later Bishop of Motherwell).

Between 1688 & 1850 the Catholic Church in England and Wales was divided into areas known as Districts, each led by a bishop known as a Vicar Apostolic. Dioceses were formed from 1850 onwards. Three Edmundian students became cardinals, two became archbishops, and forty became bishops. In addition, nine non-Edmundian bishops were consecrated at the College. The three Vicars Apostolic who were involved with the events leading up to the establishment of the College, Richard Challoner, James Talbot and John Douglass, never actually worked or studied at the College, and are not included in the list of Edmundian bishops below. In the list, their archdioceses are shown in bold, titular dioceses are in *italics*, and those marked with an asterisk (*) were consecrated in the former College Chapel at St Edmund's.

Francis Cardinal Bourne

Edmundian Cardinals

* His Eminence Thomas Weld, *Amycla 1826-37*, Kingston (Ontario) 1826-37 (coadjutor), Cardinal 1830-27

His Eminence Herbert Vaughan (1855-61), Salford 1870-92, **Westminster 1892-1903**, Cardinal 1893-1903

His Eminence Camillo di Rende (1800s), Tricarico 1877-79, **Benevento 1879-97**, Cardinal 1887-97

His Eminence Francis A Bourne (1875-80), *Epifania 1896-1935*, Southwark 1897-1903 (coadjutor from 1896), **Westminster 1903-35**, Cardinal 1911-35

Edmundian Archbishops

Most Rev Henry O'Callaghan (1843-61), Hexham & Newcastle 1888-89, *Nicosia 1889-1904*

Most Rev Edward Myers MA (1893~1932), *Lamus 1932-56*, Westminster (auxiliary) 1932-51, **Westminster 1951-56 (coadjutor)**

Most Rev Fulton J Sheen (1924-25), New York (auxiliary) 1951-66, Rochester (New York) 1966-79, **Caesariana (Newport) 1969-79**

Most Rev Derek J H Worlock (1934-44), Portsmouth 1965-76, **Liverpool 1976-96**

Edmundian Bishops

* Rt Rev Gregory Stapleton DD (1795-1801), *Hiero-Caesarea 1801-02*, VA Midland District 1801-02

* Rt Rev William Poynter DD (1795-1813), *Halia 1803-27*, VA London District 1812-27

* Rt Rev Peter Bernardine Collingridge OFM, *Thespia 1807-29*, VA Western District 1809-29

* Rt Rev Thomas Smith, *Bolina 1810-31*, VA Northern District 1821-31 (coadjutor from 1809)

Rt Rev Thomas Jumentier (1799-1802), Bishop in France c.1815

* Rt Rev James Yorke Bramston, *Usula 1823-36*, VA London District 1827-36

Rt Rev Thomas Penswick (Old Hall Academy), *Europum 1824-36*, VA North District 1831-36 (coadjutor from 1824)

Rt Rev Jean C R D'Ancel (1795-1802), Bayeux 1827-36

* Rt Rev Daniel McDonnell (1808-10), *Olympus 1829-44*, VA Trinidad 1829-44

* Rt Rev William M Morris OSB, *Troy 1832-72*, VA of Capo di Buono Speranza (South Africa) 1832-72

* Rt Rev Thomas Griffiths (1805~34), *Olena 1833-47*, VA London District 1836-47

Rt Rev Charles M Baggs (1822-24), *Pella 1844-45*, VA Western District 1844-45

Rt Rev Edward Barron DD (1814-18), *Constantia 1842-54*, VA The Two Guineas 1842-1854

Rt Rev James Danell (1835-43), Southwark 1871-81

Rt Rev William Weathers DD (1843-69), *Amycla 1872-95*

Rt Rev James Laird Patterson (1870-80), *Emmaus 1880-1902*

Rt Rev Gonzalo Canilla (1867-69), *Lystrensitanus 1881-98*, VA Gibraltar 1881-98

Rt Rev John E Luck OSB (1849-58), Auckland 1882-96

Rt Rev William Giles (1844-47), Philadelphia unknown-1913

Rt Rev John Vertue (1845-48), Portsmouth 1882-1900

Rt Rev John Butt (1846-49), *Melos 1885-99*, Southwark 1886-97, Sebastopolis 1897-99

Rt Rev George M Lenihan OSB (1876-77), Auckland 1896-1910

Rt Rev James Bellord (1858-70), *Milevum 1899-1905*, VA Gibraltar 1899-1905

Rt Rev John Baptist Cahill (1855-63), *Thagora 1900-10*, Portsmouth 1900-10

Rt Rev Peter E Amigo (1878-92), Southwark 1904-49

Rt Rev Patrick Fenton (1855~87), *Amycla 1904-18*

Rt Rev William A Johnson (1859-61), *Arindela 1906-09*

Rt Rev Georg Schmid von Gruneck (1872-74), Chur (Switzerland) 1908-32

Rt Rev William L Keatinge (1877-78), Bishop in Ordinary to H M Forces 1917-34

Rt Rev Bernard N Ward (1868~1916), *Lydda 1917-20*, Brentwood 1917-20

Rt Rev Arthur H Doubleday (1880-85), Brentwood 1920-51

Rt Rev James Dey (1900-02), Bishop in Ordinary to H M Forces 1934-46

Rt Rev Thomas E Flynn (1917-24), Lancaster 1939-61

Rt Rev James D Scanlan (1922-29), *Cime 1946-76*, Dunkeld 1949-55 (coadjutor from 1946), Motherwell 1955-64, Glasgow 1964-76

Rt Rev John E Petit MA (1916-18), Menevia 1947-73

Rt Rev Joseph E Rudderham (1919-21), Clifton 1949-79

Rt Rev Charles A Grant (1921-23), *Alinda 1961-89*, Nottingham (auxiliary) 1961-67, Northampton 1967-89

Rt Rev Francis Thomson (1940-46), Motherwell 1964-87

Rt Rev Patrick J Casey (1926-29), *Sufar 1965-99*, Westminster (auxiliary) 1965-69, Brentwood 1969-99

Rt Rev B Christopher Butler (1968-86), *Novabarbara 1966-86*, Westminster (auxiliary) 1966-86

Rt Rev John B Kakubi (1958-60), Mbarara (Uganda) 1969-present

Rt Rev Philip J B Harvey (1933-39), *Baanna 1977-2003*, Westminster (auxiliary) 1977-2003

Rt Rev David E Konstant (1943-54), *Betagbara 1977-present*, Westminster (auxiliary) 1977-85, Leeds 1985-present

Rt Rev James J O'Brien (1948~75), *Manaccenser 1977-present* , Westminster (auxiliary) 1977-present

Rt Rev John P Crowley (1959-65), *Tala 1986-present*, Westminster (auxiliary) 1986-92, Middlesbrough 1992-present

Rt Rev Patrick O'Donoghue VG (1961-67), Tulana 1993-present, Westminster (auxiliary) 1993-2001, Lancaster 2001-present

Rt Rev Declan R Lang (1968-75), Clifton 2001-present

Rt Rev George M L Stack (1966-72), *Gemelle di Numidia 2001-present*, Westminster (auxiliary) 2001-present

Bishop David Konstant on St Edmund's Day in 1993

Cardinal Herbert Vaughan: Founder of the St Joseph's Missionary College
Herbert Vaughan; born 15 April 1832; staff 1855-61; died 18 June 1903

Herbert Cardinal Vaughan

Five of Herbert Vaughan's seven brothers also became priests – two later bishops – and all of his five sisters became nuns. He was ordained in Italy in 1854 and his first post after ordination was Vice-President of St Edmund's.

He aimed to establish a missionary training college, embarked on a fund-raising tour in the Caribbean, South America and elsewhere, and after his return to England oversaw the building of a new college in Mill Hill in north London. Rome then assigned the evangelisation of the recently-freed black population of the southern states of the USA. Herbert Vaughan travelled to America with his first four missionary priests, leading to the establishment of a mission in Baltimore, Maryland.

He was next appointed Bishop of Salford. He was connected with the Rescue and Protection Society, a philanthropic organisation working with Catholic children in the north of England, the purchase and editorship of the Catholic newspaper *The Tablet*, and – following his ordination as Archbishop of Westminster in 1892 – the foundation of Westminster Cathedral. He was head of the Missionary Society and was able to witness the expansion of missionary activity from Mill Hill, including the establishment of additional training colleges in the Netherlands and the Tyrol, and missions to South India, West Pakistan, Brunei, New Zealand and Uganda.

Rev Adrian Fortescue BD PhD DD: Priest & scholar
Adrian Fortescue; born 14 January 1874; staff 1919-23; died 11 February 1923

Dr Adrian Fortescue

In 1891, Adrian Fortescue entered the Scots' College in Rome, and due to his musical talent was soon appointed organist. He was awarded his PhD in 1894 when he entered the Theological Faculty at Innsbruck University. He was ordained priest in 1898, and by 1905 he had passed doctoral examinations in Moral Theology, Dogma, Church History, Canon Law, Arabic and Biblical Science. In 1905 he was awarded the degree of Doctor of Divinity, making him the very rare recipient of a triple doctorate.

After holding a number of temporary positions, in 1907 he was appointed rector of the new parish of Letchworth, Hertfordshire, the world's first "garden city" founded just three years earlier. He oversaw the construction of a temporary church in 1908, which was used up until the 1960s and is now the parish hall. As well as running the parish he wrote many books.

In his study there were four desks, upon each the manuscript of a book which he was writing, and he would work at each desk depending on his mood. He was also an artist, calligrapher, composer and adventurer.

Adrian Fortescue was professor of Church History at St Edmund's for four years. He died of cancer at a relatively young age. His funeral must have been one of the most impressive given to a parish priest – the cortege is said to have stretched for nearly a mile. His vestments are now kept at St Edmund's.

Archbishop Derek Worlock CH: Archbishop of Liverpool

Derek John Harford Worlock; born 4 February 1920; Douglass & Allen Hall 1934-44; died 8 February 1996

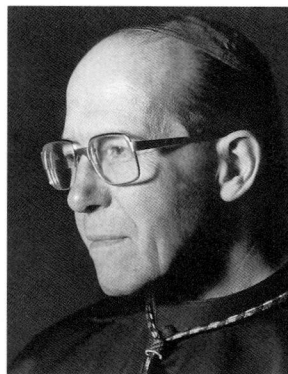

Archbishop Derek Worlock

Arguably one of the best known Edmundians, Derek Worlock was ordained to the priesthood in 1944 in Westminster Cathedral, and not long afterwards was appointed private secretary to Cardinal Griffin. He assisted successive Cardinals for some 19 years. He attended every session of the Second Vatican Council between 1962 and 1965, the year in which he was appointed Bishop of Portsmouth. Whilst in Portsmouth he set about renewing parishes, as well as undertaking the work of developing ecumenical relationships and the building of over thirty new churches in his Diocese.

In 1976 he was appointed Archbishop of Liverpool. Important events in his Cathedral included the Papal Visit in 1982 and the launch in 1990 of the Council of Churches for Britain and Ireland. Archbishop Worlock contributed to the work of reconciliation after the Toxteth riots in 1981, and in the aftermath of the football stadium tragedies at Heysel in 1985 and Hillsborough in 1989.

Archbishop Worlock was committed to evangelisation, and collaborated with his fellow Church leaders, as demonstrated by the books *Better Together* and *With Hope in our Hearts* which he and his Anglican counterpart Bishop David Sheppard jointly produced.

In July 1992 he underwent major surgery for lung cancer but survived to celebrate the fiftieth anniversary of his ordination to the priesthood two years later. In January 1994, along with David Sheppard, he was awarded the Freedom of the City of Liverpool. He was made Companion of Honour in the 1996 New Year's Honours List, but sadly died of cancer just a week before he was due to receive the honour.

Mgr Daniel Gilbert VG DD: Founder of Providence Row shelter

Daniel Gilbert; born 11 July 1827; student 1843-53; died 18 February 1895

Mgr Daniel Gilbert

After his ordination in 1853, Daniel Gilbert spent almost all his priestly life based at Moorfields in London.

In response to the poverty and homelessness he witnessed in the City and East End of London, in 1858 he worked with the Sisters of Mercy from Wexford to open a night shelter, which backed on to a small alley-way called Providence Row. By 1860 the demand for places had out-grown the available space. They bought land in Spitalfields and built a refuge to house the growing number of homeless people. That charity has now grown to become The Providence Row Housing Association, which only recently relocated to Bethnal Green, and receives govern-ment funding to run modern hostels and housing units for the homeless.

In additional to his charitable work, Daniel Gilbert held the post of Vicar General in Westminster for 25 years.

Mgr Canon Clement Parsons: Founder of two schools
Clement Henry Parsons; born 2 June 1892; student 1903-15; staff 1966-68; died 6 March 1980

Canon Clement Parsons

While he was at St Edmund's, Clement Parsons received some prizes for Scripture but his Latin was poor and special coaching was arranged – ironically he was later to coach others in Latin himself as well as teaching New Testament Greek.

He was ordained to the priesthood in 1915. Whilst still a deacon he was appointed to the Vaughan School in Kensington, a new fee-paying day grammar school, where he taught only in the mornings, and in the afternoons worked at the headquarters of the Association of the Propagation of the Faith (APF). Exhausted by his labours, in 1919 he was released from his work at the school, and transferred to St John's Wood as curate where he was to baptise another Edmundian, Derek Worlock, later Archbishop of Liverpool. Over the next few years, Clement Parsons travelled widely in support of the APF.

In 1924 he was appointed as curate at St Alban's, Finchley, but was soon put in charge of the parish upon the death of the parish priest under whom he worked. The Catholic population in this part of London had expanded rapidly since the early 1900s, but the provision of Catholic schools had not kept pace.

Fr Parsons obtained permission from Cardinal Bourne to form a school, and in September 1926 formal classes began in the church hall with just 18 boys. Within two years, having outgrown the church hall, a mansion with grounds was purchased in Woodside Park further north. In spite of depression and unemployment, the Catholic community continued to expand and the numbers in the school grew until 1939. Finchley Catholic Grammar School was recognised by the Board of Education and became first a direct grant, then a maintained school, and in 1944 a new Education Act led to the abolition of fees and the County of Middlesex helped to fund it. Many boys went on to the diocesan seminary at Allen Hall at St Edmund's.

In 1949, Fr Parsons founded the Challoner School. It is said that the first the diocesan authorities knew of this new fee-paying day school was when they received the first school magazine the following year!

Clement Parsons became a well-known and respected figure in the Finchley area. He retired from the parish in 1958, and went to Chorleywood as parish priest, where he lived until 1966. That year he returned to St Edmund's where he acted as Spiritual Director in Allen Hall until 1968, and edited *The Edmundian* magazine until 1973. Preferring to be known as Canon rather than Monsignor, he spent his final years at the College and died, after a long illness, in the sixty-fourth year of his priesthood. He is buried in the crypt under the College Chapel.

Fr Thomas Byles

Rev Thomas Byles MA: Hero of The Titanic
Roussel Davids Byles; born 26 February 1870; staff 1895-99; died 14 April 1912

The eldest son of a Congregationalist minister, Roussel Byles was educated at Leamington College and Balliol College, Oxford, obtaining his degree in 1894. He initially decided to become an Anglican minister, however he became less convinced of the Anglican Church's claims and, in 1894, entered the Catholic Church, taking Thomas as his baptismal name. Soon afterwards, he accepted a position as tutor to the second son of Prince von Waldburg-Wolfegg-Waldstein.

By now known as Thomas, he was determined to study for the Catholic priesthood, however he found the seminary at Oscott too stressful and so took up a position as a professor at St Edmund's, where he both taught and continued his studies. In 1899 he was sent to study at the Beda in Rome, the English seminary established primarily for converts and late vocations, and he was ordained in 1902. After various appointments, Fr Byles was assigned to the parish of St Helen's in Ongar, Essex, in 1905.

Fr Thomas was to bless the marriage of his brother William in the USA, and purchased a White Star Line ticket. At the last minute, his passage was changed to the Line's newest and grandest ship, the *Titanic*. The ship set sail on its maiden voyage on 10 April 1912, and on the following Sunday, 14 April, Fr Byles offered what were to be his last two Masses, one in the Second Class Lounge, followed by another for Third Class passengers. Ironically, he preached on the need to have "a lifeboat in the shape of religious consolation at hand in case of shipwreck."

The Titanic

Eyewitness accounts confirm leadership and courage with which he acted after the *Titanic* struck an iceberg. Fr Byles assisted in bringing third-class passengers trapped below decks up to the lifeboats and helped them to board. He heard over one hundred confessions, before giving general absolutions as the vessel was about to sink.

As panic set in, he is reported to have said "Be calm, my good people", raised his hand, and instantly people were calm. He began reciting the Rosary, and was joined by members of many different religions. A sailor warned the priest of the danger and twice begged him to board a lifeboat, but Fr Byles refused.

Thomas Byles perished in the freezing water. His body was never recovered.

William and his wife did not postpone their wedding: instead it was a simple ceremony, after which they changed into mourning attire and returned to the church for a Requiem Mass for Fr Byles. Later in 1912, in an audience with the newlyweds, Pope Pius X remarked that Fr Thomas Byles was "a martyr for the Church".

A memorial brass to Fr Byles has been erected at St Edmund's in Monument Lane, and his final brave acts have been recorded in the 1997 film *Titanic*, in which he is played by the actor James Lancaster.

Parish Priests of Old Hall Green

When the Old Hall Green Academy was established in 1769, **Fr James Willacy** was appointed in charge of the parish. The school chapel, located within the loft of the south wing of Old Hall, was the only Mass centre in Hertfordshire and became available for all Catholics who could attend. In 1793 a small chapel was built adjacent to Old Hall, followed in 1818 by the building which now contains the squash courts. The current parish church was built in 1911.

There have been 59 different parish priests of Old Hall Green, serving for an average total time of three years and eleven months. The longest serving was Fr Willacy, and there have been many who have served the parish for just a few months.

1769-1792 – Rev James Willacy (1769-92)
1792-1810 – Rev John Potier (1785-1810)
1810-1815 – Rev Richard Horrabin (1801-15)
1815-1818 – Rev Thomas Griffiths DD (1805~34)
1818-1819 – Rev Louis Havard (1795-1819)
1819-1824 – Rev John White (1807~24)
1824-1827 – Rev John Hutchison (1816-28)
1828-1830 – Rev John Clarke (1817~30)
1830-1838 – Rev Charles Threlfall (1818~38)
1838-1839 – Rev George Rolfe (1818~43)
1839-1840 – Rev William Crook (1838-41)
1840-1842 – Rev Patrick O'Dwyer (1839-42)
1842-1845 – Rev John Geary (1838-45)
1845-1848 – Rev John Ainsworth (1834-48)
1848-1849 – Rev John Larkin (1848-49)
1849-1851 – Rev Walter McAvila (1839-51)
1851-1859 – Rev Alfred W Delman (1840-50)
1859-1861 – Rev William A Johnson DD (1859-61)
1861-1864 – Rev Thomas Parkinson (1838-40)
1864-1864 – Rev John Wyse (1864-65)
1864-1865 – Rev Charles Bullen (1864-65)
1865-1871 – Rev Robert Swift (1836~71)
1871-1874 – Rev Charles Collingridge (1871-74)
1874-1875 – Rev Henry Joyner (1874-75)
1875-1876 – Rev Anthony Glattfelter (1875-76)
1876-1878 – Rev Philip Gun Munro (1860-79)
1878-1879 – Rev Joseph W Redman DD (1867~79)
1879-1882 – Rev John Noonan (1879-82)
1882-1883 – Rev Alfred Roche (1871~83)
1883-1883 – Rev James Horan (1883-83)

1883-1884 – Rev Daniel O'Sullivan (1883-84)
1884-1885 – Rev John H Pape (1874~85)
1885-1897 – Rev Charles Jones (1875~97)
1897-1899 – Rev William C Donlevy (1885~99)
1899-1902 – Rev Edward J Watson MA (1883~1902)
1902-1907 – Rev Francis Stanfield (1850~1907)
1907-1908 – Rev D L McGowan (1907-08)
1908-1911 – Rev Charles J Sims (1888~1911)
1911-1915 – Rev James Ridyard (1897~1915)
1915-1916 – Rev Edward Melly (1915-16)
1916-1916 – Rev William Duff (1898~1916)
1916-1919 – Rev John P Arendzen PhD DD MA (1916~54)
1919-1920 – Rev Edward J Mahoney (1905~54)
1921-1921 – Rev John Fleming (1915~21)
1921-1924 – Rev John G McGrath (1906~24)
1924-1924 – Rev James Fitzpatrick (1920-24)
1924-1924 – Canon David Dunford (1891~24)
1924-1937 – Rev Clement Rochford (1919~43)
1937-1939 – Rev Richard Crofton-Sleigh (1927-39)
1939-1943 – Rev Clement Rochford(1919~43)
1943-1944 – Rev J Michael Ware (1933~44)
1944-1945 – Rev Francis J Kelly (1929~45)
1945-1965 – Rev Michael J Lynam (1937~65)
1965-1977 – Rev Richard E D Johnson BA (1965-77)
1977-1978 – Rev James A McCormick (1946~78)
1978-1984 – Rev Thomas Gardner (1952~84)
1984-1993 – Rev Harold E Hamill (1948-54)
1993-1997 – Rev Francis I Press (1993-97)
1997-present – Rev Jeremy Davies

Gradually other new places of Catholic worship in Hertfordshire were served from St Edmund's. These included St Albans (1840), Hertford (1848), Ware (1870), Buntingford (1914), Hare Street (1917), Puckeridge (1921) (with the current church later built in 1926), Much Hadham (1939), Furneaux Pelham (1948) and Walkern (1949).

chapter 6

Military service

From the earliest years the College has been well represented in the armed forces. As early as 1795 there was a family of six Edmundian brothers who all served in the Army or Navy. John Whyte (1795-98) became an officer in the 13th Regiment of the Honourable East India Company service and was later Judge Advocate, Francis Whyte (1795-98) was a lieutenant in the 46th Regiment, Nicholas Whyte (1795-98) was a Commander in the Royal Navy, twice in action, Edward Whyte (1795-99) was a Captain in the Royal Navy, Marcus Whyte (1796-1800) was the Vice-Consul at Lima in Peru, and Henry Whyte (1803-09) a midshipman, was in action at the taking of the Rivoli. It was later that Captain Edward Whyte whose persistent and efforts in 1817 finally led to the Act of Parliament, which made it legal for Catholics to hold military commissions.

The Honorable Michael Browne (1801-09) was in the 40th Regiment of Foot. On the afternoon of 18 July 1815, he was severely wounded in both legs on the battlefield of Waterloo. An enemy officer lieutenant was halted by the wounded Englishman. The story is that the two officers immediately recognised each other – they had been at St Edmund's together – and Michael Browne's life was saved!

But many Edmundians were not so fortunate and lost their lives in the service of their country. Fr Michael Canty (1845-53) and Fr Denis Sheahan (1842-47) were both military chaplains who lost their lives in the Crimean War. Denis Cronly Dillon (1879-88) was in South Africa when Mashonaland and Matabeleland were being subjugated. In December 1893, he was a member of a patrol which was cut off by a large number of Matabele, a Zulu race. Thirty-four men faced hundreds of Zulu, and formed a circle behind the bodies of their dead horses. As their ammunition gradually ran out the tribesmen came nearer. When the last shot was fired the Zulu rushed in with their spears and massacred all the Englishmen. John Cunningham (1879-82) served in the Imperial Light Horse Regiment and died in the Boer War.

Ensign Everard March Phillipps VC: Killed during the Indian Mutiny
Everard Aloysius Lisle March Phillipps; born 28 May 1835; student 1847-49; died 18 September 1857

In 1854 Everard March Phillipps sailed for India to join the 11th Bengal Native Infantry. When the Mutiny broke out in 1857, Phillipps' regiment was amongst the first to revolt. When the Queen's proclamation against the insurgents came, he had to read it out as he could speak the native tongue. Riding boldly forward while the bullets whistled round him, he began to read the proclamation, but before he got to the end of the first sentence his horse was shot from under him, and he fell to the ground, himself wounded by a stray bullet. Undeterred, he sprang to his feet and read through the whole proclamation from beginning to end before taking cover.

On the desertion of the Bengal Infantry, he then joined the 60th Rifles. He performed many gallant deeds, and in the months before his death he was wounded three times. He was killed during the assault of the city of Delhi. Ensign Phillipps was awarded the Victoria Cross fifty years after *Ensign Everard March Phillipps*

his death "for many gallant deeds which he performed during the siege of Delhi". Established in 1856, and Great Britain's highest award, the Victoria Cross (VC), was awarded for most conspicuous bravery, a daring or pre-eminent act of valour, self-sacrifice or extreme devotion to duty in the presence of the enemy.

First World War Roll of Honour

Number who died: 73
The rank and unit, if applicable, is given after the name, followed by the date of death in italics

A Thomas Bantock (1908-08), Lt, 6th Battalion Royal Fusiliers *During November 1915*

Arthur G Bourchier (1905-09), 2nd Lt, Royal Berkshire Regiment *9 May 1915*

Cecil J Boyes-Varley (1903-07), 6th Manchester Regiment *During 1915*

Siegfried Brockbank (1908-09), 7th Middlesex Regiment *5 June 1915*

Thomas Brownrigg (1914-15) *During September 1918*

Donald L Carden (1910-13), 2nd Devons *24 April 1918*

Bernard Cary (1892-94), 1st Battalion London Scottish *10 May 1917*

Rev Herbert C F Collins (1894-1901), Black Watch *9 April 1917*

George Conolly (1909-10), 46th Saskatchewan Regiment *3 June 1917*

William J Corcoran (1900-01), Capt, Duke of Cambridge's Own *24 October 1914*

Desmond J Crowley (1904-09), HMS India *8 August 1915*

Henry R Cruise (1897-1901), Capt, 1st King's African Rifles *22 April 1916*

Oswald Dawes (1908-11), 2nd Lt, 14th Yorks & Lancs *8 May 1917*

A G H L Bernard de Forceville (1907-08), Lt, French Army *During March 1915*

Charles de la Pasture (1890-92), Capt, Scots Guards *19 October 1914*

Austin E Deprez (1894-1902), Capt, Royal Field Artillery *12 April 1918*

Edward J Dillon (1904-08), Lt, Royal Field Artillery *12 April 1918*

Albert Dunphy (1916-17) *During 1918*

Leonard A Edens (1908-10), 2nd Lt, Royal Flying Corps *March 1918*

Clifford Farrow (1912-14), 2nd Lt, 2nd Battalion Dorset Regiment *9 April 1918*

Gerald Fitzgerald (1903-06), 2nd Lt, Northumberland Fusiliers *1 July 1916*

John E Foreman MRCS LRCP(1897-1900), Royal Army Medical Corps *9 July 1917*

Christopher R Fowler (1905-07), Honourable Artillery Company *13 March 1915*

Alfred I Frost (1895-97), Lt, Middlesex Regiment *1 July 1916*

Henry C Gouldsbury (1897-98), Capt, Royal Berkshire Regiment *27 August 1917*

Athole Gudgeon (1894-99), Lt, HMS Ettrick *27 August 1917*

H E Redmond Hamilton (1894-97), Capt, Canadian Railway Corps *19 May 1917*

Thomas M Horgan (1896-99), Sgt, Royal Inniskilling Fusiliers *26 August 1914*

Francis Hughes (1874-78) *Date unknown*

Reginald I Hughes (1902-05), 1st Canadian Brigade *29 December 1915*

Sidney St J Hunt (1908-14), Queen's Westminster Rifles *1 May 1917*

Henry Hussey (1886-89), 1st Canadian Brigade *13 June 1916*

Thomas Hussey (1874-80) *Date unknown*

Louis Isnardi-Bruno (1907-11), Italian Army *24 May 1917*

Raphael Kerry (1916-17), Royal Garrison Artillery *13 April 1918*

Henry Kilduff (1902-07) *23 July 1918*

Rev Simon Stock (Francis) Knapp DSO MC (1873-77), Military Chaplain *1 August 1917*

William R C P Lee (1904-04), 2nd Lt, 7th Battalion Royal Fusiliers *10 July 1915*

Osmund H Lewis (1886-88), Honourable Artillery Company *22 June 1915*

Christopher Lockwood (1908-11), Sgt, Australian Expeditionary Force *24 September 1917*

Henry Lovell (1909-17), Royal Marines *6 April 1918*

Richard Lynch (1897-99), 11th King's Liverpool Regiment *7 August 1915*

Archibald H Mankelow MC (1904-05), Lt, 39th Garhwal Rifles *14 May 1915*

Joseph L Mann (1910-16), Honourable Artillery Company *15 March 1917*

John V McCarthy (1911-13), Canadian Expeditionary Force *10 April 1917*

E James H Meynell (1910-12), Capt, division unknown *4 October 1918*

Bertram St Clair Miller (1904-08), 2nd Lt, Régiment de Génie de Combat *Date unknown*

Stewart Moore (1901-03) *2 September 1918*

Joseph A Morgan (1912-15), 2nd Lt, Royal Flying Corps *30 May 1917*

Mark O Nugent (1904-06), Asst Paymaster, HMS Hampshire *5 June 1916*

Herbert P Oates (1899-1905), 2nd Lt, King's Liverpool Regiment *20 September 1917*

Godwin S O'fflahertie (1910-12), 2nd Lt, Royal Flying Corps *Date unknown*

Francis J Page DCM (1896-97), Lance-Sgt, 16th Lancers *5 November 1914*

Edward E Parker (1890-96), 1/21st London Regiment *7 July 1917*

G Huntly Philip, 2nd Lt, 15th Royal Hampshires *11 November 1916*

Alban W Powell (1905-05), 2nd Lt, 8th Queen's Regiment *21 August 1916*

Vincent J Power (1905-09), King's Liverpool Regiment *During July 1916*

B Hubert J Pownall (1900-01), 2nd Lt, Royal Warwickshire Regiment *23 July 1916*

Merrick O Prismall (1905-08), 2nd Lt, Royal Flying Corps *20 December 1917*

George B Rayner (1895-97), 2nd Lt, Essex Regiment *14 May 1915*

Oswald Rutt (1910-14), 10th Battalion Royal West Kent *8 May 1918*

Francis R Ryan (1905-08), 5th (Royal Irish) Lancers *10 August 1915*

John D Smee (1900-01), Sgt, Queen's Westminster Rifles *22 October 1915*

Gilbert K Smith (1899-1905), Lt, 5th Middlesex Regiment *13 March 1915*

R Cuthbert Stowell (1901-05), 2nd Lt, 3rd King's Own Lancasters *20 November 1917*

Wilfred Stowell (1901-06), 2nd Lt, 3rd Battalion Prince of Wales Leinster Regiment *21 March 1918*

Louis Tysmans (1915-16) *8 October 1918*

Philip E Ward (1902-02), Lance-Cpl, 10th Liverpool Scottish *26 February 1916*

Cyril Waxman (1914-15), 2nd Lt, Royal Flying Corps *26 April 1918*

Charles W Weidner (1902-04), 2nd Lt, Royal Field Artillery *4 June 1917*

Maxwell H Williams (1909-13), 2nd Lt, London Regiment *19 September 1917*

Stuart D Williams (1909-13), 2nd Lt, Household Battalion *3 May 1917*

Francis J Woods (1887-94), Pte, 10th Royal Fusiliers *15 July 1916*

RIP

Captain William Corcoran   *Henry Hussey*   *Captain Redmond Hamilton*

First World War Honours

A description of each honour is given in italics. In some instances the citation or a description of the acts carried out are stated.

Companion of the Order of St Michael & St George (CMG)
Established in 1818 by King George III; conferred upon British subjects for services abroad

Lt Col Jonas W Leake (1888-90), Royal Army Medical Corps
Rev Emmanuel M Morgan (1873-74), Chaplain to the Forces

Distinguished Service Order (DSO)
Established in 1886; awarded to military officers for individual instances of meritorious or distinguished service in war; recipients usually received it for combat against the enemy

Major Wilfrid F S Casson (1888-94), 27th Light Cavalry
Capt Oswald W McSheehy (1897-1900), Royal Army Medical Corps
Francis Knapp (Rev Simon Stock OCD) (1873-77), Chaplain to the Forces
Rev Joseph L Whitfield (1891-1906), Chaplain to the Forces

Distinguished Service Cross (DSC)
Established in 1914; awarded to naval and marine warrant officers and officers of the rank of Commander or below for the performance of meritorious or distinguished service before the enemy

Observer Lt H Albert Furniss (1895-1907), Royal Naval Air Service

Lt B Thomas McNabb (1895-96), Royal Naval Volunteer Reserve
  "in recognition of his gallantry in going overboard and securing a line to a drifting mine after attempts to sink it by gunfire had failed, owing to a choppy sea and considerable swell which made accurate shooting impossible."

Military Cross (MC)
Established in 1915; awarded to commissioned officers of the rank of Captain or below, and warrant officers, for distinguished and meritorious service in battle; for additional acts of bravery, a straight silver bar was awarded

Rev Francis P Bickford (1899~1946), Chaplain to the Forces
Capt John F Bourke (1898-1906), Royal Army Medical Corps *later Major Bourke*
Capt Arthur V Gompertz (1901-04), Royal Engineers *later Colonel Gompertz*
2nd Lt Osmund Goulden (1904-11), West Kent Regiment *later Sergeant Goulden*

2nd Lt J Francis Hagarty (1912-15), 182nd Brigade, Royal Field Artillery
  Military Cross & Bar
  " for conspicuous gallantry and devotion to duty in extinguishing a fire in his battery position during a heavy barrage which had ignited an ammunition dump. He was aided by another officer and their joint efforts undoubtedly averted a serious explosion. He was severely wounded in the operation."

Capt Cecil F Haigh (1902-05), Territorial Army *later Brigadier Haigh*
Military Cross & Bar
He was one of the first to join the Territorials (in fact he was the 64th). He was keen on marathon races and marches – will full uniform and rifle, from London to Brighton. He received the MC in 1917 & Bar in 1918. On the latter occasion he carried two wounded men from an exploding ammunition dump. In 1943 he was in charge of the Turkish and Iraq Command, organising all the supplies to Russia from the south. After the War he served in the Control Commission in Germany before his retirement.

Francis Knapp (Rev Simon Stock OCD) (1873-77), Chaplain to the Forces

2nd Lt William J Leahy (1911-14), Royal Engineers
"for conspicuous gallantry and devotion to duty in charge of working parties. He rallied them under heavy fire and by his personal courage and determination kept them at work until the two strong points upon which he was engaged were completed. He displayed the greatest fearlessness and boundless energy."

Rev William W Leonard (1899-1911), Chaplain to the Forces
Lt *(temporary Capt)* John V Macartney (1898-1901), Prince of Wales' Leinster Regiment (Royal Canadians)

Lt Archibald H Mankelow MC (1904-05), 39th Garhwal Rifles
"for conspicuous gallantry at Neuve Chapelle. He shewed great determination and ability throughout the operations, handling his machine guns against enemy … with great effect"

Lt Stewart Moore (1901-03), 50th Canadian Expeditionary Force
Lt Philip J McKevitt (1910-15), 17th Lancashire Fusiliers *later Colonel McKevitt*
Capt Kevin R O'Brien (1904-08), 1/7 London Regiment
Rev Daniel F Roche (1902-12), Chaplain to the Forces

Capt Edmund C Staples (1902-06), 11th Rajputs, Indian Army
"for conspicuous gallantry and devotion to duty. He was in command of Brigade Machine Guns and, although wounded himself, and with only one wounded man to help him, he continued to work one of the guns at close range and under heavy fire for about an hour until the action closed. At the end he was working the gun alone as the man helping him was a second time wounded."

Lt Francis Tordiffe (1891-95), 2nd British Colombia Regiment (Canadian Expeditionary Force)
2nd Lt Edward Villa (1914-14), Notts & Derby Regiment

Distinguished Conduct Medal (DCM)
Established in 1854; awarded to enlisted personnel, non-commissioned officers and warrant officers of any nation, in any branch of the service, for distinguished conduct in battle

Dominic P B Hegarty (1909-13), London Regiment
"for conspicuous gallantry and devotion. Being wounded, he lay out for five days with three wounded comrades, attending to their wounds, and feeding them by

collecting food and water from the dead. Finally he succeeded in reaching our lines, and after his wounds had been dressed, he insisted upon guiding the stretcher party to where the wounded men lay."

Lance-Sgt Francis J Page (1892-96), 16th Lancers
 "for most conspicuous gallantry at Wulverghem on November 5th, 1914, in assisting in leading a body of forty unattached men in a successful charge against the enemy, in which he was mortally wounded."

Military Medal (MM)
Established in 1916; awarded for individual or associated acts of bravery

Cpl Edward J Dillon (1904-08), Royal Field Artillery
Frederick W Dixon (1909~23), Honorable Artillery Company
Brigadier Ernest J Hogan (1900-03), Royal Field Artillery

Officer of the Order of the British Empire (OBE)
Established in 1917; awarded in recognition of the people who were helping the war effort both as combatants and as civilians on the home front

Rev Albert B Purdie (1900-1913), Chaplain to the Forces *later Headmaster*

Cross of St George, 4th Class (Russian)
Established in Russia by Emperor Alexander I in 1807; divided into four classes by Emperor Alexander II in 1856; bestowed upon non-commissioned officers and enlisted men for extreme acts of bravery in the face of the enemy; recipients automatically received promotion to the next highest rank, were exempt from any form of corporal punishment, and paid no taxes upon retirement from military service; from 1913, living recipients received a stipend for having received the award

Dominic P B Hegarty (1909-13), London Regiment

Legion of Honour
Established by Napoleon in 1802; awarded as a general military and civil order of merit conferred without regard to birth or religion provided that anyone admitted swears to uphold liberty and equality

Capt Robin Grey (dates unknown), Warwickshire Royal Artillery & Flying Corps

Croix de Guerre
Established in France in 1915; awarded for bravery to military personnel mentioned in dispatches

Observer Lt H Albert Furniss (1895-1907), Royal Naval Air Service
Capt Robert J Rodwell (1906-11), Royal Field Artillery

Second World War Roll of Honour

Number who died: 45
The rank and unit, if applicable, is given after the name, followed by the date of death in italics

Peter O D Allcock (1931-37), Flying-Officer, Killed in action *19 December 1941*

David A L Appleton (1918-23), Gunner, Killed on active service *1 November 1940*

Raymond C Bingham RE (1931-35), Major, Killed on active service *During November 1940*

E Raymond Boshell (1927-34), 2nd Lt, Killed in action *6 June 1944*

John G Boshell (1927-32), Lt, Killed on active service *During November 1943*

John F Bourke MC (1898-1906), Major, Missing *Date unknown*

Michael R I Boyle (1921-30), Sqn-Ldr, Royal Air Force *During April 1944*

Peter J Brady (1930-33), O/Seaman, Killed in action *During December 1942*

Timothy E A Brophy (1934-38), Pte, Killed in action *26 June 1944*

Alfred A Burgess (1931-34), Pte, Killed in action *1 August 1944*

Colin R J Connors MBE RE (1910-14), Capt, Killed on active service *Date unknown*

Richard J Cussen (1930-40), Pilot-Officer, Killed in action *29 March 1942*

Desmond P Dore RE (1939-40), Lt, Killed in action *29 May 1944*

John J B Farrow, Major, Killed in action *During 1944*

* Andreas Frölich (1939-39), Died in a concentration camp *Date unknown*

Philip A L Gompertz (1929-35), Capt, Killed in action *Date unknown*

E Osmund Goulden MC (1904-11), Sgt, Killed on active service *24 April 1944*

John H R Greenwood (1914-17), Capt, Indian Army *During December 1943*

Eric L J Hayward DFC (1926-35), Sqn-Ldr, Killed in action *Date unknown*

Shane E Kearney (1932-36), Lt, Killed in action *27 March 1945*

William J Lee (1928-32), rank unknown, Killed on active service *Date unknown*

John C L Lucas (1931-37), Gunner, Killed in action *29 October 1942*

P G Rex Mahony (1926-32), Lt, Killed in action *During 1944*

Alan S D J McGavin (1930-37), Capt, Killed in action *28 November 1942*

Patrick C McNair (1934-38), Pilot-Officer, Killed in action *During 1942*

Hugh J A McNair (1935-40), 2nd Lt, Killed in action *30 May 1944*

Francis B Mitchell BEM (1934-35), Sgt, Killed on active service *Date unknown*

Peter A Offord (1939-41), Flt-Sgt, Killed in action *24 December 1944*

Flying-Officer Peter Allcock   *Sergeant Osmund Goulden*   *Flight-Sergeant Peter Offord*

Alan G Porter (1925-33), Major, Killed in action *Date unknown*

* Geoffrey C T Repton (1930-32), Pte, Missing *Date unknown*

Ian M A Ross (1931-40), rank unknown, Killed on active service *16 December 1944*

John Segrue (1897-1901) *During 1943*

Walter F Sicé (1930-32), rank unknown, Died of illness contracted on active service *16 January 1946*

Donald W Smith MC (1934-37), Major, Killed in action *1 March 1945*

E Charles Splane (1926-33), Flying-Officer, Killed in action *During June 1944*

George D Stevens RN (1924-28), Petty-Officer, Killed in action *During 1940*

Henry E Tindall (1936-38), Gunner, Killed in action *18 June 1940*

Francis Vance (1940-41) *18 October 1944*

Eric F J von Bock (1932-41), Flying-Officer, Killed on active service *5 December 1944*

Peter L Watson RN (1934-35), Midshipman, Killed in action *21 January 1940*

Philip L West MM (1928-31), Sgt, Killed in action *During August 1941*

John E Westfield (1935-36), Sgt-Pilot, Killed on active service *Date unknown*

John H White DFC (1924-32), Wing-Cdr, Killed in action *Date unknown*

Maurice P White (1924-33), Sub-Lt (A), division unknown, Missing *Date unknown*

Claud M Wright (1934-36), Sqn-Ldr, Killed on active service *Date unknown*

RIP

* The names of Andreas Frölich and Geoffrey Repton are inadvertently omitted from the Second World War honours board in Monument Lane

Second World War Honours

Member of the Order of the British Empire (MBE) (Military Division)
Established in 1917 with the Military Division in 1918; awarded to non-combatants for services to the war

Capt Colin R J Connors (1910-14), Royal Engineers Colin
Connors came to St Edmund's in 1910 and left in 1914 at the age of seventeen to join the Sherwood Foresters. He served in France and was promoted to Captain. Demobilised in 1920, he became a respected civil engineer and surveyor in Leeds. As a reserve officer, he was again mobilised in 1939 and joined the Royal Engineers. He volunteered for bomb disposal work, even though this meant reverting to the lower rank of lieutenant. He was given the task of clearing mines from beaches and other places which had been laid down in the time when invasion threatened. In 1944 he was awarded the MBE (Military Division) for his exceptional services to this dangerous work. However shortly afterwards, when there remained just a few mines in the area he was engaged in clearing, he was blown up in a tragic accident. He left a widow and ten children.

Rev Daniel McGowan (1931-37), Chaplain to the Forces

Distinguished Service Cross (DSC)
Established in 1914; awarded to naval and marine warrant officers and officers of the rank of Commander or below for the performance of meritorious or distinguished service before the enemy

Lt John Craig (1930-39), Royal Naval Volunteer Reserve

Military Cross (MC)
Established in 1915; awarded to commissioned officers of the rank of Captain or below, and warrant officers, for distinguished and meritorious service in battle

2nd Lt Richard A J Cheffins (1925-28), Middlesex Regiment (DCO) *later Captain Cheffins*
"For gallantry in France and Flanders"
"Second Lieutenant Cheffins led his guns into action across a piece of bullet swept ground, and maintained them in action in the face of heavy enemy fire. His disregard for danger was a fine example to his men, and his action was instrumental in saving a company of infantry which had been surrounded."

Major Donald W Smith (1934-37), Royal Norfolk Regiment Donald William Smith was in Challoner (1934-37). He was killed in battle on 1 March 1945 whilst leading his company against a key position dominating a town on which the whole German defence relied. The position was stormed, but Donald lost his life while it was accomplished. Shortly before his death, he had received a citation letter signed by Field-Marshal Montgomery for bravery and initiative in action.

Rev Daniel McGowan (1931-37), Chaplain to the Forces

Air Force Cross (AFC)
Established in 1918; awarded to officers and warrant officers for an act or acts of valour, courage or devotion to duty whilst flying but not in active operations against an enemy.

Sqn Ldr Charles R J Hawkins (1922-27), Royal Air Force "For meritorious service."
Wg Cdr V Gordon Lane DFC (1929-33), 103rd Squadron
Wg Cdr Allan R Wright DFC (1934-38), 92nd Squadron

Military Medal (MM)
Established in 1916; awarded for individual or associated acts of bravery

Philip L West (1928-31), Sgt, Royal Engineers (died of wounds)

Distinguished Flying Cross (DFC)
Established in 1918; awarded to officers and warrant officers for an act or acts of valour, courage, or devotion to duty performed while flying in active operations against the enemy; for additional acts of valour, a straight silver bar was awarded

Sqn Ldr V Gordon Lane AFC (1929-33), 103rd Squadron *later Wing-Commander Lane*
   "For gallantry displayed in flying operations against the enemy, carried out in daylight
   successfully, despite heavy and accurate anti-aircraft fire and fighter opposition."

Flt-Lt Eric L J Hayward (1926-35), 101st Squadron
   "This officer is a pilot of exceptional ability, and has performed his operational
   tasks with a high degree of efficiency. He has carried out numerous sorties as captain of aircraft, successfully bombing many important and heavily defended targets
   and placing mines in enemy waters. In December 1941, F/Lieut Hayward carried
   out a daring daylight attack on an oil refinery, scoring direct hits from only 300
   feet. He has always shown great courage and determination."

Wg Cdr John H White (1924-32), Royal Air Force
   John White, whose father, uncles & brother were all educated at St Edmund's was
   in St Hugh's & Talbot (1924-32). Joined the Royal Air Force in 1936 and with the
   outbreak of war worked in both the UK and abroad as an instructor. In 1943 he was
   awarded the DFC for courage and devotion to duty on operations, and was later
   promoted to the rank of Wing Commander. At the time of his death he was
   employed on pathfinder operations.

Sqn Ldr Michael R I Boyle (1921-30), Royal Air Force
Flt Lt Peter O Kershaw (1931-31), Royal Air Force
Flying Officer Thomas C McNamara (1935-40), Royal Air Force

Flt Lt Allan R Wright 92nd Squadron *later Squadron Leader Wright* **and Bar**
"This officer has been continually engaged in operational flying since May 1940. He has led his flight and sometimes his squadron with great skill and determination. Flight-Lieutenant Wright has destroyed at least sixteen enemy aircraft. On one occasion he flew his damaged aircraft back from France, making a successful landing despite extreme difficulties. His keenness and devotion to duty have been outstanding."

Sqn Ldr Jack S Belton (1932-35), 77th Squadron **and Bar**
"This officer maintained a high standard of keenness and devotion to duty. His cheerful disposition and outlook has always been an asset to squadron morale."

Flight-Lieutenant Allan Wright

British Empire Medal (BEM)
Replaced the Medal of the Order of the British Empire (1917-1922) and had a military and a civil division; awarded for meritorious service mainly to non-commissioned officers

Sgt Arthur H Cole (1917-18), Kent Special Constabulary
"When an RAF plane crashed near Sergeant Cole's home, the pilot was trapped and was hanging by his harness upside down. Cole immediately ran to his assistance and, although expecting the plane to blow up at any moment, freed the pilot from his gear and dragged him away. The petrol tank exploded a minute later."

Sgt Francis B Mitchell (1934-35), Royal Air Force
"Sgt Mitchell was the wireless operator/air gunner of an aircraft which, whilst engaged on a navigation flight, crashed into a hill side in sparsely populated mountain country. The pilot was killed and the remainder of the crew seriously injured. Sgt Mitchell, though suffering from severe and painful injuries, crawled on hands and knees for a distance of two to three miles, over treacherous countryside during a thick fog to obtain assistance. The time taken was about three hours. As a result of his courage and devotion, the rescue of the other members of the crew was made possible by nightfall. There is no doubt that, but for his efforts, they would have succumbed to their injuries."

Mentioned in Command Orders

Capt Raymond C Bingham (1931-35), Royal Engineers *later Major Bingham*
"The General Officer Commanding-in-Chief wishes to bring to notice the determination and gallantry shown by Captain R C Bingham in dealing with unexploded bombs in the area allotted to him. He showed a fine example to his section of fearlessness, disregard for danger and devotion to duty, and by his excellent work was the cause of reducing to a minimum the loss of production in certain establishments."

Midshipman Peter Watson (1934-35) became the first Edmundian casualty of the Second World War when the destroyer Exmouth was sunk by U-boat in 1940. As a boy aged 15 he was taught Chemistry by the Headmaster, Fr Sherlock. After explaining a point to him, the Headmaster finished with the words, "Elementary, my dear Watson". "Quite, my dear Sherlock" he replied, and saw with relief that the Headmaster had a sense of humour!

Flying-Officer Peter Allcock (1931-37) was one of the 'Few'. Shot down in flames in August 1940, and severely burned, he was back in the air the next year in the Middle East. He lost his life in December 1941, when on patrol in his Hurricane bomber, which bore on its fuselage the shield of St Edmund and the college colours.

Francis Clayton: Escaped from prisoner-of-war camp
Francis Theophilus Clayton; born 9 January 1918; Douglass & Allen Hall 1934-38

After leaving St Edmund's, Francis Clayton completed his training as an Observer (navigator and bomb-aimer) at Kinloss and was commissioned as a Pilot Officer in the Royal Air Force in December 1940. After two sorties with IX Squadron, in 1941 he was posted with 51 Squadron at Dishforth, York. He was involved in the bombing of a German battleship the *Scharnhorst* whilst it was in Brest Harbour.

On 6 August 1941, he was one of a crew of five who took off on a mission to attack Frankfurt. The plane was shot down by a night-fighter and crashed at Heeze, 8 km south east of Eindhoven. Francis was captured and became a prisoner-of-war. Whilst being held at Oflag 21B in Poland he was caught in an escape tunnel and was put into solitary confinement for thirty days. He was then transferred to Stalag Luft III at Sagan, 160 km south east of Berlin. It was from this same camp in March 1944 that many aircrew escaped, but of the total re-captured, fifty were subsequently murdered by the Nazi Gestapo and SS, as dramatised in the 1963 film *The Great Escape*.

Francis was at Stalag Luft III when the long march of over 200km back into Germany. However in early April 1945, he escaped from Luckenwalde and headed south east through two armoured battlefronts, via Juterbog and Wittenburg, crossed the Elbe and then went west to Bitterfeld, where he was met by the US Army having walked for nearly 80km.

After the War he worked in Chile, becoming consular assistant at the American Embassy in Santiago until 1959, when he joined his parents in Australia. There he became lecturer in Poetics and Film Creativity at the Queensland College of Art in Brisbane.

Francis is a member of the RAF Escaping Society, Air Crew Association and The Edmundian Association and he lives in retirement in Queensland, Australia.

Squadron Leader Jocelyn Millard AE KSG

Jocelyn George Power Millard; born 23 February 1915;
Douglass 1928-31

Squadron Leader Jocelyn Millard

Jocelyn Millard was in Fighter Command from September 1940 until March 1941 with No.1, 242 & 615 Squadrons, all three being well-known for particular reasons. No.1 Squadron was formed during the First World War and is still operational, 242 Squadron was commanded by Douglas Bader who was his commanding officer when Millard joined, and 615 was the County of Surrey Auxiliary Squadron, known as "Churchill's Own", as he was the Honorary Commodore.

His greatest fear was of a mid-air collision – an inevitability in a sky full of aircraft. His squadrons, based at Wittering, Lincolnshire, and at Coltishall, Norfolk, flew Hurricanes during the Battle of Britain. When they scrambled, they flew in a very tight arrowhead formation, only a few feet away from each other. In an interview with the Daily Mail in 2000, he said " When you lost a friend you felt bad, but you never talked about it. None of us discussed the men who died. And every one of us was afraid – whoever says he wasn't is lying – we just didn't show our feelings."

He believed that the downfall of some of the pilots was that they went into combat after having a few too many the night before. He was fortunate in that his plane was never badly hit and that he managed to avoid colliding with anyone.

Having been assessed as an above-average pilot-navigator, he was made flying instructor in 1941, and taught the new crop of young fighter pilots coming in to replace those who had been killed.

He possesses the only known remaining complete headgear from the Battle of Britain, exactly as it was when he did his last sortie in Fighter Command in 1941. Apparently there are still some 1940 flying helmets and goggles around, but there are no canvas oxygen masks, nor tumbler-switch type of microphones.

He retired from the RAF in 1947 and afterwards worked for the Ministry of Civil Aviation, and later for the Ministry of Defence. He has been awarded the Silver Medal of Merit of the Guild of St Stephen (awarded for sixty years of service to Church as an altar server), the Papal Medal *Bene Merenti*, the Papal Cross *Pro Ecclesia et Pontifice*.

Jocelyn Millard lives in retirement in Letchworth, Hertfordshire, and is a Life Patron of The Edmundian Association.

Sir Neville Stack KCB CVO CBE AFC: Air Chief Marshal

Thomas Neville Stack (junior); born 19 October 1919; St Hugh's & Challoner 1930-36; died 26 January 1994

"Jimmy" Stack was the son of Neville (senior) (1909-11), who was a celebrated air pioneer and test pilot who made the first flight out to India in a light aircraft. He also used sometimes to arrive at St Edmund's by plane rather than car.

It seemed inevitable that Jimmy would join the Royal Air Force. He won the Sword of Honour at Cranwell, and then immediately served in the Second World War. He was on flying boat patrols throughout the war and was mentioned in dispatches for his professionalism. His expertise in maritime reconnaissance kept him in the same field for some years afterwards, on the Staff of Coastal Command Headquarters and as Chief Instructor at the Joint Anti-Submarine School.

He was again on active service in the 1950s, commanding a transport wing in Singapore, supporting ground troops in Malaya. His Air Force Cross was

Sir Neville Stack (Photo © Ministry of Defence)

awarded in 1957 in recognition of the work carried out by his squadrons in supplying British patrols, including the newly reconstituted SAS, operating in the jungle against Communist insurgents and keeping their lines of communication open. At the same time Jimmy Stack and his men carried out their own psychological warfare, dropping leaflets to isolated villages and sometimes even using loud hailers to get the message across.

After this, Jimmy Stack was involved in mobile operations with the Parachute Brigade in Africa and the Middle East. One of his tasks was to transport paratroopers to Jordan to help protect King Hussain and following the 1958 coup in neighbouring Iraq and the murder of King Faisal. After two years as Deputy Captain of the Queen's Flight, he was back in action in the Far East, this time as a group captain organising support for British troops in North Borneo at the time of confrontation with Indonesia. He was by now acknowledged to be one of the RAF's leading experts on support flying. He returned in 1965 to become Senior Air Staff Officer (SASO) in Flying Training Command. As such he helped to launch the RAF's display team the Red Arrows, which had been formed shortly before his arrival.

He was Commandant of Cranwell between 1967 and 1970, then spent two years in Ankara as Britain's military representative at the Central Treaty Organisation. He returned to Britain to become Commander in Chief, RAF Training Command, and then in 1976 he was appointed Air Secretary, responsible for managing the RAF's career structure. He retired from the RAF in 1978.

He then entered a totally different field as the director-general of the Asbestos International Association, to counter what it saw as ill-informed criticism, a job he did until 1989.

Capt Paul Rogers BA: Murdered in Northern Ireland
Paul Rogers; born 4 October 1941; staff 1977-79; died 19 April 1979

Between 1964 and 1976 Paul Rogers held teaching posts in four schools, notably at St Paul's, where he taught for six years. He was particularly distinguished as a fencing instructor, and was for a number of years Honorary Secretary of the Schools Fencing Union.

He was a member of the Territorial Army, when in 1976 he resigned his teaching post and joined the Ulster Defence Regiment (UDR). He served as an officer in the UDR for a year before concluding that his true vocation lay after all in schoolmastering. He came to St Edmund's in 1977 as an English master, Assistant Housemaster of Stapleton and an officer in the CCF. He still assisted with the training of new recruits, and it was whilst he was undertaking this activity that he lost his life.

Paul Rogers was murdered by Irish Republican Army terrorists during the Easter holidays of 1979. The armoured Land Rover in which he was travelling was specifically targeted by a sniper. Learning of the event on the television evening news, the death of their teacher or colleague came as a shock to many Edmundians.

Fr Phelim Rowland VG RAChD: Principal Roman Catholic Chaplain to the Army
Phelim C Rowland; born 9 December 1949; Allen Hall 1969-74

Phelim Rowland became a chaplain to the Navy in 1979, serving in Scotland, Portsmouth and at the Royal Naval College at Dartmouth, before transferring to the Army, where he has served alongside British soldiers in Northern Ireland, Germany, Bosnia & Kosova. He counselled frontline servicemen during the Falklands War. At the height of the conflict in May 1982, he held a memorial service onboard HMS Yarmouth for the survivors of the Exocet missile attack on HMS Sheffield.

Marcus Hayakawa

Marcus Hayakawa: Queen's Medal
Marcus James Hayakawa; born 7 February 1978; Poynter 1991-96

After leaving St Edmund's, Marcus Hayakawa studied International Relations at Sussex University. He subsequently gained an MA in Governance at The Institute of Development Studies. In a gap year he worked on an environmental project in Uganda for six months and travelled in Jordan, India and Nepal. He proceeded to the Royal Military Academy at Sandhurst and in 2002 received the Queen's Medal, which is awarded to the cadet who achieved the highest score in military, practical and academic studies. He has represented the Academy at rugby, swimming and boxing and is commissioned into the Royal Engineers.

Some other Edmundians in military service

Brigadier-General **Stanhope Pedley** CB (1878-79) served on the North-West Frontier in 1897 and 1898. From 1912 to 1916 he commanded the 2nd Battalion of the The Royal West Kent Regiment, and in 1915 went to Mesopotamia and took part in the Battle of Nasiriyah. He then went to France to command the 15th Battalion of the Durham Light Infantry, and in 1917 was given command of the 34th Infantry Brigade.

Major-General **Simon Beardsworth** CB BSc (1940-47) was in command of the 1st Royal Tank Regiment between 1970 and 1971. He was made Deputy Commandant of the Royal Military College of Science in 1980. He was Vice Master General of the Ordnance.

Major **Patrick O'Brien** TD (+2 clasps) KHS MA FCIPD FCMI FRSA (1949-53) was involved with the Territorial Army from 1956 to 1983. He had a career in industry, and is currently Deputy Lieutenant of the London Borough of Barnet.

Brigadier-General **Jan Johnson** BS Juris Doctor (1959-61) was formerly an F-16 fighter pilot. He is now retired from the US Army.

Flying Officer **Joseph Jackson** (1970-77) was killed in 1984 when his Jaguar jet fighter crashed in the Nevada Desert during a "war games" exercise.

Major **Louis Tuson** MBE (1973-83) received his award in 2001 for his work on the British Army staff in Washington DC.

Major Louis Tuson

Wing Commander Andy Offer: Leader of the Red Arrows
Andrew Charles Offer; born 17 January 1966; Junior House & Challoner 1977-84

Wing Commander Andy Offer

Having been awarded an RAF Flying Scholarship, Andy Offer joined the RAF straight from St Edmund's. After flying training, he was selected to become a first-tourist flying instructor at Linton-on-Ouse, teaching students barely younger than himself. His aerobatic career began when he was the solo Jet Provost Display Pilot for 1989. He later completed weapons training at Chivenor, in north Devon, and was then posted to No 3(F) Squadron at Gutersloh and Laarbruch in Germany. He participated in operational sorties policing northern Iraq following the 1991 Gulf conflict.

On returning to the UK, Andy Offer was posted to the Harrier conversion unit at Wittering where, in between his instructional duties, he flew over in over fifty aircraft displays. He was selected to join the Red Arrows aerobatic display team and he was a team member for the 1996, 1997 and 1998 seasons. He returned in 2000 to become the youngest officer ever to command the Red Arrows.

He is currently serving at RAF Staff College in Shrivenham.

Bishop Richard Challoner

Current Chairman of Governors Ivor O'Mahony (1945-53) (left), with Mrs Margarita Lehrian & former Chairman John Gillham, in front of a portrait of former Chairman George Lehrian (1941-49)

Toby Gribbin (1996-2003) (left), former Deputy Head Boy, with Bishop George Stack (1966-72) & Bill Gribbin (1968-91), former Housemaster of Griffiths

First Communicants (from left) Etiosa Igbinedion (1997-2002), Emma Proctor (1996-98), James Bennett (1996-98) & Antonino Faranda (1997-present) with Fr Michael Pinot de Moira in 1998

Cardinal Basil Hume, 23rd President of the College, at the end of Mass in honour of the 750th anniversary of the canonisation of St Edmund, in Westminster Cathedral on St Edmund's Day in 1996

D

Jeremy Janion (1957-64) on the cover of Rugby World magazine (Photo © Rugby World)

Charlie Smith at work on the cricket field

Giles Kershaw (1961-66) during his flight around the world via the North and South Poles (Photo © Doug Thost Photography)

David Kay (1975-82), when Chairman of The Edmundian Association, presenting a framed print by Jim Odell (1968-93) to Cardinal Basil Hume, 23rd President of the College, on St Edmund's Day in 1993

Astrid O'Reilly & Paul Bartlett, Head Girl & Head Boy 2003-2004

Fr Michael Pinot de Moira

chapter 7

Public life & commerce

Since the early days of the College, students have gone on to fill senior roles in the legal profession, in diplomat and public service and in commerce. This chapter mentions some of those who became well known public figures.

Henry Stonor: County Court Judge
Henry James Stonor; born 14 March 1820; student 1832~37; died 24 April 1908

Judge Henry Stonor

From the outset Henry Stonor took first place in his class, and at the end of the year carried off the prize for Classics. He was then away from the College, probably through illness, for a year. It took him a whole further year to establish himself one again at the head of the class, but he succeeded in carrying off the Classics prize at the end of Poetry and in Rhetoric.

He was called to the Bar at Middle Temple in 1842. In 1858 he was appointed Chief Commissioner of the West Indian Encumbered Estates Commission, an office which he held until his appointment as County Court Judge in 1865. He is said to have been particularly scholarly in giving his judgements, with his proficiency in the classics occasionally manifesting itself in an apt quotation. He was generally regarded as the best lawyer among the County Court judges of London, and although he was firm and even stern at times, his courtesy and consideration towards those practising before him made him very popular. He retired in 1905.

Having shown an interest in the fortunes of St Edmund's for more than three quarters of a century, on his death Henry Stonor left the College an oil painting of his relative, the Douay professor Alban Butler, author of the famous *Lives of the Saints*, together with his own copy of the publication.

John Adams: Judge
John Granville Adams; born 28 January 1911; Talbot 1925-30; died 21 February 2001

After leaving St Edmund's, John Adams studied Law at Cambridge and wrote the Cambridge Letter in *The Edmundian* magazine during the early 1930s. His legal career was interrupted by the Second World War. He became a Captain in the London Irish Rifles, serving in various places including Italy, and being wounded in action in 1943.

In 1945, he served in the administrative section of the army in occupation in Malaya, and was inaugurated as President of the Superior Court in the State of Perak with the powers of a High Court judge. By 1951 he was a judge in Singapore, with the rather dubious distinction of being known as "Hanging John".

Michael Johnstone: District Judge

Michael Anthony Harry Johnstone; born 12 June 1936; Junior House & Challoner 1947-54; died 10 October 2001

During his time at the school, Michael Johnstone was more interested in reading that in physical activities, however this led him into a legal career.

He started his professional life as an articled clerk with a firm of solicitors in Uxbridge. Upon hearing of Michael's chosen career, the Headmaster Fr Britt-Compton is said to have remarked to his father "Well, Mr Johnstone, better your money than mine!" However, the money was well-spent, as his career covered the disciplines of solicitor, barrister and finally District Judge at Highbury Corner Magistrates' Court

He was an independent man of high integrity who had great empathy with the troubled defendants who came before him, and during his time on the bench, some of Michael's judgements attracted the attention of national tabloid newspapers. One headline stated "Judge cannot tell his Arsenal from his elbow" whilst another was "I like a drink myself, JP tells alcoholic thief"! Of course there was always a serious point behind the headlines. In the latter case Michael pointed out to the shoplifter involved that *he* also drank – in moderation – but did not also

Judge Michael Johnstone

have a drugs problem, and he deferred sentencing to give the defendant an opportunity to show that he could come off alcohol and drugs.

One Boxing Day, Michael went into court to find 26 defendants waiting there, but the prosecution had not shown up, so Michael let them all go. This caused some subsequent consternation, but Michael had acted quite properly, and the defendants certainly approved of his judgement!

His great interest from an early age was naval and military history. He travelled extensively visiting nearly 70 historical battle sites all over the world, recording and photographing avidly.

He retired in July 2001, but died suddenly just three months later, whilst on holiday in Cremona, Italy, following in the footsteps of Napoleon. His name lives on through the Michael Johnstone Library Fund at the Royal Naval Museum, where he was a frequent visitor.

Some other Edmundians with careers in the legal profession

The Honorable Sir **William Shee** (1814-17) was the first Roman Catholic judge since the Emancipation Act; he was also Member of Parliament for Kilkenny between 1852 and 1857. Sir **Stanley Batchelor** (1881-87) was appointed secretary of the Council of India in about 1899, and later became a judge of the Bombay High Court; he was knighted in 1914. **George de Cabral** (1929-33) was Chief Magistrate in Trinidad and Tobago, and in 1976 was about to take up a new appointment as Chief Justice of the Windward Islands when he died. **Malcolm Davis-White** (1969-78), a recently-appointed Queen's Counsel, is a barrister specialising in company law.

Everard Green: Somerset Herald
Everard Green; date of birth unknown; student 1864-65; died 1926

While at St Edmund's, Everard Green briefly considered studying for a clerical life, but he later entered the profession of heraldry.

"Thank you ever so much, dear Dragon, for putting me through it all so nicely" the Prince of Wales was alleged to have said at the end of his elaborate investiture ceremony at Caernarvon Castle. 'Dragon' was the shortened form of 'Rouge Dragon, Pursuivant at Arms' which was retained by Everard Green's friends long after he had been promoted to the rank of Somerset Herald.

He is said to have been eminently fitted for his job. His wide knowledge of people worth knowing, his extraordinary memory, and his skill as a raconteur, made him the most entertaining of people. The President of the College, Mgr Bernard Ward, used to say how welcome he was as a guest in great country houses: "on a rainy day he could by himself keep the whole party amused from morning to night".

Everard Green (left), Rouge Dragon, at the Proclamation of King Edward VII

Charles Goulden OBE MD MChir FRCS: Surgeon-Oculist to Queen Mary
Charles Bernard Goulden; born 20 August 1879; student 1888-96; died 20 September 1953

After graduating from Downing College, Cambridge, Charles Goulden was house surgeon at the Middlesex Hospital and Moorfields before his first consultant post in 1909 as an ophthalmic surgeon at Oldham Royal Infirmary. He joined the Royal Army Medical Corps during the First World War, for which services he received the OBE. His exceptional ability was so much appreciated by his colleagues during the War that in 1919 he was elected to the staff of the London Hospital and became Dean of the Medical School at Moorfields.

Between 1937 and 1948, Charles Goulden was surgeon-oculist to Queen Mary. During the Second World War he was ophthalmic consultant to the Ministry of Health. He was also consultant in ophthalmology to the Ministry of Pensions and consultant ophthalmic surgeon to the London Hospital, the Queen Alexandra Military Hospital, St Vincent's Orthopaedic Hospital, and the Hostel of St Luke. He was president of the Ophthalmological Society, twice the Montgomery Lecturer of the Royal College of Surgeons, and wrote many publications, including a textbook on refraction.

He was Lay Vice-President of The Edmundian Association between 1936 and 1953.

Sir George Delisle Gray VRD MA MD FRCS: Surgeon
St George Bernard Delisle Gray; born 1892; student 1904-1907; died 26 December 1968

"Dolly" Gray – as he was familiarly known among his contemporaries at the College – came from a medical family and himself took up the same profession, pursuing his studies at the Strand School, Guys Hospital and Oporto University. In later life he was appointed Surgeon Commander to the Royal Naval Volunteer Reserve and Councillor member of the Guild of Catholic Doctors.

Sir Edward Henry KCB: Fingerprint pioneer

Edward Richard Henry; born 26 July 1850; student 1864-66; died 19 February 1931

After his time at St Edmund's, Edward Henry went to University College, London, where he studied English, Latin, Physics and Mathematics. After graduating in 1869, he worked as an insurance clerk at Lloyds of London. In 1871 he started studying law at the Society of the Middle Temple, London. Two years later he passed the examinations for entry into the Indian civil service, and in 1873 was appointed as a civil servant in Bengal.

In September 1873, he left for India, where the Government of the North West provinces appointed him as an Assistant Magistrate Collector. He quickly became fluent in Urdu and Hindi as he presided over the courts where tax claims and disputes were adjudicated.

In April 1891, Edward Henry was appointed as Inspector General of the Bengal Police. In 1892 the police force adopted the anthropometric measuring system for the identification of criminals. Around the same time, he became interested in the work concerning the use of fingerprints to identify criminals. In January 1896, he issued an order to the Bengali Police that criminal record forms should not only display a prisoner's anthropometric

Sir Edward Henry

measurements but also the prisoner's rolled fingerprint impressions. He devised a classification system between July 1896 and February 1897. The Henry fingerprint system enabled fingerprints easily to be filed, searched and traced against thousands of others. The simple system found world-wide acceptance within a few years.

In March 1897 a commission was set up in Calcutta to examine both identification systems. It came to a unanimous verdict in favour of Edward Henry's fingerprint system and in July 1897 fingerprinting was introduced to British India by the Governor General. Three years later he was invited to London to address the Belper Committee which has been set up to look into the problems of personal identification for the police. The panel sent him to the colony of Natal in South Africa to help reorganise the local police force and establish a one-man fingerprint bureau at Pietermaritzburg, which proved to be an outstanding success.

In 1901 Edward Henry was recalled to Britain, and on 31 May was appointed Assistant Commissioner of Scotland Yard in charge of the Criminal Investigation Department. On 1 July 1901, the first fingerprint bureau in the UK was established at Scotland Yard. The first successful conviction in the United Kingdom using fingerprints was in a burglary case in 1902 and the burglar, Harry Jackson, was jailed.

On 11 March 1903, Edward Henry was appointed Commissioner of Scotland Yard and in 1906 was knighted. In 1910 he was made Knight Commander of the Order of the Bath (KCB). In 1912, he was the victim of an attempted murder on the doorsteps to his Kensington house. Although three shots were fired, only one hit the Commissioner and he survived. On 31 August 1918, he resigned as Commissioner following a strike that lasted over 44 hours by 11,000 Metropolitan and City of London Police Officers. He was made a baronet in November 1918.

He died from a heart attack and was buried in the cemetery adjoining All Souls Church, South Ascot. His grave was renovated by the Fingerprint Society in 1994.

Sir Leo Curtis: Mayor of Melbourne

Edward Leo Curtis (née Leonard Beaumont); 13 January 1907; St Hugh's 1914-18; died 20 February 2001

He was a student in St Hugh's from 1914 until 1918 under the name Leo Beaumont, the second son of an English mother and an Australian father. Leo Curtis came to St Hugh's on the outbreak of the First World War, but his mother died when he was 10 and his father two years later. As there were no close relatives in England, he and his only brother were passed first to unknown relations in New Zealand and then, after two years, to more unknown relations in Sydney, Australia. His formal schooling ended when he was 16.

Soon after their arrival in Sydney, his brother, James, died in a dentist's chair. His first job was as a copyboy on a newspaper. During the following five years he held nine positions, each a little better than the last. In 1929 Leo Curtis was appointed manager of a handbag shop in Melbourne. Although the Depression was deepening, he possessed the flair of a first class salesman and put live canaries in the shop window: pedestrians stopped in droves. This humble beginning marked the starting point of his expanding retail empire called Bradman Stores, which eventually grew to a chain of 40 outlets in Victoria, New South Wales and Queensland.

Sir Leo Curtis

The growth and consolidation of the Curtis empire took place over 25 years and was accompanied by involvement in various trading and community activities. In 1955 he offered his services to Melbourne City Council; his election was a foregone conclusion and he served for 20 years. He was elected, unopposed, as Lord Mayor of Melbourne in 1963. One of the greatest moments he recalled was when he hosted a civic reception for *The Beatles* in 1964.

He retired from business in 1988 and indulged his interests in a cattle farm, golf and poker. In a preface to his proposed autobiography he wrote: "I have had a long and eventful life, containing a great deal of happiness and more sadness than most are asked to bear."

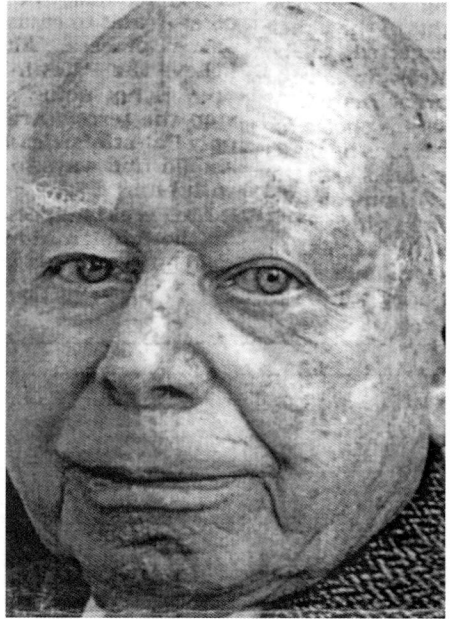

Bernard Molloy: Member of Parliament

Bernard Charles Molloy; born c.1840; student 1850-55; died 1916

Bernard Molloy was the brother of the composer James Lynam Molloy. After leaving St Edmund's he finished his education in London, France and Germany, and then in 1867 joined the Papal Army. He later became a captain in the French army and earned a gold medal for bravery during the Franco-Prussian War.

On the end of hostilities he studied Law and was called to the Bar in 1872. He tried several times to be elected as an MP, and eventually became the Member for King's County between 1880 and 1890. However, he spent much of his time as an MP indulging in his private passion for gold extraction, and spent prolonged periods out of the country.

Bernard Molloy

Sir Andrew Armstrong Bt CMG: Diplomat

Andrew Clarence Francis Armstrong; born 1 May 1907; College & Challoner 1920-25; died 21 December 1997

Sir Andrew Armstrong

Andrew Armstrong applied for a Pacific posting in the Colonial Administrative Service in 1929 after reading Economics at Cambridge. At his interview, he was asked whether the fact that a diplomat in the Solomon Islands had recently been killed, and probably eaten, by the local inhabitants made any difference to him. It did not, and he got the job.

He worked first from Ocean Island (now called Banaba) joining the staff of the Resident Commissioner of the Gilbert and Ellice Islands (now Kiribati and Tuvalu), which are scattered across thousands of miles of ocean. The normal transport between the islands was by Gilbertese sailing canoe, at which Andrew Armstrong became a proficient helmsman.

In January 1930, he married Phyllis Waithman, who travelled to join him on Ocean Island, but she tragically died just ten days after arrival from burns received when a primus stove exploded in her face.

On leave in Fiji two years later, Andrew Armstrong met the Governor's secretary, Laurel Stuart, and they married soon afterwards. Returning to the Gilbert and Ellice Islands he took up an appointment as a District Officer. His responsibilities were varied, as he his roles included being the judge, head of police, director of prisons, postman and wireless operator.

After serving for over twelve years in the western Pacific, he was transferred to West Africa and was posted to Nigeria in 1941. During the voyage to Lagos, whilst in an unescorted convoy of four passenger liners, his ship was bombed and sunk off the coast of Sierra Leone. He was picked up by the Navy, and landed at Lagos with nothing but the borrowed shirt and shorts he stood up in.

Andrew Armstrong first served as a District Officer in northern Nigeria, working in Bida, Zaria and Abuja, and he became fluent in the Hausa dialect. Later, as a Senior District Officer, he specialised in mining and worked in the Secretariat at Kaduna. Much time was spent touring the outstations. Armstrong travelled for days at a time in an old army lorry along the dirt roads, camping out at night. He would call on the headmen of as many villages as possible, mediate in disputes, and take steps to resolve local problems.

Armstrong often remarked that the advent of Paludrine, the anti-maleria drug, heralded the end of real comradeship. Prior to its availability, everyone was kind to everyone else, as one never knew when one might be struck down and urgently in need of assistance!

In the run-up to Nigerian independence, Andrew Armstrong was Permanent Secretary to the Federal Ministry of Mines and Power, helping to prepare for the transition to self-government.

He retired in 1961 and in 1987 succeeded his cousin as the 6th Baronet, Armstrong of Gallen Priory.

Sir Alan Burns GCMG: Diplomat

Alan Cuthbert Burns; born 1888; student 1900-03; died 29 September 1980

Entering the Colonial Civil Service, Alan Burns was appointed to the Treasury and Customs Department of St Kitts in the Leeward Islands. In 1911, he was appointed deputy coroner and Justice of the Peace.

In 1912 he was transferred to Southern Nigeria and in 1914 became Assistant Secretary there. A little later he joined the West African Regiment and in 1915 was adjutant of the Nigeria Land Contingent and served with the Egba Expedition of 1918.

In 1924 he left Africa for a time to become Colonial Secretary in the Bahamas, where he administered the government of the islands during several periods.

In 1929 he returned to Nigeria as acting Chief Secretary and on various occasions was Deputy to the Governor.

Sir Alan Burns (right) when Governor of the Gold Coast in 1941

He remained there until 1934 when he was appointed Governor of British Honduras.

Having completed his term he was invited in 1940 to become assistant Under Secretary of State in the Colonial Office, where he was particularly concerned with the leasing of British bases to the United States. In 1941 he was appointed Governor of the Gold Coast (now Ghana) and he held this post until his retirement from the Colonial Service in 1947.

In the Gold Coast, he was responsible for introducing the "Burns constitution", under which, for the first time in any African territory, unofficial members were placed in a majority in the Legislative Council. In the conditions of the time, this was a notably progressive measure, and although this constitution was soon swept away by the tide of political development which in a decade transformed the Colony into the independent State of Ghana, it was the pioneer work of Burns that set the course.

After his retirement from the Governorship, Alan Burns worked as permanent United Kingdom representative on the Trusteeship Council of the United Nations, and devoted considerable energy to writing about his experiences. In his lifetime he wrote many books: *History of Nigeria* (1929), *Colour Prejudice* (1948), his autobiography *Colonial Civil Servant* (1949), *In Defence of Colonies* (1957), *History of the British West Indies* (1954), and *History of Fiji* (1963).

He was made a CMG in 1927, created KCMG in 1936, and advanced to GCMG in 1946. Alan Burns married Kathleen Hardtman in 1914, and they had two daughters. He served as Lay Vice-President of The Edmundian Association between 1960 and 1966, and was a governor of St Edmund's from 1969 until 1976.

Dr Felipe Benavides OBE: Conservationist

Felipe Diego Alberto Benavides; born 7 August 1917; Challoner 1934-34; died 21 February 1991

Son of the Peruvian Ambassador to the United Kingdom, Felipe Benavides first became interested in conservation while he was at the London School of Economics. He served as a secretary at his father's embassy and rendered useful services to Britain and France after the entry of Peru into the war in 1943.

As a businessman Felipe Benavides represented the British construction company George Wimpey; among the various contracts he procured for the company was the construction of the port of Salaverry near Trujillo,

A vicuna

north of Lima.

But it was as a wildlife conservationist that Felipe Benavides was to achieve international fame. In 1965 he became an international trustee of the Worldwide Fund for Nature, but after 12 years resigned in protest at their policy regarding the endangered vicuna. The vicuna is a cameloid native of the Andean High Plateau, a royal animal of the Incas and an aristocratic relation of the llama. When he first took an interest in its plight in the 1950s, the vicuna was threatened with extinction by commercial poachers, as its wool is reputed to be the most valuable in the world.

Felipe Benavides then used his connections in Great Britain, the chief manufacturing country of cloth made from vicuna wool, and in the United States, the chief consumer, to implement import controls. With help, he then persuaded the Peruvian Government to set up national parks and protected reserves for the vicuna.

It is as a result of these efforts that the vicuna population rose dramatically from 5,000 to 60,000, and the world's most precious wool could be shorn from the animals without the need to kill them.

Felipe Benavides was appointed OBE in 1963, and in 1975 was first winner of the *J Paul Getty Wildlife Conservation Prize*.

Bruce Kent MA PhD: Peace campaigner

David Bruce Kent; born 22 June 1929; Allen Hall 1952-58

Ordained as a catholic priest in 1958, and retiring from the active ministry in 1987, Bruce Kent first became involved with the international peace movement in 1958 through his work with Pax Christi in Britain. He has at various times been the General Secretary and Chairperson of the Campaign for Nuclear Disarmament (CND), and is now its Vice-President. He is President of the London Region of the United Nations Association, Chairperson of the Culture of Peace Committee and of the British overseas development agency War on Want. He is a member of Amnesty, Compassion in World Farming, the Campaign to Free Vanunu, and many other organisations. His publications include *Building the Global Village* (1991) and his autobiography *Undiscovered Ends* (1992), in which he talks about his time at St Edmund's from an unusual perspective. He has travelled to many places around the world in the cause of peace based on justice.

William Scholl CBE: Shoe designer & businessman

William Howard Scholl; born 24 September 1920; Talbot 1931-1937; died 15 March 2002

The third son of an American of German descent, William Scholl went abroad to learn French and German, returning to read Modern Languages at Christ's College, Cambridge. He was on holiday in America when the Second World War broke out and unable to return to Britain. He joined the US Army, where his language skills were put to good use when he was made an intelligence officer interrogating prisoners of war.

The Dr Scholl family firm, founded in 1906 by his uncle, an American doctor and also called William, originally specialised in chiropodists' equipment and foot care products such as corn plasters. Another uncle, Frank Scholl, joined the business in 1910 and moved to London soon after, heading a new company selling Scholl products in Europe. When William returned to Britain after the war and joined the firm, he devel- *William Scholl*
oped its range of foot care products.

The original Dr Scholl sandal, developed in the late 1950s, was based on a Finnish design, refined and marketed through the company as a health product and sold with the slogan "Looking good and doing you good". The Scholl sandal was designed specifically to exercise the feet and legs, support the arch, tone muscles and prevent foot problems. But the sandal had a wider appeal, and it became the ultimate hippie accessory. Made from carved wood with a leather strap across the front, it was worn by millions of women worldwide. In the mid-1960s sales reached two million pairs a year. William Scholl had inadvertently created a fashion icon and by the mid-1960s an estimated half of all British women owned a pair of Scholl sandals.

In 1971 Dr Scholl's became a public company, and seven years later a brand of Schering Plough Health Care Products. William became president of the international consumer products division and worked until his retirement in 1984. He learned to windsurf age the age of 65, and enjoyed skiing into his seventies. He became a proficient pilot and once flew himself to America. It was on his pilot's training flights that he first saw the Isle of Man, which he though was so beautiful that he later made his home there. He devoted much of his time in retirement to the Dr Scholl Foundation, a charitable body which he had directed since 1961. The Foundation has given around £140m to charitable causes; he was appointed CBE in 1998 for his charity work.

James & Robert Floris: Perfumiers

James Floris; born 1803; student 1813-18; died 1868 & Robert Floris; born 1805; student 1814-18; died 1862

Juan Famenias Floris came to England from Menorca in 1730 and set up a barber's shop in the fashionable Jermyn Street in London. He began importing ornate Spanish combs and oils and essences, and gradually the shop was turned over to the sale of fragrances, and tortoiseshell and ivory hair ornaments. Documents from the period refer to the House of Floris as "Combmakers To HRH The Prince Of Wales." James and Robert Floris were the grandsons of the founder who together steered the business in a period of particular success overseas. One of their clients was Florence Nightingale who, in a letter to James in 1863, thanked him for a "sweet-smelling nosegay".

James's son – also called James – was at St Edmund's between 1852 and 1854, however he was never to enter the family business as tragically he died in a boating accident at the age of 19.

Some other Edmundians who have been honoured for their public service

Companion of the Order of the Bath (CB)
Col George L K Hewett (1850-55)

Commander of the Order of the British Empire (CBE)
James J R Bridge (c.1900)
Lt Col Paul A J Hernu (1917-19)
Brigadier Charles Hince (1984-92)
Gp Capt Stuart E MacKenzie (1921-29)
Charles R J Weston Cubides (1947~52)

Companion of the Distinguished Service Order (DSO)
Very Rev William J A Le Grave (1858-74)
Lt Col William H Murphy (1885-89)
Very Rev John M Scannell (1860~99)

Member of the Order of the British Empire (MBE)
Jeremy N S Burne (1969-78)
Rev William J Campling (1930-35)
Rev G Andrew A Dorricott (1947-49)
Rev Edward J Hinsley (1925-35)
Alan E C McGavin (1901-02)
Maurice McGowan (1933-39)
Peter G Morgan (1956-63)

Officer of the Order of the British Empire (OBE)
Rev John A Coughlan (1928-38)
Clarence P Erskine-Lindop (1937-38)
Mgr Canon Charles Flood (1915-26)
Very Rev Robert J McCliment (1907~22)
Rev Christopher B McKenna (1926-30)
Canon Francis O'Farrell (1888-89)
Wg Cdr Andrew C Offer (1977-84)
John W A Ollard (1904-05)
Rev Alberto J Parisotti (1895-1911)

Andrew Keenan OBE

chapter 8

Publishing & broadcasting

Many hundreds of Edmundians over the years have had their written works published or have entered the world of broadcasting. Some of them had long and prolific writing careers and established themselves as leading authorities in their own spheres of interest. This chapter highlights just a few of them.

Archbishop Fulton Sheen PhD DTheol: Television evangelist
Fulton John Sheen; born 8 May 1895; staff 1924-25; died 9 December 1979

Fulton Sheen was born in Illinois, was ordained priest in 1919, and then studied philosophy at universities in the United States and Europe.

It was during this time that he taught at St Edmund's for a year. In 1926, he began teaching at the Catholic University of America, and published his first book *God and Intelligence in Modern Philosophy*. Bishop Sheen also wrote *Communism and the Conscience of the West* (1948), *Peace of Soul* (1949), *Life is Worth Living* (1953), and *The Priest is Not His Own* (1963).

As early as the 1920s, he was a vigorous opponent of communism in his writings and on *The Catholic Hour*, an American national radio program. During the 1950s, he became widely known as a television personality as host of his series called *Life is Worth Living*, viewed by 30 million people each week. He received 8,000 letters a day.

Archbishop Fulton Sheen

In 1950, he resigned as professor at the Catholic University of America to direct the Society for the Propagation of the Faith in the United States, an international mission aid society. A year later he was named titular bishop of Cesariana.

In 1966, he was appointed bishop of the diocese of Rochester, New York. He resigned from that position in 1969 and was named titular archbishop of Newport, Wales.

He was one of the best-known spokesmen for the teachings of the Roman Catholic Church, and remained active in broadcasting until his death. As an author of 69 books, along with many other articles, he brought Catholic doctrine to millions of people around the world.

Laurence Meynell: Author
Laurence Walter Meynell; born 1899; St Hugh's & College 1908-17; died 14 April 1989

Writing more that one hundred books, Laurence Meynell had a long and prolific literary career. He left St Edmund's to serve in the Honourable Artillery Company during the First World War. Following that, he tried teaching, advertising and estate agency. He also travelled a great deal in Europe and, on foot, over much of England and Wales.

During those travels he started writing, and whilst he was in Paris in 1924 he wrote his first novel *Mockbeggar*, which won the Harrap Fiction Prize.

Under his own name and under the nom de plume Robert Eton, he continued to compose occasional novels, which reflected his observation of the changing society around him. He wrote children's books, some under the names Stephen Tring and Valerie Buxton. These included *Policeman in the Family* (1953), *Animal Doctor* (1956), *District Nurse Carter* (1958). He also wrote biographies, including one about Brunel, and several books about cricket.

However, the majority of his work was crime fiction, such as *The Door in the Wall* (1937), *His Aunt Came Late* (1939), and a series of private eye stories featuring a character called Hooky Hefferman.

Laurence Meynell served in the Royal Air Force throughout the Second World War, and was mentioned in dispatches. Between 1955 and 1957 he edited a series of books called *Men of the Counties*, and from 1958 to 1960 was Literary Editor of *Time and Tide*.

He was married twice: first, in 1932, to Shirley Ruth Darbyshire, herself also a writer, and, after her death in 1955, to the actress Joan Belfrage.

The cover of one of Laurence Meynell's books

Thomas Harper: Legal journalist
Thomas Shirley Harper; born 27 June 1922; Douglass & Allen Hall 1935-40; died 14 June 1983

After leaving the College, Tom Harper trained in medicine before moving into journalism. He joined the Law Society as Assistant Editor of the *Gazette* in 1950, and became its editor in 1956. During the 15 years he was with the *Gazette* he earned considerable respect for his ability as a journalist, and his legal knowledge was remarkable in view of his lack of any formal legal training. He resigned in 1965 to become the first Editor of the *New Law Journal*, which he was able to establish in a comparatively short time as an independent and controversial weekly legal publication.

In 1972 Tom Harper left the *New Law Journal* to concentrate on freelance writing, and he was for some time a consultant to the National Council for Civil Liberties. He also lectured part-time, first at the University of Kent and later at Bedford College, London. From 1976 to 1979, he was a member of the Royal Commission on legal services, to which he devoted himself with great zeal, taking particular interest in the question of legal services available to prisoners.

Brigadier Martin Gompertz: Author
Martin Louis Alan Gompertz; born 1886; student 1900-03; died 29 September 1951

On leaving St Edmund's, Martin Gompertz joined the 3rd Battalion of the Hampshire Regiment, and in 1906 transferred to the Indian Army and later served in the First World War. He was later appointed Brigade Major of the Delhi Brigade and was wounded in active service. In 1932 he was promoted to the rank of Colonel, in 1938 he was appointed Commander of the Thai Brigade in India, and in the following year retired from active service.

Under his own name and under the pseudonym of "Ganpat", Brigadier Martin Gompertz wrote numerous books including *Harilek, Roads of Peace, Fairy Silver* and *The Sleepy Duke*. He also wrote various magazine articles.

Canon Frederick Oakeley: Poet & translator
Frederick Oakeley; born 5 September 1802; Divinity student 1846-48; died 29 January 1880

The son of the governor of Madras, Frederick Oakeley was originally ordained as an Anglican clergyman before transferring to Roman Catholicism in 1845. For many years he worked among the poor of Westminster. His most well known translation is that of four of the six verses of *Adeste Fideles*, written in Latin, to its English version *O Come All Ye Faithful*.

Adeste Fideles was transcribed by John Francis Wade, a music teacher in Douay, between 1740 and 1743, in a manuscript called *Cantus Diversi*. The original manuscript is on display in the College Museum.

Canon Frederick Oakeley

It has become one of best known and most performed pieces played during the Christmas season, and it is now sung in over one hundred different languages throughout the world.

Canon Mark Tierney FRSA FRS: Historian & antiquarian
Mark Aloysius Tierney; born September 1795; student & staff 1810-19; died 19 February 1862

After his ordination in 1818, Mark Tierney remained at St Edmund's for a further year as professor and Procurator. He then served as an assistant priest at Warwick Street, London, and afterwards at Lincoln's Inn Fields until his ill health forced him to move to a country parish in Sussex. In 1824 he was appointed as chaplain to the Duke of Norfolk at Arundel, where he spent the rest of his life, devoting himself to historical and antiquarian studies. His chief object was to bring out a new edition of Dodd's *Church History of England*.

His work as an antiquarian received public recognition, and in 1833 he was elected a Fellow of the Society of Antiquaries and, in 1841, a Fellow of the Royal Society. He also acted as secretary to the Sussex Archaeological Society.

Mark Tierney also wrote *The History an Antiquities of the Castle of Arundel* (1834) and several controversial pamphlets, and for a time he acted as editor of the *Dublin Review*.

Canon Daniel Rock DD: Antiquarian & ecclesiologist
Daniel Rock; born 31 August 1799; student 1813-19; died 28 November 1871

At St Edmund's, Daniel Rock came under the influence of Fr Louis Havard (1795~1819), from whom he acquired his first interest in liturgy, and was a close friend of Mark Tierney (1810-19). He was then chosen as one of the first students sent to the newly repoened English College in Rome, where he remained till he took his degree in 1825. He had been ordained priest a year earlier.

Returning to London, Daniel Rock became assistant priest at St Mary's, Moorfields, until 1827, when he was appointed as domestic chaplain to John, Earl of Shrewsbury, whom he had met whilst in Rome. He resided at Alton Towers in Staffordshire until 1840, with the exception of two years during which Lord Shrewsbury's generosity enabled him to stay at Rome collecting materials for his great work *Hierurgia or the Holy Sacrifice of the Mass*, which was published in 1833. Daniel Rock had previously published two shorter works *Transubstantiation vindicated from the strictures of the Rev Maurice Jones* (1830) and *The Liturgy of the Mass and Common Vespers for Sundays* (1832).

In 1840 he became chaplain to Sir Robert Throckmorton of Buckland in Berkshire, and while there wrote his greatest book *The Church of Our Fathers*. This work, which profoundly influenced liturgical study in England and which caused his recognition as the leading authority on the subject, was published in three volumes between 1849 and 1854.

Daniel Rock was a prominent member of the *Adelphi*, an association of London priests who were working together for the restoration of the hierarchy. When this object was achieved, he was elected one of the first canons of the Diocese of Southwark in 1852.

Shortly afterwards, he ceased parochial work, and later went to live near the South Kensington Museum in which he took the keenest interest and to which he proved of much service. His introduction to the *Catalogue of Textile Fabrics* in that Museum was separately reprinted in 1876 and was of great authority. He also contributed frequent articles to the *Archeological Journal*, the *Dublin Review*, and other periodicals. For many years before his death, he held the honourable position of President of the Old Brotherhood of the English Secular Clergy.

James Molloy: Poet, author & composer
James Lynam Molloy; born c.August 1837; student 1851-55; died 4 February 1909

James Molloy attended St Edmund's along with his brother Bernard who later became an MP. After leaving the College, he went to the Catholic University in Dublin, graduated in 1858, and then continued his studies in London, Paris & Bonn, being called to the Bar in 1863, however he never practiced Law.

He started writing and publishing songs which soon became popular in concert halls. Initially concentrating on operettas, he later rose to popularity with his songs *The Old Cottage Clock, Bantry Bay* and *The Kerry Dance*. In 1894 he had his greatest success of all *Love's Old Sweet Song*, a song since very popular with sailors. He also wrote a book in 1874 called *Our Autumn Holiday on French Rivers*.

James Molloy

Peter Phillips: Author
Peter James Phillips; born 13 July 1932; Talbot 1946-48

Peter Phillips (far left) with some of his nine children and closest family

Peter Phillips was born London when his Australian father was working as a journalist in England. The family returned to Australia in 1936 on a German boat (on which the crew taught Peter to say "Heil Hitler") but came back to England in 1946 when his father was made editor of *The Australian Associated Press* in Fleet Street. His brother David Phillips was concurrently in St Hugh's.

He returned to Australia in 1949, soon undertaking medical studies at Melbourne University and working elsewhere, including as surgical registrar again in England at the North Middlesex Hospital. He finally returned to Australia in 1965, and became a general surgeon in Echuca, a small town in northern Victoria, where he worked for 35 years. During that time he was involved in Aboriginal Health, and helped to set up a clinic at a nearby Aborigine settlement.

Peter Phillips has published seven books: *Disaster First Aid* (1966), a history of the paddle steamers on the Murray River *Riverboat Days* (1974), a history of Echuca Hospital *To Comfort Always* (1976), an illustrated history of medical quackery *Kill or Cure* (1978), *Redgun & Paddlewheels* (1980), *Riverboat Ways* (1983), and *Journey of a Country Surgeon* (1988) (written under the pseudonym Richard Wallace).

Peter married Beatrice Benson in 1962 and has nine children. He is a member of The Edmundian Association, and lives in semi-retirement in Victoria, Australia.

Brother Nigel Cave IC: Author
Nigel Terence Adrian Cave; born 10 March 1954; staff 1977-84

Coming to St Edmund's from the Royal Military Academy at Sandhurst, Nigel Cave was an energetic history master and Assistant Housemaster of Poynter. He led several groups to visit the First World War battlefields in Flanders. He left the College to join the Institute of Charity, a religious order known as the Rosminians, founded in 1828 by Antonio Rosmini, an Italian Philosopher and priest.

Since that time, he has become a leading world authority on the First World War, and the *Battleground Europe* series of books, which he has written, co-written and edited, now runs to some fifty titles. These include *A Guide to Battlefields in France & Flanders* (1990), *Santuary Wood & Hooge* (1993), *Beaumont Hamel* (1994), *Vimy Ridge* (1996), *Serre* (1996), *Gommecourt* (1997), *Hill 60* (1998), *Delville Wood* (1998), *Polygon Wood* (1999), *Mons* (2000), *Bazentin Ridge* (2001), *Bourlon Wood* (2002), and his latest book *Le Cateau* (2003).

Nigel Cave also works for the Canadian government as a part-time historical adviser on their Great War sites, and helps to run their guide training programme. Based at Stresa, near Milan on Lake Maggiore in Italy, he is archivist for the Rosminians. He is an honorary member of The Edmundian Association.

Mgr Ronald Knox: Satirist, essayist, novelist & translator
Ronald Arbuthnott Knox; born 17 February 1888; staff 1919-26; died 24 August 1957

With a prolific writing career spanning over fifty years, Ronald Knox is perhaps best known for his translation of the *Bible*. He converted to Catholicism in 1917, and in a privately printed book *Apologia* (1917), and in *A Spiritual Aeneid* (1918), he explained his religious search and his rejection of the contemporary Anglican Church. He was ordained a Roman Catholic priest in 1918.

After teaching at St Edmund's, he was a chaplain to the Catholic undergraduates at the University of Oxford, and then moved to Shropshire, where he worked as a private chaplain to Lord and Lady Acton at Aldenham Park.

Mgr Ronald Knox

The Belief of Catholics (1927) established Knox as one of the foremost Catholic voices in England.

Ronald Knox was a prominent figure of the Detection Club, which was formed in the 1930s by a group of British mystery writers including such well-known authors as Agatha Christie, Dorothy L

Sayers and G K Chesterton. The members of the club agreed to adhere to a code of ethics in their writing, so as to give the reader a fair chance at guessing the guilty party. With its major writers he published in the early 1930s *Scoop* (1930) and *Behind the Screen* (1931), which both appeared in *The Listener* and originally were to be broadcasted.

Ronald Knox's first mystery novel was *The Viaduct Murder* (1925): in the story a group of golfers discover the dead body of the local atheist below a railway viaduct. The pipe-smoking insurance investigator Miles Bredon, the hero in Ronald Knox's series, was introduced in *The Three Taps* (1927). At that time he worked in Oxford, where he typed his books between early morning Mass and lunch. Miles Bredon's investigations continued in *The Footsteps at the Lock* (1928), a story about two scheming cousins, *The Body in the Silo* (1934), *Still Dead* (1934) in which a body vanishes and appears again, and *Double Cross Purposes* (1937) about a treasure hunt set in the countryside of the Scottish Highlands. After six mystery novels he stopped writing them because his bishop ordered him to spend his time with more dignified pursuits!

The Body in the Silo is considered to be Ronald Knox's best mystery, though some critics considered his plots implausible. In this story, the murderer kills the wrong man, an influential politician whose body is removed to a silo. The blundering murderer then also ends up dead.

During the Second World War, Ronald Knox headed a committee that provided Catholic books for servicemen. When Lord Acton decided to move with his family to Southern Rhodesia, Ronald Knox moved to Mells in Somerset, where he took up chaplaincy for Katherine Asquith.

St Jerome's fourth century Latin *Bible* had remained the official Catholic version for many centuries, and the bishops of England and Wales requested him to make a new translation. Knox's version of the *New Testament* was published in 1944, the *Old Testament* in 1949 and 1950. The complete text, with hundreds of revisions suggested by the overseeing committee, was published in 1955.

Ronald Knox's biography was written by Evelyn Waugh in 1959.

Eric Braun: Biographer of show business celebrities
Eric Douglas Hugo Braun; born 31 March 1921; Challoner 1934-38

As a correspondent for *The Stage*, Eric Braun travelled across Britain by bicycle. He does not drive and has clocked up more than 300,000 miles on his bicycle (or rather 22 bicycles) since 1951 – a greater distance than most people ever drive in their cars. He was once fined £25 for cycling along the M5 motorway near Exeter. He cycled to Capri to meet Gracie Fields and, on another occasion, to Paris to interview Marlene Dietrich.

His first major biography was *Deborah Kerr* (1978). Between 1984 and 1987, he was the ghost writer of three best-selling books for the late actress Beryl Reid, including the book *So Much Love*. In 1992, while he was writing his biography of the actress Doris Day, his home was broken into and his sheepdog drugged. All that was stolen was a folder containing material about President Ronald Reagan which he was intending to use in the book.

At the age of 75, Eric Braun cycled from New York to Memphis, Tennessee, to research his definitive work *The Elvis Film Encyclopaedia* (1997). His latest book *Frightening the Horses: the Rise and Fall of Gay Cinema* was published in 2001.

Eric Braun

Henry Oxenham: Controversialist & poet
Henry Nutcombe Oxenham; born 15 November 1829; student 1859-60; died 23 March 1888

The son of a master at Harrow, Henry Oxenham went to Balliol College, Oxford, took Anglican orders in 1854, but became a Roman Catholic in 1857. At first his thoughts turned towards the priesthood, and he spent some time at the London Oratory and St Edmund's, but being unable to surrender his belief in the validity of Anglican orders, he proceeded no further than minor orders in the Roman Catholic Church.

In 1863 he made a prolonged visit to Germany, where he studied the language and literature, and formed a close friendship with Dollinger, whose *First Age of the Christian Church* he translated in 1866. Henry Oxenham was a regular contributor to the *Saturday Review*. A selection of his essays was published in *Short Studies in Ecclesiastical History and Biography* (1884) and *Short Studies, Ethical and Religious* (1885). In 1876 he also translated the second volume of Bishop Hefele's *History of the Councils of the Church*, and published several pamphlets on the reunion of Christendom. His *Catholic Doctrine of the Atonement* (1865) and *Catholic Eschatology and Universalism* (1876) were standard works.

Paul Roche: Poet & translator
Donald Robert Paul Roche; born 25 September 1916; Douglass & Allen Hall 1934-43

Paul Roche is a poet and a translator of Greek and Roman classics. He studied for the priesthood at St Edmund's and in Rome but was unsuited to a vocation, preferring instead to tour around London on his bicycle, wearing beads and jewellery. He dyed his hair orange and his beard purple and began mixing with the fashionable artistic set of his time.

He has published several books of poetry, and has been poet-in-residence at various American universities. He now lives in Majorca.

Paul Roche

Etienne Dupuch: Journalist & publisher
Leon Etienne Henry Dupuch; born 23 May 1931; Douglass 1949-50

The Dupuch family is synonymous with publishing in the Bahamas. Etienne was the grandson of Leon Dupuch, who founded *The Nassau Daily Tribune* in 1903, and the son of Sir Etienne Dupuch, who edited the same newspaper for 72 years – the current world record.

Etienne Jr was in Douglass for one year before entering the newspaper world as a reporter, photographer and cartoonist. In 1960 he started producing annually *The Bahamas Handbook*, a comprehensive guide containing everything from tourist advice to investment information, and has later published maps, handbooks and dining guides.

Etienne Dupuch

Some other Edmundian writers, publishers & broadcasters

Kevin Bocquet

Mark Byrne (1992-94), a former international athlete, was diagnosed with Non-Hodgkin's Lymphona whilst working as a PE teacher at St Edmund's. His book *I Kicked the Devil in the Shins* describes the extraordinary events of his life that followed.

Kevin Bocquet (1960-70) regularly appears on national television as the North of England Correspondent for the BBC.

David Malsher (1984-91) is Managing Editor of *Motor Sport* magazine.

Kevin Mayhew (1956-59) is a publisher of church music and Christian books.

Martin Haven (1968-78) is a television sports commentator.

Adrian Gilbert (1962-67) is an author of esoteric mystical books.

Peter Blackman (1964-71) is director of the Churches' Advisory Council for Local Broadcasting.

Oliver McTernan

Martin Chick (1969-76) wrote the textbook *Industrial Policy in Britain 1945-1951: Economic Planning, Nationalisation and the Labour Governments* in 1997.

Oliver McTernan (1960-72), a former priest who now concentrates on radio broadcasting and lecturing, has written a number of books, his latest recently published being *Violence in God's Name: The Role of Religion in an Age of Conflict*.

Hubert Richards (1949-65), a former professor of scripture in Allen Hall, has written 14 books and composed numerous hymns.

Inigo Gilmore (1978-80) is a reported for the *Daily Telegraph*

chapter 9

Art, music & drama

Thomas Bowman: Actor
Thomas Horne Bowman; born 14 November 1920; Talbot 1933-38; died 8 January 1997

Thomas Bowman's Bentley outside his residence in New York State in 1990

At school Thomas Bowman participated in rugby, cricket and the Officers' Training Corps (in the Corps of Drums), but he did not have particularly scholarly interests. He was considered to be extrovert and sometimes a little brash. On one occasion, when he was fielding at cricket, he misjudged a high catch and the ball landed full on his face. He had to drink liquid food through a straw for some days. The Talbot House photograph of 1935 (see page 42, far right in the photograph) shows him shortly after the incident.

After leaving St Edmund's he went to Westminster Art School. Then came the Second World War, when he was in No.12 Paratroop Regiment, and became a Lieutenant in the Commandos. He was wounded in 1940. One day during the early years of the war he arrived at the College in full battle dress – complete with revolver, grenades and spare ammunition!

Thomas Bowman is said to have distinguished himself on the beaches at Dunkirk when he walked amongst his exhausted men, oblivious of enemy fire, keeping them awake and as alert as possible, in the hope of being evacuated.

Later in his life, he and his Bentley motor car moved to the United States of America, where he embarked upon a career in acting. He had an apartment in Manhattan and a country residence in New York State. As well as appearing on stage, he used his distinctive baritone to make voice-overs for American and British radio and television commercials. Perhaps his most memorable was the advertisement for the 1985 film *Ghostbusters*.

By then Thomas had become a little eccentric in his attire – he neither wore a tie nor used any of his shirt buttons, preferring to wear his open shirts tied in a knot at the naval, exposing his midriff – even in sub-zero temperatures.

He was very proud of his time in the Commandos: his country residence was adorned with the Commando "knife" symbol.

Philip Barraud: Photographer
Philip George Barraud; born 1859; student 1871-72; died 1929

Philip Barraud was the son of Henry Barraud and the brother of Mark Barraud (who painted the mural which runs the length of the Ambulacrum). From the later 1880s, Philip and his elder brother Francis ran a photographic studio in Liverpool. In 1906 he presented to the College a large framed photograph he had taken of Pope Pius X, who was canonised in 1954. There cannot be many photographic studios which can claim a Saint among their patrons! Philip's son Eric Barraud (1907-11) was a member of The Edmundian Association; he died in 1982.

Francis Barraud: Artist

Francis James Barraud; born 16 June 1856; student 1871-72; died 29 August 1924

Nipper was a mongrel born in Bristol in 1884 and so named because of his tendency to nip the backs of visitors' legs! When his first master Mark Barraud died destitute in Bristol in 1887, Nipper was taken to Liverpool by his younger brother Francis, who was a painter. Nipper discovered the phonograph, a cylinder recording and playing machine and Francis Barraud "often noticed how puzzled he was to make out where the voice came from." Nipper died in September 1895, but the scene must have been indelibly printed in Barraud's brain, for it was three years after Nipper died that he committed it to canvas.

In 1898 Barraud completed the painting and registered it on 11 February 1899 as 'Dog looking at and listening to a Phonograph.' Barraud then decided to rename the painting 'His Master's Voice' and tried to exhibit it at the Royal Academy, but was turned down. He had no more luck trying to offer it for reproduction in magazines. "No one would know what the dog was doing" was given as the reason! Next on Barraud's list was The Edison Bell Company, leading manufacturer of the cylinder phonograph, but again without success. "Dogs don't listen to phonographs," the company said.

Francis Barraud making copies of his painting of Nipper

Barraud was given the advice to repaint the horn from black to gold, as this might better his opportunity for a sale. With this in mind, in the summer of 1899 he visited the offices of the Gramophone Company, with a photograph of his painting and a request to borrow a brass horn. The manager asked him if the picture was for sale and if he could introduce a machine of their own make, a Gramophone, instead of the phonograph in the picture.

The Gramophone Company paid £50 for the altered painting and a further £50 for the full copyright. This painting made its first public appearance on The Gramophone Company's advertising literature in January 1900, and later on some novelty promotional items, however, 'His Master's Voice' did not feature on the Company's British letter headings until 1907. The painting and title were finally registered as a trademark in 1910.

Meanwhile Francis Barraud spent much of the rest of his working life painting 24 replicas of his original, as commissioned by The Gramophone Company. The original painting hangs in the offices of EMI, the successor of the Gramophone Company. It is one of the most widely recognised and valuable trademarks in the world.

Michel Cazabon: Artist

Michel Jean Cazabon; born 20 September 1813; student 1826-30; died 20 November 1888

Michel Cazabon is renowned for his paintings of Trinidad scenery and for his portraits of planters, merchants and their family in the 19th century. He was the son of Francis Cazabon, a former slave migrant from Martinique, and was born at his parents' estate on the outskirts of San Fernando. He was recognised as a prodigy by the age of nine, and was sent, at great personal sacrifice by his parents, to be educated at St Edmund's.

View of Port of Spain from Laventille Hill
Painted by Michel Cazabon

On leaving school he went to Paris with intention of studying medicine, but switched to art. He returned to Trinidad in 1850 with his French wife and two daughters.

His major publications included a series of eighteen Lithographs of Trinidad scenes entitled *View of Trinidad, 1851*, a second series of local scenes entitled *Album of Trinidad* (1857) and a series of sixteen scenes entitled *Album of Demerara* (1860).

In 1860 he migrated to Saint-Pierre in Martinique. He moved to Trinidad in 1870, where he taught art at Queen's Royal College and St Mary's College. He lived the last years in relative poverty and died in 1888 of a heart attack whilst painting.

John O'Connor: Musician

John Kevin O'Connor; born 11 May 1949; Douglass 1960-66

John O'Connor

Starting out as a guitarist, John O'Connor became interested in recording. He did demos for songwriters and started his own recording studio in London, called Bark Studios, which is still running today.

All sorts of musicians recorded their material there, from folk to pop, and R&B to Indian classical. He drew the line, however, at punk when some of the artists started spitting on the control room window! Running the studio prevented him from working on his own music, and therefore he recruited a studio manager so that he could concentrate on writing and playing his own material.

In 1982, he co-wrote a song called *Arthur Daley (E's Alright)* based on a character played by George Cole in the television series *Minder*. The record was performed by The Firm and got to number fourteen in the UK charts.

A few years later, in 1987, he co-wrote another novelty song for The Firm. Loosely based on an old German folk song, *Star Trekkin'* put to music the antics of the Starship Enterprise from the television and film series *Star Trek*. John O'Connor approached a few record companies but none was prepared to release the single. So he started his own label, produced 500 copies of the song, and sent them to radio stations. He ended up with a Number One hit in the United Kingdom, as well as in Europe, Australia and Japan. *Star Trekkin'* ended up selling over one million copies. Entering the

UK charts at number 74, within a week it had risen to number 13, the second biggest climb in the history of the charts. The record was at the top of the charts in the UK for two weeks.

After this, John O'Connor moved to the USA, where he still continues to write and perform. He has recorded under the name Eko – Sanskrit for 'one' – for the American new age company Higher Octave, and has albums including *Future Primitive* (1991), *Eko Logical* (1992), *Alter Eko* (1994), *Celtica* (1996) and *Evolution* (2002). He is also one of the principal composers for the comedy cartoon series *King Of The Hill*.

Sir Ralph Richardson: Actor
Ralph David Richardson; born 19 December 1902; student 1917-17; died 10 October 1983

Spending only a short time at St Edmund's, Ralph Richardson was moved between several schools in his childhood. He started adult life doing bland office work, but an inheritance enabled him to embark upon his chosen career as an actor.

Richardson was recognised, during his lifetime, as one of the prime performers of the Bard of his generation. He made 75 films, and received two Oscar nominations and a British Academy Award. He was knighted for his contributions to the arts, and had a career on stage, screen and radio which spanned 60 years.

Sir Ralph Richardson

Martin Faulkner: Actor & dancer
Martin David Faulkner; born 6 June 1964; Junior House & Talbot 1975-82

Through his interest in Latin American and ballroom dancing, Martin Faulkner, a graphic designer and illustrator by training, made a brief foray into the world of television.

As the actor Johnny Martin, he appeared as an extra in many television programmes, including *Poirot, Campion, The Bill* (as a drugs squad officer), *Brush Strokes* and *Lovejoy*. He was also to be seen in advertisements for Dulux paint, Persil washing powder, the Halifax Building Society, and the Escom chain of electrical shops (in which he played the character "The Man from Escom"). He appeared on the stage in *Puttin' on the Ritz* in London, Dublin and Guernsey.

Johnny Martin

His photograph appeared in *The Daily Telegraph* as he danced the jitterbug at the Barbican Centre during *We'll Meet Again*, a musical review in 1989 commemorating the fiftieth anniversary of the outbreak of the Second World War.

Aiden Turner: Soap opera actor
Aiden John Turner; born 2 April 1977; St Hugh's & Douglass 1985-93

After leaving St Edmunds, Aiden Turner attended catering college and worked part-time in a bar. He was then a chef for two years before spending time travelling around the world. Whilst he was in Australia, he was approached to do some modelling work. He continued modelling after returning to the UK and also took acting classes. This led to auditions for commercials, and small parts in television programmes. He appeared in advertisements for Head & Shoulders shampoo and Coca Cola.

Aiden Turner

Aiden Turner moved to the USA to be closer to his girlfriend and, shortly after arriving there, his agent put him forward for a screen test for the soap opera *All My Children*. Although he did not get the part for which he was auditioning, the programme's producers were so impressed that they created a new character called Aidan Devine especially for him.

He has become so well recognised in the USA that he now gets mobbed by autograph hunters, and even has his own official fan club.

Some other Edmundians involved in art, music & drama

Chizoba Akudolu (1986-92) is an actress who has appeared in various television commercials, in the theatre and in short films.

Patrick Jansen (1977-84) and his brother **Paul Jansen** (1980-87) played the lead role in the West End stage version of *Oliver Twist* in the 1980s.

Jim Odell (1968-93), a former art master, drew a set of contemporary pencil sketches of the College in to commemorate the bicentenary of the establishment of the foundation of St Edmund's.

Patrick Doherty (1975-78) is a professional actor appearing mainly in theatrical productions.

Jim Odell

The Barbarini Pine by William Giles

Dr **William Giles** (1844-47), who spent most of his adult life in Rome as Vice-Rector and then Rector of the Venerable English College, was an accomplished artist.

Dominick Baron

Dominick Baron, a current student at St Edmund's, had his first big television acting role in the hospital drama *Casualty*, in which he played a boy who had bleach thrown in his face. More recently he appeared in the series *William and Mary*, playing a tearaway boy called Terrence.

chapter 10

Sports achievements

Walter Swinburn: Jockey

Walter Robert John Swinburn; born 7 August 1961; St Hugh's 1972-74

Born the son of Wally Swinburn, a successful Irish jockey, Walter Swinburn first saw success in horseracing on *Paddy's Luck* at Kempton in 1978.

He became famous when he won the 1981 Derby by a record ten lengths riding the ill-fated *Shergar*. He rode nearly 1,400 winners, including *All Along* in the 1983 Arc de Triomphe and *Shahrastani* in the 1986 Derby.

In February 1996 he suffered a serious fall from *Liffey River* at Sha Tin racecourse in Hong Kong, but by later that year had recovered to ride more winners. Despite suffering from an eating disorder over the next few years, Walter Swinburn went on to further success. For example, in 1998 he won 51 races in the UK and collected the Italian Oaks and the Coronation Stakes.

He surprised many people by announcing his official retirement as a jockey in 2000. Today works as a racing commentator on Channel 4.

Walter Swinburn
(Photo © Channel 4)

Sport has always been a part of life at St Edmund's. Records suggest that cricket was introduced in 1852 and football in 1896. Rugby football started in September 1920. The following pages include lists of the sports team captains recorded in The Edmundian magazine since 1930.

Captains of Cricket

1852-1855	– Edmund Tunstall (1845~94)	1889	– Hugh B O'Rourke (1881-89)
1856-1861	– James Purcill (1852-62)	1890	– James Driscoll (1883~1902)
1862-1865	– Thomas Morissey (1855-65)	1891	– William C Donlevy (1885~99)
1866-1867	– Thomas G Moore (1858-67)	1892-1893	– Charles J Sims (1888~1909)
1867-1868	– Peter Kernan (1857~76)	1894	– Joseph B Newton (1887-94)
1869	– Reginald Fowler (1859~71)	1895	– Maurice FitzGerald (1893-96)
1869-1871	– Thomas Butterworth (1864-71)	1896-1897	– James Goggin (1890~1912)
1871-1873	– John Boase (1868~85)	1898	– John Runalls (1896-99)
1873-1875	– James Morrissey (1868-75)	1899-1900	– Austin A J Askew (1894~1917)
1875-1876	– Patrick Dillon (1868-76)	1901	– Charles F Foley (1894-1900)
1876-1877	– Robert Lynch (1874-78)	1902	– Andrew Arthur (1894-1905)
1877-1879	– William Sullivan (1873-82)	1903-1905	– Kenneth F L Wigg (1898-1910)
1879-1883	– Albert Coughlan (1876-83)	1906	– H Albert Furniss (1895-1907)
1884-1885	– Ferdinand C Le Quilbecq (1876-86)	1907	– Basil E Booker (1897-1912)
1886	– William J Dunn (1884-86)	1908	– Francis P Bickford (1899~1946)
1887	– William A Bolger (1885-87)	1909	– Louis C Conolly (1906-10)
1888	– John J Wren (1884~98)	1910	– Austin M Oates (1899-1915)

1911-1912	– Augustine A Pimley (1904-12)	1973	– Simon J Gillham (1966-73)
1913	– George Perkes (1906-17)	1974	– Patrick J Ryan (1967-74)
1914	– John E Howell (1908-18)	1975	– Roberto C E Solari (1969-75)
1915	– Michael J Wilson (1910-18)	1976	– Brian F Wight (1968-76)
1916	– Seymour Paton (1914-16)	1977	– Douglas G H Ansley (1968-77)
1917	– Laurence A W Meynell (1908-17)	1978	– C William (Liam) Shevlane (1971-79)
1918-1920	– Geoffrey Cammiade (1911-20)	1979	– Simon J C Rossi (1969-79)
1921	– H J Leslie Biggie (1914-22)	1980	– Peter J Frost (1975-80)
1922	– Joseph E McEntee (1916-27)	1981	– David P A Doyle (1977-81)
1923	– Vincent I McCarthy (1918-29)	1982	– Christopher J Witte (1975-82)
1924	– Francis I Dias (1919-24)	1983	– Michael B Wight (1976-83)
1925	– William T M Hecquet (1921-25)	1984	– Guy W Kerrell-Vaughan (1978-84)
1926	– Kenneth L Kershaw (1921-26)	1985	– Simon M A Cousins (1978-85)
1927-1928	– Nicholas J Kelly (1924~61)	1986	– Mark A Everett (1979-86)
1929	– Stuart E MacKenzie (1921-29)	1987	– Alexandre H M Uyt den Bogaard
1930	– Michael R I Boyle (1921-30)		(1982-87)
1931	– Joseph P Doyle (1927-37)	1988	– Daniel F Balado-Lopez (1981-88)
1932	– James I Cosgrove (1926-32)	1989	– Justin R S Devine (1981-89)
1933	– E Charles Splane (1926-33)	1990	– Ediri Sideso (1982-90)
1934-1935	– Albert Stanley (1929-36)	1991	– Chineme E E Ezeoke (1984-91)
1936	– Thomas N Stack (1930-36)	1992	– Simon J Logue (1983-92)
1937	– Alan S D J McGavin (1930-37)	1993	– Steven W Hughes (1989-93)
1938	– Brian D H de F Hick (1929-39)	1994	– David A Logue (1983-94)
1939	– Brian W M Bayliss (1931-39)	1995	– Thomas J Gillham (1988-95)
1940	– Patrick A L Barnes (1936-41)	1996	– Jonathan J R Hilliard (1988-96)
1941	– Eric F J von Bock (1932-41)	1997	– Richard J S Gillham (1990-97)
1942	– Peter C J Rossi (1934-42)	1998	– Paul J Adshead (1991-98)
1943-1944	– Frederick A Miles (1939~67)	1999	– Michael P Collins (1992-99)
1945	– Denis R Nottingham (1939-51)	2000	– George M Beckley (1993-2000)
1946-1947	– Neil A Muldoon (1940-47)	2001	– Thomas O M Marks (1995-2002)
1948	– John R Sweeney (1943-54)	2002	– Patrick T Loughrey (1992-2002)
1949	– Robert H Hines (1943-49)	2003	– J Toby Gribbin (1996-2003)
1950	– John J A Pulton (1945-50)		
1951-1952	– John C A Bex (1946-52)		
1953-1954	– Ian F Stewart (1945~64)		
1955-1956	– Patrick R Sheridan (1946-56)		
1957	– Christopher N Reed (1947-57)		
1958	– Derrick I P Price (1952-59)		
1959	– Andrew D Toomey (1950-60)		
1960	– Stephen G Street (1954-60)		
1961	– Colin J Allen (1959-63)		
1962-1963	– Christopher J B Slade (1953-63)		
1964	– Christopher J Gillham (1958-64)		
1965	– Peter A Knight (1954-65)		
1966	– George H Rocco (1958-66)		
1967-1968	– Michael J Stone (1962-68)		
1969	– Kieron S Heath (1962-69)		
1970	– H H Lawrence Ross (1963-70)		
1971	– Roger H B Wright (1964-71)		
1972	– Robin A Bieber (1963-72)		

Kieron Heath
Captain of Cricket 1969

Derek Lindsay: Cricketer
Derek Stanislaus Lindsay, born 3 September 1922, Challoner 1936-40,
died 28 October 1998

Born in Burma, Derek Lindsay spent his early years in the Andaman
Islands in the bay of Bengal where his father was in the Colonial
Service. His mother died when he was six and his early education was
in India. He came to the College, after his aunts in England had offered
to look after him in the holidays. By the time he left in 1940 he had
rewritten the batting records and won the Batting Cup three years in
succession.

Derek Lindsay

He is considered to be the best batsman produced by the College in 150
years of Edmundian cricket. As a member of the First XI from 1937 (aged
14) to 1940 he scored eight centuries for the College over three seasons. He
would dearly have liked to have become a professional cricketer but the war put paid to that.

The Edmundian of the last years of the 1930s is littered with references to his other sporting activities in rugby, fives, tennis and hockey. As an adult he had an exceptional career as a hockey player,
being awarded his county colours for Middlesex in 1951.

The memorabilia of Derek Lindsay's sporting achievements at St Edmund's have been donated to
the College and are displayed on various occasions.

Laurie D'Arcy
Cricket Coach 1962-1981

Jeremy Gillham – Secretary
of the Old Edmundian
Cricket Society

Jeremy Janion: England international rugby player
Jeremy Paul Aubrey George Janion; born 25 September 1946; St Hugh's & Challoner 1957-64

After leaving St Edmund's, Jeremy Janion started playing rugby for Bedford & Eastern Counties. He
made a rapid advance to international rugby, in which he made his debut in the match between
England and Wales on 16 January 1971. He appeared on the cover of Rugby World magazine in 1971;
a copy of that cover is reproduced on page E. Later that year he went on the England tour of Japan
and the Far East. In 1972 he toured South Africa with England, and played in the defeat of the
Springboks. In total he was capped twelve times during his international career. His last match was
against Australia on 31 May 1975. An accountant by profession, Jeremy Janion is based in London
and is director of a number of commercial companies he has set up.

Simon Geoghegan: Ireland international rugby player
Simon Patrick Geoghegan; born 1 September 1968; Junior House & Talbot 1980-87

Twenty years after Jeremy Janion played for his country, Simon Geoghegan made his international rugby debut, on 2 February 1991 when Ireland played France. His regular team was London Irish. Between 1991 and 1996 he accumulated a total of 37 caps. Injury forced him to end his playing career at the height of his success, and he played his last international against England on 16 March 1996.

Simon Geoghegan

Captains of (Rugby) Football
Rugby was introduced in September 1920

1896-1897 – James Goggin (1890~1912)	1939-1939 – John D Sharpe (1932-39)
1897-1900 – Francis Parker (1889-1900)	1939-1940 – Humphrey F McElligott (1933-40)
1900-1901 – Patrick O'Reardon (1895-1901)	1940-1941 – David J Norris (1936-47)
1901-1902 – Herbert C F Collins (1894-1902)	1941-1942 – Francis J Hannon (1937-42)
1902-1904 – Francis Rusher (1895~1908)	1942-1943 – Michael G Garvey (1940~84)
1904-1905 – Kenneth F L Wigg (1898-1910)	1943-1944 – Denis R Nottingham (1939-51)
1905-1906 – H Albert Furniss (1895-1907)	1944-1946 – Alexander M Gilroy (1938-46)
1906-1907 – Basil E Booker (1897-1912)	1946-1947 – Eric H Cunnington (1941-47)
1907-1908 – John P Bird (1900-08)	1947-1948 – Peter Lux (1941-48)
1908-1909 – A George Bourchier (1905-09)	1948-1949 – George P Lehrian (1941-49)
1909-1911 – Augustine A Pimley (1904-12)	1949-1950 – Michael F W Tilden (1946-50)
1911-1912 – Thomas N O'Connell (1903-14)	1950-1951 – Francis W Daley (1947-52)
1912-1913 – George Perkes (1906-17)	1951-1952 – Paul A Webb (1943-52)
1913-1914 – John E Howell (1908-18)	1952-1953 – Patrick A Burgess (1945-53)
1914-1915 – Michael J Wilson (1910-18)	1953-1954 – Ian F Stewart (1945~64)
1915-1916 – Frederick W Dixon (1909-23)	1954-1956 – John D Crowley (1949-56)
1916-1917 – Laurence W Meynell (1908-17)	1956-1957 – Christopher N Reed (1947-57)
1917-1918 – Frederick Melendez (1911-18)	1957-1958 – John D (Sam) Langham Service (1947-58)
1918-1919 – Geoffrey Cammiade (1911-20)	1958-1959 – David A R Peel (1951-59)
1919-1921 – H J Leslie Biggie (1914-22)	1959-1960 – Roger McGlynn (1956-60)
1921-1922 – Joseph E McEntee (1916-27)	1960-1961 – David J B Bett (1951-61)
1922-1923 – Frederick Berrington (1918-23)	1961-1962 – Derek C Lance (1957-62)
1923-1924 – Charles P Carr (1919-29)	1962-1964 – Christopher J Ryan (1953-64)
1924-1925 – Conway Kershaw (1921-25)	1964-1965 – F Timothy Harrison (1956-64)
1925-1926 – Roger J Quin (1920-26)	1965-1966 – Adrian B Gillham (1960-65)
1926-1927 – Dudley H Biscoe (1923-27)	1966-1967 – Aidan F M Heathcote (1960-67)
1927-1928 – Nicholas J Kelly (1924~61)	1967-1968 – James M Boshell (1961-68)
1928-1929 – Stuart E MacKenzie (1921-29)	1968-1969 – Michael J Stone (1962-68)
1929-1930 – Michael R I Boyle (1921-30)	1969-1969 – John C Sidery (1962-69) to Dec
1930-1931 – Alexander C Groves (1927-37)	1970-1970 – H H Lawrence Ross (1963-70) from Jan
1931-1932 – Edmund F Fletcher (1927-32)	1970-1971 – Ronald W Anderson (1964-71)
1932-1935 – Sydney M Thornton-Grimes (1930-36)	1971-1972 – Barrie F Duncan (1963-72)
1935-1936 – James A Porter (1927-36)	1972-1973 – Simon H O'Neill (1966-73)
1936-1937 – Denis J P Calnan (1934-37)	1973-1974 – John Fisk (1969-74)
1937-1938 – Allan R Wright (1934-38)	1974-1975 – Roberto C E Solari (1969-75)

1975-1976	– Gerard M Delaney (1971-76)		1990-1991	– Bankole A Odunuga (1984-91)
1976-1977	– Julian A Lott (1970-77)		1991-1992	– Mark E A Anderson (1985-92)
1977-1979	– C William (Liam) Shevlane (1971-79)		1992-1993	– Matthew O Davies (1988-94)
1979-1980	– David L Hughes (1974-80)		1993-1995	– Thomas J Gillham (1988-95)
1980-1981	– Brian A Mulholland (1971-81)		1995-1996	– Peter C D Young (1989-96)
1981-1982	– Martin A R Collier (1979-82)		1996-1997	– Richard J S Gillham (1990-97)
1982-1983	– Paul A Rennie (1973-83)		1997-1998	– Martin L Docherty (1992-98)
1983-1984	– Mark H Copping (1974-84)		1998-1999	– Stuart J Cullinan (1992-99)
1984-1985	– Gavin N Turney (1978-85)		1999-2000	– Patrick J Cullinan (1993-2000)
1985-1986	– Mark A Everett (1979-86)			James Weaver (1994-2000)
1986-1987	– Robert J Boos (1982-87)		2000-2001	– Aubrey G Smith (1992-2001)
1987-1988	– Martin J S Da Costa (1981-88)		2001-2002	– Christopher J Georganas (2000-02)
1988-1989	– Andrew A Haji-Hannas (1982-89)		2002-2003	– Zubeen J Khan (2001-03)
1989-1990	– Ediri Sideso (1982-90)		2003-2004	– Lewis G Skittrall (1998-present)

Hector Ryan: Tennis Player

Hector James Gaffney Ryan; born 24 September 1911; Challoner 1924-29; died 19 June 1968

After leaving St Edmund's, Hector Ryan entered Trinity College, Dublin, qualified as a solicitor and became one of the senior partners in Whitney, Moore and Keller in Dublin. He was on the Irish Lawn Tennis team for some years and in their Davis Cup team in 1938.

Hector Ryan tragically died whilst travelling with his wife and family in Italy, when he was knocked down by a car when crossing the road.

Hector Ryan

Captains of Tennis

1930-1931	– C Horace Zino (1922-31)		1952-1953	– Patrick A Burgess (1945-53)
1931-1932	– Gerard E Mallett (1926-33)		1953-1954	– Timothy Gleeson (1945-54)
1932-1933	– P Alexander Zino (1924-33)		1954-1955	– John D Crowley (1949-56)
1933-1934	– John A Denny (1930-34)		1955-1956	– Thomas M Wiszniewski (1950-56)
1934-1935	– Arthur J Armfield (1931-35)		1956-1957	– Douglas R J de Broekert (1954-57)
1935-1936	– C Mandeville Wright (1934-36)		1957-1958	– Colin J F P Jones (1959-58)
1936-1938	– John D Sharpe (1932-39)		1958-1959	– Jolyon S Baldwin (1953-59)
1938-1939	– Antony R D Arden (1930-39)		1959-1960	– John S West (1955-60)
1939-1940	– Thomas Gibian (1939-40)		1960-1962	– Edward D Burgess (1957-62)
1940-1941	– *not recorded*		1962-1963	– Christopher J Ryan (1953-64)
1941-1942	– Alexander Firks (1937-42)		1963-1964	– F Timothy Harrison (1956-64)
1942-1943	– E Mervin Shipsey (1941-44)		1964-1966	– John P Laydon (1960-66)
1943-1944	– *not recorded*		1966-1968	– Terence P Keane (1963-68)
1944-1945	– Peter A Shipsey (1941-45)		1968-1969	– John C Sidery (1962-69)
1945-1946	– Simon J Beardsworth (1940-47)		1969-1970	– Jerzy K (George) Dziedzic (1963-70)
1946-1948	– Antony K Harrison-Thomas (1943-48)		1970-1971	– Edward H Mohan (1964-71)
1948-1949	– Richard F Artesani-Lyons (1946-49)		1971-1973	– Timothy Carswell (1968-73)
1949-1950	– Michael P A Pinot de Moira (1944-present)		1973-1974	– S Christopher Milburn (1967-74)
1950-1951	– H Michael Burgess (1945-51)		1974-1975	– Fabio M Perselli (1971-75)
1951-1952	– Robert H T Brown (1946-52)		1975-1976	– Peter B West (1972-76)

1976-1978 – Stuart R Jackson (1971-78)
1978-1980 – David L Hughes (1974-80)
1980-1981 – Michael K Hodges (1971-81)
1981-1982 – Grant M Branton (1975-82)
1982-1983 – Gerhard A Wallbank (1976-83)
1983-1985 – Kean B Wong (1981-85)
1985-1986 – Kean K Wong (1981-86)
1986-1987 – James S Davies (1980-87)
1987-1989 – Kean L Wong (1984-89)
1989-1990 – *not recorded*
1990-1991 – Michael J Von Speyr (1986-91)
1991-1992 – *not recorded*
1992-1993 – Clare L Edwards (1991-93)
              S Lawrence Iregbulem (1991-93)
1993-1994 – Sarah A (Lucy) Edwards (1992-94)
              Quinton D Haddon (1987-94)

1994-1995 – Robert A Beckley (1988-95)
              Charlotte S E Cade (1990-95)
1995-1996 – Sophie Perry (1989-96)
1996-1997 – Matilda R Beckley (1990-97)
              Alexander C Ross (1995-97)
1997-1998 – Shiu Fung (Donald) Mak (1996-98)
1998-1999 – Anna F Lillywhite (1992-99)
              Matthew C T Robins (1994-99)
1999-2000 – Antonia I (Tina) Mortensen (1990-2000)
              Cedric Tay (1999-2000)
2000-2001 – Victoria E Foster (1994-2001)
2001-2002 – Natalie M Kersey (1991-2002)
2002-2003 – Stefan Bratu (1999-2003)
              Claire E Thornton (1992-2003)

Captains of Fives

1930-1931 – Gerard E Mallett (1926-33)
1931-1932 – James D Rochford (1924-32)
1932-1933 – P Alexander Zino (1924-33)
1933-1934 – Michael Keelan (1930-35)
1934-1935 – Raymond C Bingham (1931-35)
1935-1936 – T Neville Stack (1930-36)
1936-1937 – Peter O D Allcock (1931-37)
1937-1938 – Brian D H de F Hick (1929-39)
1938-1939 – Denis J L Knight (1931-39)

1939-1940 – *not recorded*
1940-1941 – John L S Whitney (1936-42)
1941-1942 – John Aurely (1937-42)
1942-1945 – *not recorded*
1945-1946 – Neil A Muldoon (1940-47)
1946-1947 – *not recorded*
1947-1949 – Robert H Hines (1943-49)
1949-1952 – John C A Bex (1946-52)

Captains of Shooting

1937-1938 – Allan R Wright (1934-38)
1938-1939 – Antony R D Arden (1930-39)
1939-1940 – John Broom (1936-40)

Captains of Swimming

1947-1948 – Antony K Harrison-Thomas (1943-48)
1948-1949 – Christopher A Nascimento (1946-49)
1949-1951 – Christopher Dobner (1946-51)
1951-1971 – *not recorded*
1971-1972 – Christopher H Thomas (1967-72)
1972-1973 – Kevin J McCallion (1968-73)
1973-1974 – *not recorded*
1974-1976 – Gerard M Delaney (1971-76)
1976-1977 – G Anthony Robinson (1967-77)
1977-1979 – *not recorded*
1979-1980 – Nicholas R Tuson (1973-80)
1980-1981 – Charles R D Allen (1973-81)
1981-1984 – *not recorded*
1984-1985 – Richard S Park (1980-85)
1985-1986 – Guy J Garden (1979-87)

1986-1987 – Curtis J Allcorn (1978-87)
1987-1988 – Andrew P Lawrence (1981-88)
1988-1989 – Emma M K Devine (1985-89)
              Malcolm G Stone (1983-89)
1989-1990 – Caroline D A Anderson (1988-90)
              Gillian L McCann (1987-90)
1990-1991 – Roger A James (1985-92)
1991-1992 – *not recorded*
1992-1994 – Dominic P Hayakawa (1987-94)
1993-1994 – Elizabeth T Brooke-Powell (1989-95)
1994-1995 – Geraldine M Downer (1991-95)
              Christian J J Laguea (1993-95)
1995-1996 – Charlotte A Bonnett (1989-96)
1996-1997 – Hugh T Parsons (1989-97)
1997-1998 – Charlotte Dewson (1989-98)

1998-1999 – Helen L Stafford (1992-99)	2001-2002 – Robert T Kennedy (1995-2002)
1999-2000 – Simon J Constant (1992-2000)	Natalie M Kersey (1991-2002)
Rachel A Matthias (1993-2000)	2002-2003 – Dimitar Bitolsky (1999-2003)
2000-2001 – Victoria E Foster (1994-2001)	2003-2004 – Alan H Miller (1997-present)
	Aimee H Foster (1997-present)

Captains of Badminton

1952-1953 – J Ivor O'Mahony (1945-53)	1988-1989 – Kean L Wong (1984-89)
1953-1954 – A John Sheridan (1946-54)	1989-1990 – Siu Heung (Paul) Lau (1985-90)
1954-1955 – Charles E Carey (1946-55)	1990-1991 – Peter J Readman (1985-92)
1955-1956 – Paul A Hypher (1948-56)	1991-1992 – not recorded
1956-1957 – Peter J Hines (1947-57)	1992-1994 – George P Sobek (1987-94)
1957-1988 – not recorded	1994-1995 – Pak Ho (Pedro) Lee (1991-95)

Nicholas Nieland: Athlete

Nicholas Peter Russell Nieland; born 31 January 1972; Junior House & Stapleton 1983-90

Nick Nieland became a junior international javelin thrower after leaving St Edmund's, and won the British Universities title in 1993 with a throw of 74.50m. He went on to compete in the World Student Games. In 1996 he won the Amateur Athletics Association title with a throw of 83.06m and was selected for the Olympic Games. He made his personal best of 83.68m in 1999. In 2002 he won a bronze medal at the Commonwealth Games.

He works for an investment bank in London, having graduated in chemistry from Bristol University.

Nick Nieland

Captains of Athletics

1959-1960 – Andrew D Toomey (1950-60)	1981-1982 – Stephen J McGrory (1977-82)
1960-1962 – Derek C Lance (1957-62)	1982-1985 – not recorded
1962-1964 – Christopher J Ryan (1953-64)	1985-1986 – Augustine U F Imevbore (1984-86)
1964-1965 – Antony Convery (1958-65)	1986-1987 – Simon J P Maynard (1979-87)
1965-1966 – Adrian L Reading (1957-66)	1987-1988 – Christopher J Boos (1982-88)
1966-1967 – Michael R White (1961-67)	1988-1989 – Alan W Rodney (1979-89)
1967-1969 – David A Rozalla (1959-69)	1989-1990 – Rachel J Burke (1986-90)
1969-1971 – Ronald W Anderson (1964-71)	Nicholas P R Nieland (1983-90)
1971-1972 – Christopher D Gardiner (1965-72)	1990-1991 – Christian Pini (1984-91)
1972-1973 – Donogh P O'Brien (1968-73)	1991-1992 – Matthew J Campbell (1987-92)
1973-1974 – William A M Morris (1968-74)	1992-1993 – Alexander Biggs (1989-93)
1974-1975 – Peter A Wilson (1973-75)	1993-1994 – Pawel M Czarnecki (1987-94)
1975-1976 – Thomas C Hart (1971-76)	1994-1996 – Vincent Martorana (1989-96)
1976-1977 – Roy P D Darkin (1967-77)	1996-1997 – Patrick R James (1986-97)
1977-1978 – Alan M Hlavaty (1971-78)	1997-1998 – Amanze E Iregbulem (1993-98)
1978-1979 – Matthew T Bench (1971-79)	1998-2000 – not recorded
1979-1980 – Christopher P Miller (1972-80)	2000-2001 – Rowena L Finn (1991-2001)
1980-1981 – Martin A R Collier (1979-82)	

Captain of Cross-Country
1971-1972   – Paul A Hick (1965-72)

Captains of Hockey
1985-1986 – Catherine L De Rosa (1984-86)	1994-1995 – Elizabeth T Brooke-Powell (1989-95)
1986-1987 – Helena A Cody (1985-87)	1995-1996 – Purdey-Emma Silvester (1989-96)
1987-1988 – Miranda K Beadell (1986-88)	1996-1997 – Claire L Habershon (1990-97)
1988-1989 – Rachel F S Da Costa (1985-89)	1997-1998 – Camilla M Sinnott (1991-98)
1989-1990 – Gillian L McCann (1987-90)	1998-1999 – Claire L Kasza (1988-99)
1990-1991 – Ondine Sinfield (1986-91)	1999-2000 – Marie-Louise (Lulu) Mortensen
1991-1992 – Sara V K N Toruñ (1986-92)	(1990-2000)
1992-1993 – Jane R Gibson (1986-93)	2000-2001 – Rowena L Finn (1991-2001)
1993-1993 – Alexandra M Stevens (1987-94) *to Dec*	2001-2002 – Nicola C Pinkney (1991-2002)
1993-1994 – David A Logue (1983-94)	2002-2003 – Claire E Thornton (1992-2003)
1994-1994 – Sarah A (Lucy) Edwards (1992-94) *from Jan*	2003-2004 – Katherine A Habershon (1997-present)

Captains of Netball
1990-1991 – Jacqueline P McIntyre (1987-91)	1997-1998 – Natalie M Saleh (1991-98)
1991-1992 – Tanya C Carney (1988-92)	1998-1999 – Anna F Lillywhite (1992-99)
1992-1993 – Sarah J Pedder (1986-93)	1999-2000 – Rachel A Matthias (1993-2000)
1993-1994 – Joanna L T Drew (1987-94)	2000-2001 – Katy White (1995-99 & 1999-01)
1994-1995 – Rachel J Pedder (1988-95)	2001-2002 – Chloe F Gamby (2000-02)
1995-1996 – Sophie Perry (1989-96)	2002-2003 – Julie E Brooks (1996-2003)
1996-1997 – Matilda R Beckley (1990-97)	2003-2004 – Grace M Gamby (2002-present)

Captains of Football
1993-1994 – Robert C Homer (1987-94)	1998-1999 – Michael P Collins (1992-99)
1994-1995 – Adam C Barrow (1987-95)	1999-2000 – Simon J Constant (1992-2000)
1995-1996 – Vincent Martorana (1989-96)	2000-2001 – Damian Williamson (1994-2001)
1996-1997 – Hugh T Parsons (1989-97)	2001-2002 – Thomas M Cullinan (1995-2002)
1997-1998 – John W Norris (1989-98)	2002-2003 – David Gerty (1995-2003)

Captains of Rounders
1993-1994 – Joanna L T Drew (1987-94)	1998-1999 – Charlotte M E Ashton (1988-99)
1994-1995 – Bethan M Davies (1988-96)	1999-2000 – Claire M Kyndt (1998-2000)
1995-1996 – Emma T Czarnecka (1987-96)	2000-2001 – Alexa J Turness (1990-2001)
1996-1997 – Eliane M Young (1991-98)	2001-2002 – Alanna C Easton (1995-2002)
1997-1998 – Fern K Edwards (1991-98)	2002-2003 – Julie E Brooks (1996-2003)

Captains of Basketball
1996-1997   – Vai Cheong (Joseph) Leong (1996-98)
1997-1999   – *not recorded*
1999-2000   – Cedric Tay (1999-2000)

chapter 11

The Edmundian Association

The idea to have an association of Edmundians was first suggested in 1852, when it was proposed to be called The Edmundian Club. A temporary committee was established, chaired by Dr William Weathers (1838-68), and consisting of Charles Corney (1832-34), Dr John Crookall (1834~55), Charles Pagliano (1810-13), John Rees (1839-43), Dr Frederick Rymer (1835~69) & Fr Henry Telford (1829~56). The Edmundian Association was formally inaugurated on 28 September 1853. Its activities were suspended during the two World Wars, but in 1946 Mgr John Bagshawe (1925~52) set up a small temporary committee to revive it. Below are listed the current Patrons of the Association (a small number of loyal Edmundians acclaimed for their loyalty to and support of its work), the officers of the Association since its foundation, and those who have served as representative committee members since 1946.

Current Patrons

John M Gillham MC KCSG KCHS FCIOB *Former Parent & Chairman of Governors*
Austin Basil Jackson (1924-27) *Member of the Association for 76 years*
Mrs Joan King (1943-present) *Widow of Mr J H W King, former Headmaster*
Rt Rev David E Konstant MA (1943-54) *Bishop of Leeds*
Donald J J McEwen KCHS MA FRSA (1984-2002) *Former Headmaster*
Very Rev Mgr Canon Frederick A Miles MA (1939~67) *Former Housemaster of Challoner & Governor*
Squadron Leader Jocelyn G P Millard AE KSG (1928-31) *Veteran of the Battle of Britain*
Very Rev Canon Peter B Phillips MA (1940~67) *Former Housemaster of Douglass & Governor*

President

Between 1853 & 1986 the President of the College was also the President of the Association; see chapter 2 for their names
1986-1994 – John M Gillham MC KCSG KCHS FCIOB
1994-1999 – George P Lehrian LLB FCHIMA (1941-49)
2000-present–   J Ivor O'Mahony BSc(Econ) FCA (1945-53)

Clerical Vice-President

The position of Vice-President was inaugurated in 1853 and two Vice-Presidents are currently elected annually, one being a priest and the other a lay person

Canon Brian Frost
Vice-President 1978-82

1853-1854	– Very Rev Canon O'Neal
1854-c.1861	– Very Rev Canon George Last (1819-32)
c.1861-1869	– Rev Frederick Rymer (1835~70)
1870-1886	– Very Rev Canon John Bamber (1848~62)
1886-1904	– Rt Rev Mgr Isaac Goddard (1854~70)
1904-1908	– Very Rev Canon George Delaney (1857-66)
1908-1920	– Very Rev Canon George Carter (1857~71)
1920-1925	– Very Rev Canon Dr Edwin H Burton (1883~1918)
1926-1958	– Rt Rev Mgr Canon Charles E Brown (1885~1902)
1958-1973	– Rt Rev Mgr Canon Dr John E Howell (1908-18)
1973-1978	– Rt Rev Mgr Frederick A Miles (1939~67)
1978-1982	– Very Rev Canon Brian A Frost (1936-44)
1982-1984	– Very Rev Canon Peter J Bourne (1957-65)
1984-present	– Rev Michael P A Pinot de Moira (1944~present)

Lay Vice-President

1853-1861	–	Charles J Pagliano (1810-13)
1861-1874	–	Lawrence Dolan (senior) (1805-07)
1874-1905	–	Lawrence Dolan (junior) (1836-41)
1905-1910	–	Charles Havers (1852-58)
1910-1935	–	Sir Henry Stafford Jerningham Bt JP (1879-85)
1936-1953	–	Charles B Goulden OBE MA MD MCh FRCS (1888-96)
1953-1960	–	Col John W A Ollard OBE KCSG DL (1904-05)
1960-1966	–	Sir Alan Burns GCMG (1900-03)
1966-1973	–	J Haldane Walton-King MA (1930-76)
1973-1979	–	George P Lehrian LLB FCHIMA (1941-49)
1979-1983	–	Wing Cdr Sydney M Thornton-Grimes (1930-36)
1983-1986	–	Peter A F Fletcher (1930-37)
1986-1993	–	Kenneth R Allen (1951-56)
1993-1998	–	Richard J Winter BSc (1970-95)
1998-present	–	David J S Kay (1975-82)

Lawrence Dolan (Junior)
Vice-President for 31 years

Peter Hanlon
Chairman 1997-2003

Chairman

This position was inaugurated in 1991 and the Chairman is currently elected for up to two periods of three years

1991-1997	–	David J S Kay (1975-82)
1997-2003	–	Peter W Hanlon (1969-74)

Treasurer

This position was inaugurated in 1853 and the Treasurer is currently elected for up to two periods of three years

1853-1886	–	Charles F Corney (1832-34)
1887-1898	–	Field Stanfield (1855-57)
1898-1912	–	Henry W Franklin (unknown-1884)
1912-1923	–	Ernest Curran (1893-98)
1923-1933	–	Kenneth de H Ollard JP (1901-02)
1933-1948	–	Capt Joseph C J O'Connor (1899-1903)
1948-1954	–	Francis G Bannister (1929-35)
1954-1960	–	Edmund T J F Fletcher (1931-40)
1960-1964	–	Michael J Gaughran (1944-53)
1964-1970	–	Kennedy D Ryan (1938-41)
1970-1977	–	Paul D Keenan AIB (1949-57)
1977-1982	–	Michael S Anderson (1953-61)
1982-1982	–	Wing Cdr Sydney M Thornton-Grimes (1930-36)
		Acting temporarily
1982-1988	–	Jeremy J Tigue (1970-77)
1988-1994	–	J Ivor O'Mahony BSc(Econ) FCA (1945-53)
1994-2000	–	Frederick H P Offer (1946-51)
2000-present	–	Ronald J Gladman (1954-59)

Secretary

This role was inaugurated in 1853 and was disbanded after the Second World War

1853-c.1861 – Horatio Rymer (1835-38)
c.1861-1870 – Arthur C Ryan (1849-51)
1870-1883 – Field Stanfield (1855-57)
1883-1893 – Rev Bernard N Ward (1869~1916)
1893-1897 – Rev Edmond Nolan (1876~96)
1897-1900 – Rev Charles T Kuypers (1882~1901)
1900-1902 – Rev Edmond Nolan (1876~96)
1902-1918 – Rev Edward Myers (1893~1932)
1918-1920 – office vacant
1920-1926 – Rev Dr John G Vance (1905~26)
1926-1931 – Rev Francis D Healy (1892~1929)
1931-1940 – Rev Leonard A Clark (1917~40)

Fr Leonard Clark
The last Secretary

General Secretary

This position was inaugurated in 1947 and the General Secretary and is currently for up to two periods of three years

1947-1953 – Rev Benedict F Westbrook (1927~65)
1953-1960 – Rev Michael G Garvey (1940~84)
1960-1965 – Rev Michael P A Pinot de Moira (1944~present)
1965-1965 – Rev John V McManus (1943~65) Acting General Secretary only
1965-1966 – Rev Michael G Garvey (1940~84)
1966-1968 – Rev Patrick D Brennan (1950-56)
1968-1971 – Paul F J Ketterer (1945~71)
1971-1974 – Rev Richard More Sutherland (1949-53) Acting General Secretary only
1975-1981 – Paul D Rossi (1960-67)
1981-1987 – Richard J Winter (1970-95)
1987-1991 – David J S Kay (1975-82)
1992-1994 – David P Broughton (1979-87)
1994-1999 – Michael P O'Connor (1976-87)
1999-present – Robert P Healy (1976-86)

Three former General Secretaries: (from L to R) Richard Winter, Michael O'Connor & David Kay

Assistant Secretary

The role of Assistant Secretary was first mooted in 1875 but was not formally ratified as an office of the Association until some 118 years later in 1993; from time to time members of the committee acted as Assistant to the General Secretary

1993-1994 – Michael P O'Connor (1976-87)
1994-1998 – Annabel S Gillham (1987-94)
1998-1999 – Robert P Healy (1976-86)
Renamed Membership Secretary 1999
1999-2003 – Dr Simon M Thompson (1988-95)
2003-present – Timothy C Fuller (1967-72)

John Vaughan-Shaw & Bishop Christopher Butler at an Edmundian dinner dance

Social Secretary

This position was created in 1947

1947-1950 – Maurice W J P Fitzgerald (1923-25)
1950-1955 – Brian D H de F Hick (1929-39)
1955-1961 – Peter E Secretan (1938-47)
1961-1966 – Peter I P Hick (1937-45)

The office was temporarily suspended because no cocktail party was planned for 1967

1969-1975 – John Vaughan-Shaw (1964-present)
1975-1982 – *office vacant*
1982-1985 – Christopher J Waters (1971-78)
1985-1988 – Richard A Vass (1973-83)
1988-1993 – *office vacant*

The office was disbanded in 1993 to be replaced by that of Assistant Secretary

Sports Secretary

This role was temporarily created during the 1970s to organise rugby and cricket matches

1972-1976 – Christopher J Gillham (1958-64)
1976-1980 – Kieron S Heath (1962-69)

Representative Committee Members

A role created in 1853, some time between 1896 & 1927 number of representative committee members increased from six to eight; in 1947 it went up to nine; in 1950 the Headmaster was added as an ex-officio member; between 1968 & 1975 the Rector of Allen Hall was also an ex-officio member; there are currently twelve representative committee members

The temporary committee set up to revive the Association after the Second World War consisted of the President and Hal King (1930-76), Fr Nicholas Kelly (1924~61), Fr Peter Geraerts (1931~53) & Fr Laurence Allan (1936~60).

1947-1953 – Very Rev Canon Robert J McCliment (1907~22)	1949-1954 – Edmund T J F Fletcher (1931-40)
1947-1952 – Rev Terence D Keenan (1916-27)	1949-1950 – Rev Denis C H Britt-Compton (1926~68)
1947-1948 – Rev Charles P Carr (1919-29)	1950-1956 – Maurice W J P Fitzgerald (1923-25)
1947-1948 – Frederick I Connolly (1903-12)	1951-1957 – Rev Edward J Hinsley (1925-35)
1947-1952 – J Haldane Walton-King (1930-76)	1951-1957 – Neil A Muldoon (1940-47)
1947-1948 – Joseph E H Stallard (1920-23)	1951-1957 – William A J Hazel (1923-27)
1947-1953 – Peter C J Rossi (1934-42)	1952-1958 – Rev Joseph R Williams (1919-31)
1947-1949 – Antony R D Arden (1930-39)	1952-1955 – John P A Hatfield (1938-40)
1948-1951 – Alfred M Burgess (née Buhagiar) (1937-44)	1953-1958 – Rev Benedict F Westbrook (1927~65)
1948-1951 – Rev Joseph P Doyle (1927-37)	1953-1955 – Antony R D Arden (1930-39)
1948-1951 – Owen F Waters (1916-19)	1954-1957 – John J O'Brien (1939-41)
1948-1950 – Brian D H de F Hick (1929-39)	1955-1957 – Brian D H de F Hick (1929-39)
	1955-1955 – Charles R J Weston (1947~52)
	1956-1959 – David G Wright (1937-44)

1957-1963	–	Rev Terence D Keenan (1916-27)		
1957-1963	–	John C A Bex (1946-52)		
1957-1963	–	Peter I P Hick (1937-45)		
1958-1964	–	Rev Ronald L Shepherd (1930-42)		
1958-1962	–	Dr Charles M Arthur (1930-34)		
1958-1959	–	Very Rev Canon William J Heffernan (1903~24)		
1959-1964	–	Rev Desmond C Sheehan (1946-58)		
1960-1966	–	Rev Frederick A Miles (1939-67)		
1960-1963	–	Laurence P Moynihan (1904-05)		
1960-1966	–	John P A Hatfield (1938-40)		
1962-1968	–	Peter E Secretan (1938-47)		
1963-1969	–	Rev David E Konstant (1943-54)		
1963-1969	–	Major Patrick T (Paddy) Ryan (1932-33)		
1963-1964	–	Kennedy D Ryan (1938-41)		
1964-1970	–	Very Rev Canon Terence D Keenan (1916-27)		
1965-1966	–	Adrian J Walsh (1958-64)		
1966-1972	–	Charles E Carey (1946-55)		
1965-1968	–	Very Rev Canon Joseph R Williams (1919-31)		
1966-1972	–	George P Lehrian (1941-49)		
1966-1972	–	Bernard A France (1939-41)		
1966-1971	–	Peter I P Hick (1937-45)		
1966-1968	–	Rev Michael G Garvey (1940~84)		
1968-1975	–	Francis W Courtney (1956-62)		
1968-1971	–	Rev Richard M Sutherland (1949-53)		
1969-1976	–	Joseph I Fitzgibbon (1948-48)		
1969-1975	–	Paul D Rossi (1960-67)		
1970-1970	–	Paul D Keenan (1949-57)		
1970-1976	–	Very Rev Canon Brian A Frost (1936-44)		
1971-1978	–	Wing Cdr Sydney M Thornton-Grimes (1930-36)		
1971-1975	–	John P Laydon (1960-66)		

The 1972 AGM, scheduled for November 1972, was postponed to February 1973, with the result that committee members appear to have served an extra year

1972-1979	–	Christopher J Gillham (1958-64)
1973-1979	–	Paul E Day (1960-67) Assistant Secretary
1973-1979	–	John M C Bryant (1962-71)
1975-1981	–	Peter A F Fletcher (1930-37)
1975-1978	–	Nicholas J Bannister (1960-64)
1975-1981	–	John Vaughan-Shaw (1964-present)
1976-1980	–	Kieron S Heath (1962-69)
1978-1982	–	Very Rev Canon Peter J Bourne (1957-65)
1978-1981	–	Martin D Gratte (1957-60)
1978-1982	–	John J O'Brien (1939-41)

1980-1986	–	Peter J C McGovern (1967-74)
1980-1983	–	Martin J Molloy (1963-71)
1981-1982	–	Jeremy J Tigue (1970-77)
1981-1984	–	James C Webb (1968-77)
1981-1984	–	Julian A Lott (1970-77)
1981-1986	–	Kenneth R Allen (1951-56)
1981-1984	–	Nigel T A Cave (1977-84)
1983-1986	–	Miss Carol A Kneebone (1977-80)
1982-1988	–	Douglas W Sandilands (1971-73)
1983-1986	–	Justin B P Bull (1972-82)
1983-1986	–	Kieron S Heath (1962-69)
1984-1987	–	Miss Sarah M (Sally) Cave (1977-79)
1984-1987	–	Rev Michael J Roberts (1958~88)
1985-1988	–	Michael D Holland (1975-82)
1986-1987	–	David J S Kay (1975-82)
1986-1989	–	R Simon Duggan (1978-82)
1986-present	–	John Vaughan-Shaw (1964-present)
1986-1992	–	Jonathan L Grace (1971-80)
1988-1991	–	Miss Julia A Davies (1984-86)
1988-1994	–	Mark J Lee (1979-86)
1987-1990	–	Paul A Goodman (1954-60)
1987-1990	–	Michael J Peachey (1950-52)
1987-1992	–	David P Broughton (1979-87)
1988-1997	–	Peter W Hanlon (1969-74)
1988-1993	–	Richard J Winter (1970-95)
1991-present	–	Alexander P A Roberts (1954-61)
1989-1991	–	Thomas J E Collett (1973-80)
1991-1992	–	Michael P O'Connor (1976-87)
1992-1998	–	Robert P Healy (1976-86)
1994-1997	–	Miss Zofia A Toruñ (1986-92)
1994-1997	–	Michael A Maslinski (1962-70)
1994-1996	–	Miss Miriam T Mason (1992-96)
1994-1997	–	Christopher J Sleight (1985-92)
1994-present	–	Mrs Irena M Toruñ
1994-1997	–	Miss Sara V K N Toruñ (1986-92)
1994-2000	–	Miss Lucy Edwards (1992-94)
1996-2001	–	Mrs Patricia H Pond (1990-2001)
1996-1999	–	Dr Simon M Thompson (1988-95)
1998-present	–	Richard J Winter (1970-95)
1997-present	–	Jeremy M Gillham (1963-69)
1997-2000	–	Patrick R D Pond (1989-96)
1997-2003	–	Austin M Harney (1981-86)
2000-present	–	Frederick H P Offer (1946-51)
2000-2002	–	Richard M C Beveridge (1981-88)
2000-2003	–	Timothy C Fuller (1967-72)
2001-present	–	James E Sheridan (1999-present)
2001-2003	–	Simon C Fuller (1966-77)
2002-present	–	Philip J C Kyndt (1962-68)
2003-present	–	Ian A Stephens (1975-82)

Basil Jackson: Member of The Edmundian Association for 76 years

Austin Basil Jackson; born 8 July 1909; Challoner 1924-27

Coming to St Edmund's after time in a convent in Abingdon and a school in Hitchin, Basil Jackson recently recalled that his scholastic achievements were "nil", his great love being cricket, for which he played in the College XI in 1926 & 1927.

Basil Jackson

In September 1927, Basil returned to India to join the British mercantile firm Killick Nixon & Co with its head office in Bombay. At the outbreak of the Second World War, he was declared unfit for combat duties by the Indian Army, owing to the onset of chest trouble, and was seconded to the Auxiliary Forces. This, in conjunction with his firm's functions, included the supervision of troop ships.

Basil was almost blown up in the "Bombay Explosion" which occurred in the Victoria Docks on 14 April 1944 when the ammunition vessel *Fort Stikine* exploded. The vessel was loaded with a cargo of cotton and high explosives; it caught fire and two shattering explosions followed. Within a few minutes the whole Bombay area was aflame and covered with a thick fog. Buildings were wrecked over a wide area by the blast and fire quickly spread through the city – at one time an area of three miles square was ablaze. Gruesome scenes were witnessed on the waterfront, dead and injured were everywhere amid the wreckage of buildings, ships and vehicles. The *Fort Stikine* had been under Basil's firm's jurisdiction and he had been standing alongside it just half an hour earlier.

His service out East enabled him also to visit other countries such as the USA, Canada & Japan. Since returning to England in 1960, Basil undertook various jobs, living in London and Reading, and finally retiring to the Isle of Wight in the late 1970s. He was widowed in 1984.

Basil has been a member of The Edmundian Association since 1927 and a Patron since 1999. Despite being the second oldest living Edmundian, he keeps in close contact with developments at the College, makes frequent donations to the Library, and is a prolific letter writer.

Advanced Studies Awards

The concept of an "Award for Advanced Studies" commenced in 1964 and superseded an annual award of £10 paid by the Association representing the value of a State Scholarship. It is awarded to those who have achieved outstanding success in their Advanced Level examinations. Since 1982 it has been given to those who achieved three or more 'A' grade passes. The amount of the Award has been increased every few years: £15 (1971), £20 (1978), £40 (1983), £50 (1985), £60 (1987), £75 (1989), £150 (1990), £200 (1993), and £250 (1999). The exception was in 1975, when Douglas Easton (1969-75) received £25 for outstanding examination success. Over the years some 86 students have received a total sum of £12,110.

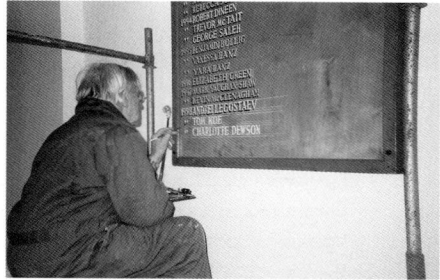

Names being added to the Advanced Studies Award honours board in 1998

1965 – Robert N Rowe (1960-65)
1966 – Anthony M Lidgate (1963-66)
1967 – John P Laydon (1960-66)
1968 – *no award made*
1969 – William A Holloway (1961-68)
1970 – *no award made*
1971 – George R Horner (1965-71)
1972 – *no award made*
1973 – Adrian A Goemans (1969-73)
   Simon H O'Neill (1966-73)
1974 – *no award made*
1975 – Douglas F Easton (1969-75)
1976 – Michael R V Barkham (1969-76)
   Martin J Chick (1969-76)
1977 – Douglas G H Ansley (1968-77)
   Stephen P Quin (1970-77)
   Martin J C Smith (1973-77)
1978 – Malcolm Davis-White (1969-78)
   Paul A Woodhouse (1971-78)
1979 – Michael J C Martin (1972-79)
   Timothy J Vyse (1972-79)
1980 – *no award made*
1981 – *no award made*
1982 – R Simon Duggan (1978-82)
   Josephine M Orchard (1980-82)
   Andrew P Shacklock (1975-82)
   Adrian C D Smith (1975-82)
   Josepha A M Wallbank (1980-82)
1983 – Peter Hobin (1976-83)
   Jonathan Hurley (1976-83)
   Andrew Webb (1976-83)

1984 – Robin J Duggan (1978-84)
   Daniel S Mills (1977-84)
   Graham K Weston (1977-84)
1985 – Alan W D Fitt (1978-85)
   Neal W Harwood (1978-85)
1986 – Wang Hei (Eugene) Wong (1982-86)
1987 – Nabil M N Badr (1985-87)
   Aidan P Casey (1982-87)
1988 – Alaster M Allum (1980-88)
1989 – Nga Ching (Eugene) Chan (1986-89)
   Siu Kay (Quintin) Kwok (1984-89)
   Kean L Wong (1984-89)
1990 – Nicholas P R Nieland (1983-90)
   John M Richardson (1980-90)
1991 – Dominic S Black (1984-91)
   Claudia D Demuth (1989-91)
   Michael F Pargeter (1986-91)
1992 – *no award made*
1993 – Roger G Elliott (1986-93)
   Robert J Hattrell (1986-93)
   Jacqueline A Noon (1986-93)
   Rebecca M Sutherland (1991-93)
1994 – Robert C Dineen (1987-94)
   Trevor M P R McTait (1987-94)
   George M Saleh (1987-94)
1995 – Vanessa M Banz (1991-95)
   Yara S Banz (1991-95)
   Benjamin A F Bollig (1988-95)
1996 – Elizabeth E Green (1989-96)
1997 – Kevin P McClenaghan (1987-97)
   Mark E Vaughan-Shaw (1989-97)

1998 – Charlotte Dewson (1989-98)
Thomas A Koe (1990-98)
Andrei Legostaev (1996-98)

1999 – William H Gilbert (1992-99)
Laura J Howard (1994-99)
Helen L Stafford (1992-99)
Matthew J Vaughan-Shaw (1991-99)

2000 – George M Beckley (1993-2000
Simon J Constant (1992-2000)
Patrick J Cullinan (1993-2000)
Po-Chu (Kevin) Hsieh (1997-2000)
Marie-Louise (Lulu) Mortensen (1990-2000)
David A Storring (1990-2000)
Katharina M Virnich (1998-2000)

2001 – Brian J Green (1994-2001)
Haichuan (Nick) Hu (2000-01)

Natasha A Marko (1996-2001)
Peter G Vaughan-Shaw (1993-2001)

2002 – Thomas O M Marks (1995-2002)
Mary Rochester (2000-02)
Jordan P Skittrall (1995-2002)
Shikai (David) Zhong (2000-02)

2003 – Stefan Bratu (1999-2003)
Julie E Brooks (1996-2003)
Hoo Ming (Henry) Cheung (2001-03)
Gao Cheng (Francis) Fang (2001-03)
David O Flynne (1995-2003)
J Toby Gribbin (1996-2003)
Sara Howard (1994-2003)
Saleh Okhovat (1998-2003)
Sophie R Wilson (1994-2003)

Andrei Legostaev
Awarded in 1998

Lulu Mortensen
Awarded in 2000

chapter 12

Personalities & a ghost

This chapter pulls together Edmundians who do not necessarily fit within any one other chapter. It is a collection of personalities who mostly have just one thing in common – that they studied or worked at the St Edmund's. It also mentions some of those who were related to well-known people. You will be pleased to know the College's official ghost does not haunt the Ambulacrum.

Chamaco: Matador
Antonio Borrero Borrero; born 28 July 1972; Junior House 1986-87

It is said that playing rugby at St Edmund's helped Antonio Borrero Borrero – "Chamaco" the matador – with his technique as a professional bullfighter.

Having inherited the title Chamaco from his father, also a bullfighter, he has been widely feted and even has streets named after him in some towns in which he has performed.

Matadors relieve bulls of their ears as trophies at the end of their fights. Over the years Chamaco can claim the following statistics:

1994:   36 bullfights, 71 ears
1996:   23 bullfights, 34 ears
1997:   21 bullfights, 29 ears
1998:   34 bullfights, 61 ears and 1 tail

Antonio Borrero Borrero

Rory McCarthy: Entrepreneur & adventurer
Rory C McCarthy; born 25 June 1960; Talbot 1976-77

In 1981, Rory McCarthy led a five-man expedition to hang-glide from the summit of Mont Blanc. The project was thwarted by the weather, and Rory was trapped on the summit for 28 hours in temperatures of -50°C and 70mph winds. After recovering, he returned to Mont Blanc and successfully flew from the summit. He set an altitude record for hang-gliding in 1984, from a hot air balloon at 34,500 feet piloted by Per Lindstrand. In 1986 he added a civilian sky-diving altitude record, again from a balloon flown by Lindstrand from 35,600 feet.

In 1997 he made the headlines with his aborted attempt to circumnavigate the world in a hot air balloon with Richard Branson. Rory McCarthy is the head of a public company with interests in telecommunications, retail and leisure. Amongst his regular weekend leisure activities is flying a Folland Gnat supersonic jet.

Edward Peppiatt BSc ARCS FRIC: Eccentric chemistry teacher

Edward George Peppiatt; born 6 May 1915; staff 1973-80; died 12 August 1983

"Three Ps, two Ts, one E, one I, one A" as he would like to remind pupils who misspelled his surname, Edward Peppiatt was one of the characters of his time at St Edmund's. Known as "Old Pepp" he taught chemistry following a career in industry as a director of pharmaceutical company Merck Sharp and Dohme, and was rarely seen outside his laboratory. His teaching methods were somewhat unconventional. Each lesson would start with a test, and if you failed, there would be a "re-test" using different questions, and even a "re-re-test". The "tests" were all individually printed on separate sheets of paper and he would staple the marked papers into students' exercise books. The whole administrative effort surrounding the "tests" meant that there was little time left for effective chemistry teaching, and class time was devoted mainly to theory with hardly any experiments.

Old Pepp chain-smoked during classes, despite the proximity of flammable chemicals, and would light his cigarettes on his Bunsen burner. On the bench in front of him during classes were three unmarked conical flasks, one containing distilled water, another containing acid, and the last one containing gin. During class, he would use two of these ingredients, together with a tea bag, to brew-up what he called "chemist's tea".

He spawned many catch phrases, but the most memorable must be "Always come to class with a full pen and an empty bladder", an object lesson in preparation which some students today might well heed.

Edward Brocard: Victim of handbag attack

Edward Francis Brocard; born circa 1890; school 1903-05; date of death unknown

Edward Brocard received adverse publicity in the national press after he was attacked on Pinner Hill Golf Course, Middlesex, in March 1929.

He was putting on the 18th green as a lady friend held the flag out of the way for him, when his wife appeared from across the fairway and struck him several times with her handbag. She was later fined £20.

Vincent Martorana (Photo © Herts & Essex Newspapers)

Vincent Martorana: Model

Vincent Martorana; born 18 October 1977; Junior House & Douglass 1989-96

Whilst still a student at the College, Vincent Martorana's photograph appeared in a local newspaper in Hertfordshire in 1996.

Shown sitting atop a pile of car tyres, he featured in an advertisement for the Mr Unique chain of tyre and exhaust garages, owned at the time by his father.

Pat McCullagh: Millionaire village tramp

Arthur Francis Patrick McCullagh; born 9 September 1917; St Hugh's & Talbot 1928-34; died 1 June 1996

"Village 'tramp' left £1.2m to charities" – so read a head-line in the *Daily Telegraph* in 1996. Pat McCullagh was born in the village of Wool in Dorset, and after his time at St Edmund's spent seven years training as a veteri-nary surgeon, subsequently practising in Devon and London. However, he gave that all up to go back to Wool to run a small engineering business from the garage and outbuildings at his bungalow, which his mother had built in the early 1920s, and at which he remained for the rest of his life.

In middle age he married Margaret, whom he survived by ten years. She transformed his life, and they set up a successful caravan park in the grounds of their home. However, he was known in the village as an eccentric who hated spending money. The bungalow became more dilapidated and he had an old wreck of a car, which he regularly drove up to the College for St Edmund's Day.

Pat McCullagh

He used to walk around the village in wellington boots, grubby old overalls with the pockets torn off, with a sack wrapped around him as an apron and a rope for a belt. He would not spend a penny if he could make something himself which would do the job. If a loaf of bread had mould on it, he would cut that end off and use the rest. He once sewed up a gash over his eye himself rather than going to hospital.

Pat McCullagh died after a short illness, but his frugality enabled him to leave £1.3m to various charities.

Francis Macerone: Inventor & eccentric

Francis Macerone; born 1788; student 1801-03; died 1846

Most of the details which follow are based on Francis Macerone's own memoirs, which were written in a des-perate attempt to raise money, and therefore must be read with that in mind.

At the height of his career, in 1814, he was Aide-de-Camp to Joachim Murat, Napoleon's King of Naples, and was his trusted envoy to the Prince Regent, to Napoleon and to Wellington. After Murat's death he became involved in many popular uprisings of the next decade, and in between these adventures he devised several promising inventions, none of which brought him any financial benefit.

In 1803 he travelled first to Rome, where his uncle was Papal Postmaster-General, and later to Naples. When the French occupied Naples in 1806, his Napoleonic sympa-thies led him to take a prominent part in the continued round of dinner parties, excursions and picnics with which some of the citizens used to entertain their conquerors.

Colonel Francis Macerone

111

He formed an archery club and then Italy's first cricket club. He also established a ladies swimming club, in a grotto at Posilipo, with himself as the instructor! He always sought to be the centre of attention, and he this achieved through a variety of escapades, such as eating live scorpions, climbing the outside of the dome of St Peter's in Rome, and keeping a coiled-up snake inside his hat during dinner parties.

His inventions included an underwater paddle-wheel, improved rockets, shells and other weapons, a project for building a canal across the isthmus of Panama, and a steam-driven road carriage.

From 1816 onwards he lived intermittently in England and South America. It was in 1831 that he became interested in steam locomotion. At a factory in Paddington, Macerone and one John Squire set about designing an improved boiler. Experimental runs with their carriage began in 1833, to Edgware, Windsor, and then finally to Hertfordshire. But hopes of making his fortune with a steam-driven road carriage were dashed with the success of the railways. Francis Macerone fell out with his business partner, and claimed that had been cheated of his patents. He and his family then lived in poverty until 1846, when he died in shabby lodgings in Hammersmith.

John Wood MA: Mathematics master
John William Wood; born c.1919; staff 1963-84

One of the most prolific and colourful characters of modern times must be John Wood, who retired after holding a number of posts at the College. He was known as Larmy – after a mathematical theorem of the same name.

He was a mathematics master, was in charge of rugby, and latterly became Careers Master. It was as an administrator that he was at his best. Whether it was co-ordinating rugby coaching, arranging the provision of referees, or planning fixtures, all were handled in his own unique style. He was at one time President of the Hertfordshire Schools Rugby Organisation.

In 1980 John Wood was asked to turn his administrative gifts to the subject of careers, and he did so with whole-hearted enthusiasm. Nothing was too much trouble for him when it was a matter of suiting the candidate to the university or to a career. He would have no hesi-

John Wood

tation in picking up the telephone, and there must have been many admissions tutors – possibly quaking in their boots – who were persuaded to admit Edmundians on courses as a direct result of John Wood's intervention.

His classes could best be described as sometimes being rowdy, and they often tested his temper. He would perch his glasses on his head whilst marking, and sometimes he would not notice that they had slipped around to the back of his head. "Where's me glasses?" he would often be heard to say. Many of his sayings or expressions are remembered by the Edmundians with whom he came into contact, like "rugby for all" and "clear a gangway".

John Wood has gone down in Edmundian folklore for falling out of a window during a class in the School Block, in a former classroom where the physics laboratories are now. Reversing along a raised dais he failed to notice the open window, and fell into the flower beds below. After picking himself up and dusting himself down, the class resumed.

Some Edmundians related to famous people

Horatio Nelson (1879-79) was a distant relation of Admiral Nelson.

David Bamford (1941-43) & **Rupert Bamford** (1933-39) were related to Joseph Cyril Bamford the inventor of the "JCB" excavator.

Paul A Rogers (1976-78) was the son of Peter Rogers, producer of the *Carry On* films.

Simon Bannister (1973-79) was the son of the actor Trevor Bannister, best known for his role as Mr Lucas in the 1970s situation comedy series *Are You Being Served?*

Owen J Brannigan (1952-57) was the son of the operatic and classical concert singer Owen Brannigan.

Simon Arden-Davis (1973-80) was the son of actress Mary Arden-Davis, who played the barmaid Pru Forrest for 30 years in the radio show The Archers

Fernando (1978-80), **Juan** (1980-82) & **Paloma** (1986-87) **Primo de Rivera** were the grandchildren of Miguel Primo de Rivera, the Spanish military dictator between 1923 and 1930.

Alfonso (1978-82) and **Fernando** (1978-82) **de Borbón Medina** were distant cousins of the Spanish royal family.

Juan Gomez-Acebo Borbón (1981-83), Viscount de la Torre, was a Spanish prince and the eldest son of present king's sister.

Lt **Gilbert Kepple Smith** (1899-1905) was a descendant of Edward III.

Christopher Baker (1981-82) was the son of diminutive actor Kenny Baker who played R2-D2 in the 1977 film Star Wars.

The father of **Joseph** (1978-84) and **Andrew Haji-Hannas** (1982-89) was Tony Costas, who was once the lightweight and welterweight wrestling champion of Cyprus.

Benedict (1910-11), **Bernard** (1907-11), **Francis** (1901~09), **Hugh** (1907-09) & **John** (1898-1902) **Tussaud** were descendants of Madame Tussaud of waxworks fame.

Stuart Collingwood (1904-13) was a relative of Lewis Carroll (Charles Lutwidge Dodgson), author of *Alice in Wonderland*, and was a descendant of Lord Collingwood who replaced Nelson in the Battle of Trafalgar.

Charles Burnand (1871-76) was the son of Sir Francis Burnand, editor of *Punch*.

Philip Weld: The Ghost of St Edmund's

Philip Weld; born 1829; student 1840-46; died 16 April 1846

Dr Edward Cox was President from 1840 until 1851, and it was during his time that a nephew of Cardinal Weld, Philip Weld was a boy in the school.

He was said to be a 'well conducted, amiable boy' and much beloved by his masters and fellow students. On 16 April 1846 there was a play day – a whole holiday – and some of the boys went on the River Lea at Rye House, near Hoddesdon. The boy had been to Holy Communion at the early Mass (having just finished his retreat), and in the afternoon accompanied one of the masters and some companions to boat on the river, a sport he much enjoyed. During this expedition, Philip Weld fell out of the boat and quickly sank to his death, the clay of the river bed holding him fast. His dead body was brought back to the College, and the President Dr Cox was very shocked. He made up his mind to visit the boy's father who was living at Southampton.

St Stanislaus Kostka

On the way he framed the words with which he would break the news to Mr Weld: "It has seemed good to Almighty God to call your son to Himself by the same element which first conveyed to him grace." But when he arrived, he was about to address the father, when he was prevented by the latter saying, "You need not say a word, for I know that Philip is dead. Yesterday afternoon I was walking with my daughter Katherine, and suddenly we saw him. He was standing by the path between two persons, one of whom was a youth dressed in a black robe." The three suddenly vanished, but he recalled every detail of the features of his son's companion. The father went on to relate how happy Philip looked.

Dr Cox was obviously very astonished. Later, when the funeral of the boy took place, Mr Weld looked around to see if any of the boys present resembled the characters he had seen with his son on that afternoon, but he could not trace the slightest resemblance in any of them.

About four months later, he and his family were visiting his brother George Weld at Leagram Hall, near Chipping in Lancashire. After going to Mass at the local church, he was in the parlour of the parish priest's house, and amused himself by looking at the pictures on the wall. He stopped before a picture which had no name written under it that you could see, and exclaimed, "That is the person I saw with Philip." The priest told him that the print was of St Stanislaus Kostka, a Jesuit saint who died when quite young. Mr Weld was deeply moved by this information, as the Weld family had always been great benefactors of the Jesuit Order, and his family were supposed to be under the particular protection of the Jesuit saints. Philip himself had an especial devotion to St Stanislaus, and moreover, St Stanislaus is the special advocate of drowned men. The parish priest presented the picture to Philip's father, who of course received it with the greatest veneration and kept it until his death.

chapter 13

Notable staff

This chapter is the outcome of a poll carried out in 2002, when members of The Edmundian Association received a questionnaire asking them to nominate their favourite Edmundian. Hundreds of replies were received and every nominee has been mentioned somewhere in this book. The vast majority of the responses came from former students who were at the College between 1950 and 1979. The ten most notable are listed in this chapter in reverse order. Tributes from some former students and colleagues have also been included.

Before listing the most liked staff, it is worth mentioning those who work behind the scenes to ensure the operation of the College. Many loyal domestic and maintenance staff have, during its history, served St Edmund's. They would merit a separate book.

Bert Willett (1915-74) was the head gardener at a time when the College grew much of its own produce; his working life spanned the horse to the tractor. Francis Jaynes (1913-60) maintained the College boilers. Ernest Berry (1919-59) used to run the Tuck Shop, which was then in the School Block; from 1950 he ran the small Post Office which was at the College Lodge, where his wife had previously been postmistress. When he died in 1959, his daughter Mrs Theresa Sole took over, and ran it until 1992.

Henry Smith (1932-70) was the head cook, famed for his apple tarts, and was a loyal and trusted servant of the College, as were his grandparents before him. Bill Sculthorp (1946-78) was variously head gardener, head groundsman and general factotum. Jack Marcham (1946-74) was head carpenter; amongst his creations were the tables in the Refectory and the window seats in the Ambulacrum.

Eileen Condon (1921-46) was sister-in-charge of the Infirmary, and was remembered with affection by many Edmundians who had been in her care. Angela Chapman (1960-96) was secretary to three Headmasters. Sally Sullivan (1885-1920) was a long-serving matron in St Hugh's.

Mrs Theresa Sole
Postmistress 1959-1992

Tony Tranter next to the College boilers in
2000

10 – Fr Denys Lucas: 1934~1964

Bill Wright (1943-51) wrote…
On D-Day, 6 June 1944, we had a Drawing class taken by Fr Lucas. On that day he told us the story of the invasion as reported on the BBC News (wireless, of course) and then said "Now draw it". If there was anything that Hugonians in 1944 could draw it was ships, tanks, guns and aeroplanes. Probably every boy had at least one near relative in the armed forces and we had at St Edmund's boys who were refugees from occupied Europe.

On many occasions during my life I have said to various people "the verb 'to be' never takes an object" and as I have said it, and as I write it now, I can hear Fr Lucas's voice in the background.

Fr Lucas died in 1995.

Fr Denys Lucas
Housemaster of St Hugh's 1949-1964

9 – Hugh Strode: 1950-1986

Fr Michael Garvey (1940~84) wrote …
Hugh Strode was a most thorough and painstaking teacher, who succeeded in passing on his own enthusiasm for History and for research to his pupils. As a result, he headed a department that was always strong, and the examination results and university awards which have marked these years are in large measure due to Hugh's high standards. Many of his pupils at university paid tribute to the excellent preparation they had received at his hands.

Hugh Strode divides his time between homes in Sussex and Sutherland, and spends his retirement enjoying his hobbies of skiing and playing golf. He is an honorary member of The Edmundian Association.

Hugh Strode

8 – Donald Tripp: 1941-1954

Canon Peter Phillips (1940~67) wrote …
Donald Tripp was a much revered teacher, presenting his subject in a way that held the interest of his pupils and inspired many of them to go on to study Chemistry in Rhetoric and at university. He had a keen sense of discipline and was scrupulously fair. He threw himself wholeheartedly into all the activities of school life. School plays showed a marked improvement in quality after he became the unofficial stage manager. With his height and reach he was a more than average tennis player, and in the fives court was a dependable doubles partner, and a difficult opponent to beat in a single game. He left to become Head of Science in a larger school in Sussex, but always maintained his links with St Edmund's. He died in 1993.

Donald Tripp

7 – May Williams: 1956~1982

Fr Michael Garvey (1940~84) wrote …
Mrs Williams gave nineteen years of service to the College, first as matron of St Hugh's and then, after a break, as matron of the newly constituted Junior House. She gave unstinting and loyal service, wherever she was, but her part in establishing Junior House in the Old Hall in 1971 was of great importance. Under Fr Pinot and Mrs Williams, "JH" began to have a life of its own and established its own tradition. Mrs Williams made it into a home, and provided maternal yet firm care. She did so with unfailing good humour and kindness. May Williams died in 1999.

Mrs Williams (back) in Top Dorm, JH, in 1978

Gavin Dorey

6 – Gavin Dorey: 1972-1991

Gavin Dorey was head of English for nineteen years, and for sixteen of those he edited *The Edmundian* magazine. As a teacher he was methodical and meticulous. He always had an appropriate turn of phrase to deal with any situation which arose in class, and was an expert at using silence to indicate disapproval of a miscreant. He motivated to examination success even those for whom English was not their strongest subject.

Gavin Dorey leads an active life in the parish of Royston, and is an honorary member of The Edmundian Association.

5 – Fr Bernard Lagrue: 1946~1993

Robert Rowe (1960-65) wrote …
Fr Lagrue was a gifted teacher of Mathematics. He ran a hobbies club, where we made model planes, and a photographic club, where we learned to develop, print and enlarge our own negatives. He would leave the radio on and we learned all kinds of facts about life in the real world – mainly from *Woman's Hour*! He also borrowed films to show us in Poetry Common Room every two weeks or so. They were a very mixed bag, mainly promotional stuff for products or institutions like the Royal Navy. We asked him once what one of them was going to be about, and he said "I believe it is in the nature of what might be called a jeu d'esprit". This catch phrase survived at St Edmund's for years.

Fr Lagrue died in 1995.

Fr Bernard Lagrue

Fr Garvey at Mass in the College Chapel

4 – Fr Michael Garvey: 1940~1984

Fr Garvey was regarded by his colleagues as a model priest-schoolmaster in the Douay tradition. By the students in the College he was regarded as firm but fair. He was sensitive to the pain of the marginalized and less successful, supporting them in various ways throughout his priestly ministry.

His retirement as Headmaster in 1984 was greeted with something like dismay by many parents who had come to rely on him and his concern for the pupils.

Fr Garvey died in 2002.

Blaise Compton (1960-66) wrote …
I liked his story of the bishop who came to perform some function in the Chapel. As you probably know such things in those Tridentine days involved many puttings-on and takings-off of the episcopal mitre, which reposed on a small credence table near the bishop's throne. The bishop's server got flustered when the bishop hissed "Mitre!" and stood there cluelessly holding it. "Put it on!" said the bishop, and the poor boy, even more confused, donned it himself. Pointing, the bishop loudly said "THIS head, not THAT head! FAThead!"

Nick Bannister (1960-64) wrote …
Scene, the early 1960s: at the foot of the stairs outside the then Poetry common room – a no talking area – a group of boys are busy talking! "Shh, I smell Garvey" said Stephen Padfield. We stop talking just before Fr Garvey comes round corner. Phew! Scene, a week later: similar group of boys talking outside the Poetry common room. Fr Garvey sweeps round corner, and says "You didn't smell me that time, Padfield!"

Stephen Quin (1970-77) wrote about "The Tripe Incident" …
While in Grammar, I think, funds were tight for the school and dinners were going downhill fast until one day we were served stewed tripe. Word quickly flashed around the room as to what this miserable looking stuff was (despite the 'no talking' rule) and no one took anything. Fr Garvey was sitting at the head table with the prefects and tried to lead the way by serving himself some, but soon realised that no one in the school was moving and a revolution was close at hand. Quick thinking, he called up the caterer (I don't remember his name) in front of the whole school, told him the food was unacceptable, ordered bread and jam to be served all round, and saved the day. Not long afterwards, the school went over to a cafeteria system.

3 – Charlie Smith: 1946-present

Charlie Smith is a permanently cheerful and happy person who is universally popular amongst staff and students alike. Working his way up from assistant gardener to become Head Groundsman, the condition of the sports fields is a tribute to his work over many years.

He is a prodigious fund of information about the College, its staff and the estate.

Charlie Smith   *Maria Smith*

Charlie and his wife Maria continue to work at the College.

2 – "Rex" King : 1930-1976

Tony Thomas (1943-48) wrote …

Rex King took over the headship in very difficult wartime circumstances as the first layman to lead the school when it was still also a seminary, with Douglass a "church boys house" and a tradition of being led by clergy. When the clergy – in the person of Fr Britt-Compton – reclaimed the Headship in 1949, King stood down without the slightest rancour and then devoted many more years to the College's welfare as a highly efficient and popular Bursar. Not too many characters would have made that transition easily. He was a stimulating teacher who would keep his mathematics classes both interested in the subject and up to scratch without anyone being aware that he also happened to be the Headmaster. As Captain, later Major, King he ran one of the best Cadet Corps in the area and introduced most of its members to aspects of disciplined activity which stood them in good stead for the rest of their lives. His practice of his faith – whether rosary after supper in the ambulacrum or unfailing occupation of his personal prie dieu beneath the rood screen in chapel – was an ever-present example to us all.

"Rex" King

John Rowe (1939-43) wrote …

On more than one occasion I remember his putting a question to a hapless pupil, possibly myself, and upon receiving no reply, would say to the whole class "Boy's a fool" or sometimes "idiot" and occasionally "imbecile", all greeted by much hilarity by the other boys. He certainly did not suffer fools gladly, but his bark was worse than his bite, and my chief memory of him is of a kind man and a fine teacher.

Paul Ketterer (1945~71), former Housemaster of Challoner, wrote …

As a teacher Rex was clear, inspired confidence in his pupils and had that invaluable talent to use the educational opportunities of a red herring profitably. I well remember his digressing off the Maths syllabus one day when Ware was suffering devastating floods with the consequent pollution from sewage. I learned more Physics that day about the principles of the U-bend in a lavatory than I ever learned in the laboratory.

As a Headmaster he was very fair but could also cut a delinquent down to size. I remember in Rhetoric I having pretensions of being promoted to Prefect the following year. Unfortunately Rex caught me visiting another study-holder during prep time. His rocket still rings in my ears. "How do you expect to discipline others, Ketterer, when you are not even disciplined yourself?"

Years later I spent 24 years as a Headmaster myself. Any success I had in facing a tricky situation was the direct result of consciously considering what Rex would have done in that situation.

As a Christian he gave a superb example of humility. I recall an incident when the First XV was playing Hertford Grammar School away. As the match was local, some members of Rhetoric were allowed to travel on the coach as supporters. Rex also drove over to Hertford in his car. It proved to be the dirtiest school match I have ever witnessed, with the referee being incapable of stamping his authority on the game. Half way through the second half Rex's patience snapped. (You must remember that he was an experienced rugby referee himself; he had even written a book on refereeing.) After yet another blatant foul by the opposition Rex stormed onto the pitch shouting "Penalty try, ref!" Then he strode over to his car and drove off. When the coach returned to the college, a messenger was waiting to send all the passengers, team and spectators, to the Headmaster's study. When we had all trooped in, Rex faced us. "What I did today was wrong. It is not an example you should follow. Gentlemen, you may go!" We left in amazement. That was an era when those in authority, particularly Headmasters, were regarded as infallible and impeccable. It was a lesson in humility we were never to forget.

1 – Fr Michael Pinot de Moira: 1944~present

Fr Pinot was voted the most popular Edmundian in the poll carried out in 2002. Apart from a brief spell as a curate in St John's Wood, he has served the College for nearly 60 years. As a student he was in the First XV and was Captain of Tennis. He became an assistant master in St Hugh's and for 20 years was the housemaster of Junior House. He has been Priest-in-Residence since 1993.

Much of Fr Pinot's work goes on behind the scenes, and countless Edmundians are indebted to him for his care and support. The value of the work he has done for the College is incalculable.

Thank you, Fr Pinot, for all you have done and continue to do.

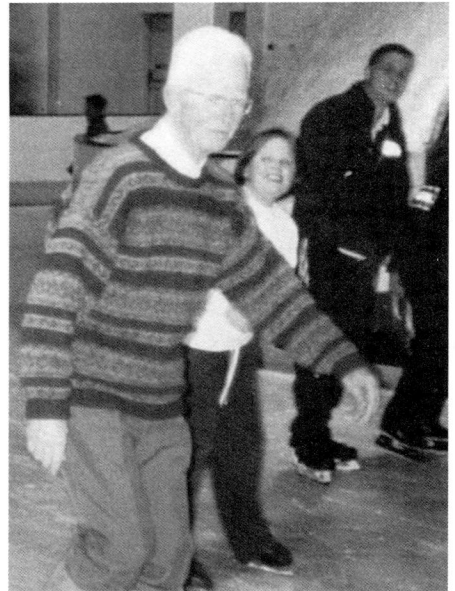

Fr Michael Pinot de Moira skating on St Edmund's Day

chapter 14

And finally...

In researching this book, it has been the intention to select one Edmundian, perhaps not familiar to many who have been at the College, who stands out as being of particular interest. The author would like to nominate the aviator and explorer Giles Kershaw (1961-66).

Giles Kershaw FRGS

John Edward Giles Kershaw; born 27 August 1948; Challoner 1961-66; died 5 March 1990

His father worked in India where he sprayed tea and rubber crops from the air, and Giles Kershaw developed a love of flying because of his father's job.

After leaving St Edmund's he wanted to join the Royal Air Force, but he failed to pass the pilot's medical examination because of his eyesight, which turned out to be amazing in view of his later achievements. A career as a pilot appeared now to be impossible, however with his parents' support he gained his Private Pilot's Licence, and he later obtained a commercial licence.

In 1974 he joined the British Antarctic Survey as a pilot, and flew for the Survey until 1979. It was during these years that he developed a deep affinity with the hostile terrain of the Antarctic.

It was Giles Kershaw's remarkable aircraft-handling ability that made these trips possible in the first place. He pioneered the Arctic and Antarctic aircraft landing system: it was not at first thought feasible to operate fixed-wing aircraft from 'civilisation' to the Antarctic, but he demonstrated that a DC4 could land on ice-fields, which he had painstakingly researched. Thus expedition members could be flown directly from Punta Arenas, Chile, to the Antarctic, then on to destinations within the continent by a Twin Otter plane.

He worked as a captain with Britannia Airways and as a first officer on Boeing 747s with Cathay Pacific. He was a pilot of enormous powers of concentration and endurance, and he could endure extremes of temperature, both of cold and of heat. He once flew for an engineering firm in Oman.

Giles Kershaw performed prodigious feats of flying in support of the Transglobe Expedition led by Sir Ranulph Twistleton-Wykeham-Fiennes in 1980-81. He was the first man to fly round the world over both the North and South Poles. During the period of the expedition he flew the equivalent of five

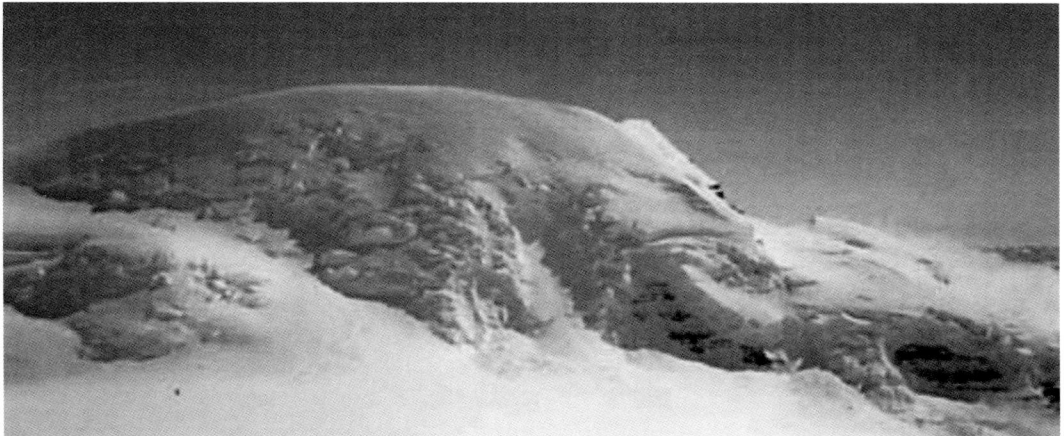

Mount Kershaw, Greenland, named after Giles Kershaw OE

times around the world. His task was to make sure that the three-man team was kept supplied with food and fuel.

He is remembered in Argentine naval circles for his rescue of three officers from the cruiser *General Belgrano*, which was later sunk in the Falklands conflict. They had become marooned on an ice-floe whilst on an Antarctic expedition.

In 1980 he also flew across thousands of miles of trackless, frozen wastes to rescue three South African scientists who were close to death, after eight days marooned on the Antarctic ice.

In November 1988, he co-piloted the first and only direct flight from Australia to land in the Australian Antarctic Territory, a distance well beyond the safe range of the Twin Otter he was flying.

Later Giles Kershaw became a founder-member of Adventure Network International, a firm which specialises in holidays for the intrepid to the South Pole. He believed that the opening up of Antarctica should not be the sole preserve of the military and government agencies, and was determined that the continent should be accessible to private enterprise. He ensured that not one piece of matter, whether organic or not, was imported into the Antarctic: all waste had to be taken out again, so the landscape would not be contaminated. (The firm continues to be run by his widow Anne, and – for the princely sum of about £20,000 – enables individuals to take a holiday to the South Pole.)

The second highest peak in Greenland is called *Mount Kershaw* after him, and a group of mountains in the Antartic has recently been renamed *The Kershaw Mountain Range.*

Giles Kershaw was tragically killed test flying a gyrocopter aircraft, which crashed on the Jones ice shelf east of Adelaide Island, off the west coast of the Antarctic peninsula. He was buried there in the ice.

He was an intrepid polar flyer, and surely one of the most interesting of *The People of St Edmund's College.*

Appendix I

Head prefects

Background

The role of Prefect was established in September 1904, at the time when the Theology students returned, and it superseded the work carried out by three "Bounds-masters". Initially there were appointed, from the oldest class in the school prior to the Seminary or from the lower years in the Seminary, six "Bounds-Prefects", a title in use for the first fifty years of the College's existence, although the name was immediately abbreviated to "Prefects". The original statement of duties of the Prefects lists the following:

1. To take the lead in all School interests which are left to the public spirit of the House
2. To set an example of obedience to rules and of high-principled conduct in those matters on which precise rules cannot be framed.
3. To enforce such obedience and such conduct on others by advice, warning, and, if necessary, punishment under the direction of the General Prefect.
4. Especially to repress all conduct incompatible with the standard required from candidates for the Church, and in the case of Lay-boys with the standard of a Catholic gentleman. Thus, for example, unbecoming language, bad behaviour in the Refectory, and in particular, all bullying, and any harmful practical jokes should be prevented.
5. In carrying out these duties to deal equally and without favour with all; and to act among themselves as a united body.

Originally at the start of their term of office each Prefects signed the Prefects Book to attest that they had read the statement of their duties and pledge themselves to endeavour to fulfil them. This now normally takes place on St Edmund's Sunday each year.

Some of the privileges enjoyed by the early Prefects included being allowed to ask for permission to have tea in their own room, to have their gas light on until 10.30pm, and to use the swimming pool when they pleased.

The original Prefects in 1904, all Church boys, were: Basil Booker (1897-1912), Stewart Caven (1897-1907), Henry Dunn (1897-1910), Albert Furniss (1895-1907), John Wall (1894~1910) & Kenneth Wigg (1898-1910). The first Lay-boys to be appointed Prefects, in 1905, were Arthur Miller (1896-1906) & Edward Stay (1904-05).

The first to be deprived of his prefectship was Daniel Roche (1902-12), on 19 February 1907, "in consequence of conduct incompatible with the standard required of prefects".

The first female Prefect was Carole Wellsted (1975-77).

Starting in 1904, in each academic year there was appointed a Head Prefect, reporting to the General Prefect or Prefect of Discipline, to act as head of the school and to organise the work of the other student Prefects. The normal term of office ran from September to the following July. Variations in this are indicated in the list below. Some Head Prefects served for more than one year.

1904-1905 – Kenneth F L Wigg (1898-1910)
1905-1906 – H Albert Furniss (1895-1907)
1906-1907 – Basil E Booker (1897-1912)
1907-1908 – Peter J Brady (1900-15)
1908-1909 – Oscar F Villinger (1901-13)
1909-1910 – Basil H Gudgeon (1908-15)
1910-1911 – Joseph J Warren (1905~24)
1911-1912 – Thomas N O'Connell (1903-14)
1912-1913 – George Perkes (1906-17)
1913-1914 – John E Howell (1908-18)
1914-1915 – James F Hunt (1907-17)
1915-1916 – Henry J Merrifield (1910-16) *to Feb*
 Albert O Hunting (1911-16) *from Feb*

No Head Prefect was appointed for the academic year 1916-1917. The reduced number of students resulting from the operation of the Military Service Act left very small choice of Prefects. The Rev James Penn (1916-17), a sub-deacon who was also on the academic staff, assisted the General Prefect as Sub-Prefect whilst awaiting his ordination to the priesthood.

1917-1918 – Peter Sidder (1914-18)
1918-1919 – Geoffrey Cammiade (1911-19)
1919-1920 – *not recorded*
1920-1922 – Joseph E McEntee (1916-27)

From 1922, when the House system was established, until 1926 when the first Headmaster was appointed, each House had its own Head Prefect.

Challoner

1922-1923 – Joseph Mallet-Paret (1919-23) *to Easter*
1923-1924 – C E Guy Pritchard (1917-24) *from Jul*
1924-1925 – Conway O Kershaw (1921-25)
1925 – Edmund J C Cowell (1921-25) *to Dec*
1926 – *not recorded*

Douglass

1922-1924 – Reginald A Crook (1917-29)
1924-1925 – Andrew Dunn (1921-25)
1925-1926 – *not recorded*

Talbot

1922 – H J Leslie Biggie (1914-22) *to Dec*
1923 – John E H Stallard (1920-23) *from Jan*
1923-1924 – Francis I Dias (1919-24)
1924-1925 – Peter A Clarke-Vincent (1917-25)
1925-1926 – Roger J Quin (1920-26) *to Apr*
1926-1927 – Dudley H Biscoe (1923-27)
1927-1928 – Nicholas J Kelly (1924~61)
1928-1929 – Stuart E MacKenzie (1921-29)
1929-1930 – Michael R I Boyle (1921-30)
1930-1931 – Alexander C Groves (1927-37)
1931-1932 – Edmund F Fletcher (1927-32)
1932 – Laurence P Janion (1925-33) *to Oct*
1932-1933 – George J R de Cabral (1929-33) *from Oct*
1933-1935 – Sydney M Thornton-Grimes (1930-36)
1935-1936 – James A Porter (1927-36)
1936-1937 – Denis J P Calnan (1934-37)
1937-1938 – Derek J H Worlock (1934-44)
1938-1939 – John D Sharpe (1932-39)
1939-1940 – Thomas P Harper (1935-40)
1940-1941 – Louis O Marteau (1937-49)
1941-1942 – John L S Whitney (1936-42) *to Mar*
1942 – Robert H Benson (1939-42) *from Mar*
1942-1943 – Michael G Garvey (1940~1984)
1943-1944 – Frederick A Miles (1939~67)
1944-1945 – Denis R Nottingham (1939-51)
1945-1946 – James T Fitzsimons (1941-46)

There was no Head Prefect from September 1946 until February 1947.

1947 – Neil A Muldoon (1940-47) *from Feb*
1947-1948 – John Galvin (1945-54) *from Dec*
1948-1949 – Jeffrey V Hernu (1939-49) *from Oct*
1949-1950 – John J A Pulton (1942-50)
1950-1951 – Francis W Daley (1947-52) *to Jun*
1951-1952 – John C A Bex (1946-52)
1952-1953 – Laurence F Udall (1950-53)
1953-1954 – Ian F Stewart (1945-54)
1954 – Bernard M A Phillips (1945-54) *to Dec*
1955 – James McDonnell (1948-61) *from Jan*
1955-1956 – John D Crowley (1949-56) *to Apr*
1956 – Patrick R Sheridan (1946-56) *from May*

1956-1957	– Christopher N Reed (1947-57)		1989-1990	– Leopoldo Ybarra Sainz de la Maza (1985-90)
1957-1958	– Patrick Carey (1948-64)		1990-1991	– DeQuincy C Prescott (1986-91)
1958-1959	– David A R Peel (1951-59)		1991	– Simon J Tagg (1985-92) *to Dec*
1959-1961	– S Guy A Scammell (1950-61)		1992	– Roger A James (1985-92) *from Jan*
1961-1962	– Derek C Lance (1957-62)		1992-1993	– Robert J Hattrell (1986-93)
1962-1963	– Christopher R Hutchison (1956-63) *to Dec*		1993-1994	– David A Logue (1983-94)
1964	– Christopher J Ryan (1953-64) *from Jan*		1994-1995	– Benjamin A F Bollig (1988-95)
1964-1965	– Michael J Hutchison (1956-65)		1995-1996	– Patrick R D Pond (1989-96)
1965	– Adrian B Gillham (1960-65) *to Dec*		1996-1997	– David J Meyer (1991-97)
1966	– Paul C McGinn (1960-72) *from Jan*		1997-1998	– Andrei Legostaev (1996-98)
1966	– Anthony M Lidgate (1963-66) *to Dec*		1998-1999	– Matthew C T Robins (1994-99)
1967	– Aidan F M Heathcote (1960-67) *from Jan*		1999-2000	– James Weaver (1994-2000)
1967	– Michael R White (1961-67) *to Dec*		2000-2001	– Peter G Vaughan-Shaw (1993-2001)
1968-1969	– John C Sidery (1962-69) *Jan to Dec*		2001-2002	– Christopher A Kyndt (1995-2002)
1970	– Anthony P Thick (1961-70) *Jan to Dec*		2002-2003	– David Gerty (1995-2003)
1971	– John M C Bryant (1962-71) *Jan to Dec*		2003-present	– Paul E Bartlett (1997-present)
1972	– Barrie F Duncan (1963-72) *from Jan*			
1972	– Henry J S Whitney (1966-72) *to Dec*			

Head Girls

1973-1974	– Martin B Smits (1967-74) *from Jan*
1974-1975	– Peter G Stone (1970-75)
1975-1976	– David H Thomas (1968-76) *to Dec*
1977	– Christopher A Sanders (1972-77) *from Jan*
1977-1978	– Timothy A P Weatherstone (1970-78)
1978-1979	– Michael J C Martin (1972-79)
1979-1980	– Peter J Frost (1975-80)
1980-1981	– Brian A Mulholland (1971-81)
1981-1982	– Martin A R Collier (1979-82)
1982-1983	– Richard A Vass (1973-83)
1983-1984	– Graham K Weston (1976-84)
1984	– Nicholas A Steele (1979-84) *to Dec*
1985	– Francis J Gunn (1978-85) *from Jan*
1985-1986	– Christopher P Carr (1984-86)

From 1986 there was a Head Boy and a Head Girl.

Head Boys

1986-1987	– Alexandre H M Uyt den Bogaard (1982-87)
1987-1988	– John S Boyle (1984-88)
1988-1989	– Odafe Sideso (1982-89)

1986	– Ailsa T C Fitzwilliam (1984-86) *to Dec*
1987	– Karla A M Boyce (1985-87) *from Jan*
1987-1988	– Yasmin K Kapadia (1986-88)
1988-1989	– Rachel F S Da Costa (1985-89)
1989-1990	– Gillian L McCann (1987-90)
1990-1991	– Alessandra Paternostro (1986-91)
1991-1992	– Tanya C Carney (1988-92)
1992-1993	– A Etive Foxworthy (1989-93)
1993-1994	– Joanna L T Drew (1987-94)
1994-1995	– Elizabeth T Brooke-Powell (1989-95)
1995-1996	– Elizabeth E Green (1989-96)
1996-1997	– Sarah A Clark (1993-97)
1997-1998	– Alice M L Gribbin (1993-98)
1998-1999	– Karen R Axford (1994-99)
1999-2000	– Marie-Louise (Lulu) Mortensen (1990-2000)
2000-2001	– Bozhidara Ianeva (1994-2001)
2001-2002	– Nicola C Pinkney (1991-2002)
2002-2003	– Elizabeth A P Archibald (1996-2003)
2003-present	– Astrid C O'Reilly (1997-present)

David Logue & Joanna Drew
Head Boy & Head Girl 1993-1994

Christopher Kyndt (right), Head Boy 2001-2002, with his
successor David Gerty

Nicola Pinkney
Head Girl 2001-2002

Appendix II

Editors of The Edmundian

The Edmundian as a printed magazine first appeared at the College's centenary celebrations in July 1893, although some manuscript copies going back to 1841 still survive in the College archives. The early editions consisted mainly of poetry and essays rather than a record of College events. Of the printed version, there have been 224 editions, and up until issue 215 it was divided into 23 volumes. There have been 18 different editors, each completing an average of just under six years, the longest serving were Fr (later Canon) Edwin Burton (1883~1918) and Gavin Dorey (1972-91), who each edited for 16 years.

1893-1894 – Rev Edmond Nolan (1876~96)
1895-1897 – Rev John J Wren (1884~98)
1898-1899 – Henry M Cross (1897~1904)
1899-1899 – Mgr Bernard N Ward (1868~1916)
1899-1914 – Rev Edwin H Burton (1883-1918)
1915-1917 – Rev Austin A J Askew (1894~1917)
1917-1918 – Rev Edwin H Burton (1883~1918)
1918-1920 – *office vacant*
1920-1926 – Dr John G Vance (1905~26)
1926-1929 – Very Rev Canon Edward Myers (1893~1932)
1929-1936 – Rev Leonard A Clark (1917~40)

1936-1937 – Rev James Stevenson (1923~37)
1937-1944 – J Haldane Walton-King (1930-76)
1944-1948 – Rev Dr Nicholas J Kelly (1924~61)
1948-1951 – Rev Laurence Allan (1936~60)
1951-1952 – J Haldane Walton-King (1930-76)
1952-1967 – Rev Peter B Phillips (1940~67)
1967-1968 – Rev Anthony E J Wheaton (1951-57)
1968-1973 – Very Rev Canon Clement H Parsons (1903~80)
1973-1989 – Gavin Dorey (1972-91)
1989-present – John A Hayes (1980-present)

Fr Edmond Nolan
First Editor

Canon Peter Phillips
Editor 1952-1967

John Hayes
Current Editor

Appendix III

Current Prizes named after Edmundians

Bishop Butler Prize
Subject: Theology
Eponym: Bishop Christopher Butler (1967-85) (see page 13)

Patrick Cullinan Salver
Subject: Contribution to Sport
Eponym: Patrick Cullinan (1993-2000)
Donated by The Edmundian Association in memory of Patrick Cullinan, a former House Captain of Pole, who tragically died on 23 November 2001

Gilbert Prize
Subject: Languages
Eponym: Canon Francis Gilbert (1890~1902)
This was not originally established as a prize, but as a bursary founded by Canon Gilbert, originally intended to provide an annual bursary of £10 towards a student's fees

John Gillham Prize
Subjects: GNVQ Art
Eponym: John Gillham, parent 1958-73, governor 1975-94, and Chairman of Governors 1986-94

Higley Prize
Subject: Creative Arts
Eponym: Fr Frederick Higley (1874-79)
This was not originally established as a prize, but as a bursary. Fr Higley served nearly all of his career as rector of Limehouse, then the poorest parish in the East End of London. Until his health began to give way at the age of 72, he had never been absent from his church on a Sunday, which meant that he had never taken a real holiday throughout his priestly life. Sadly he never lived long enough to see the completion of a new church in his parish, the construction of which he had been overseeing for many years. At one point, Fr Higley was bequeathed a substantial sum of money. Instead of spending it on his own parish, he bought the oratory that had been in the Empire Exhibition at Wembley and presented it to a new parish in another diocese, explaining that this was a "challenge" to St Teresa to help Limehouse. His hobby was gardening, and he presented St Edmund's with a large quantity of roses, bulbs, and other plants for the terraces and drives. He died on 25 September 1934.

J H W King Prize
Subject: Social Science
Eponym: Hal King (1930-76), the first lay Headmaster (see pages 20, 119 & 133)

Keith Latham Cup
Subject: Mathematics
Eponym: Keith Latham (1975-96), former mathematics master & head of mathematics

George Lehrian Prize
Subject: AVCE Advanced Business
Eponym: George Lehrian (1941-49), Chairman of Governors 1995-99

George Lehrian (1941-49) (right) in whose memory the prize for AVCE Advanced Business is named, being appointed Vice-President of Trust House Forte Executive De Luxe Hotels by Lord Forte in 1983

D S Lindsay Prize
Subject: Sports Studies
Eponym: Derek Lindsay (1936-40) (see page 95)

Canon Parsons Prize
Subject: Science
Eponym: Canon Clement Parsons (1903~68) (see page 50)

QWERTY Cup
Subject: Advanced ICT Skills
Not named after an OE called Qwerty, but in fact donated by Ken Allen (1951-56)

Paul Rogers Prize
Subject: English
Eponym: Capt Paul Rogers (1977-79) (see page 67)

D J K Walters International Prize
Eponym: David Walters (1986-97), former Deputy Headmaster, who died suddenly on 28 August 1997

Westwood Prize
Subject: Mathematics
This was not originally established as a prize, but as a bursary founded by a Miss Westwood. It was intended to provide annually £8 for pocket money, with preference for the award being given to a student from Marylebone or St John's Wood

Mary Woodcock Prize
Subject: Mathematics at University
Eponym: Mrs Mary Woodcock (1971-94), a former mathematics mistress

Appendix IV

Burials & Monuments

In the passage leading into the College Chapel, known as Monument Lane, there are stone and brass memorials (excluding the War Memorials) commemorating a total of 60 people mostly connected with the College. There are 26 Edmundians buried in the crypt, 22 elsewhere within the buildings of the Chapel, and 12 known to be buried in the graveyard. A list of those who are buried in or near the Chapel, and/or have a memorial in Monument Lane, is given below.

For each person there is provided where known their full name, date of birth, years and status at the College, date of death, the location of their grave, the location of their memorial (if they have one), and if applicable the number of the page in this book with further details about the person. Memorials have been numbered starting immediately to the left entering Monument Lane, continuing clockwise around the room, and concluding with memorials set into the floor. Where memorials are set one above another, the top one has the suffix 'a', the next one down a suffix 'b', and so on.

The large brass in a framework of carved stone on the north wall of the cloister (memorial 4), which was given by The Edmundian Association in 1885, records the names of all those buried under the church until 1965, when the memorial became full. The names represent all stages in the hierarchy of the Church from a cardinal to a tonsured cleric, and every stage in the hierarchy of the College: Presidents, priests and professors, divines and boys. The name of Edward Scholfield has been omitted.

The War Memorials (memorials 11b & 12b) were originally erected in the porch of the Galilee Chapel but were later moved to Monument Lane. They record 73 Edmundians who laid down their lives during the First World War and 43 during the Second World War (two names are missing from the latter). The complete list of the names is provided in Chapter 6.

A number of bodies were re-interred in the College Chapel, either from the vault under the former Chapel which was where the Religious Education classrooms are now, or from the church of St Mary Moorfields, which was demolished in 1899 to make way for the Metropolitan Line in London.

William Archer; date of birth unknown; student 1854-56; died 1856; crypt; memorial 4

Victor Karniah Athisayam; born 30 December 1923; staff 1971-75; died 18 May 1975; graveyard; no memorial

George Bardey; date of birth unknown; staff 1877-83; died 1883; crypt; memorial 4

Charles Barge; born 27 November 1814; student 1824-35; died 19 February 1836; crypt; memorial 4

Mgr Canon **Francis Philip Bickford**; born 12 January 1889; St Hugh's, College & Allen Hall 1899-1913; staff 1932-46; died 6 December 1968; Galilee Chapel; no memorial (see page 11)

Cardinal **Francis Alphonsus Bourne**; born 23 March 1861; student 1875-80; Galilee Chapel; memorial 4

William Henry Bower; born 8 November 1814; student 1827-36; staff 1872-1905; died 17 January 1905; graveyard; memorial 1 (see pages xii & 2)

Bishop **James Yorke Bramston**; born 18 March 1763; died 11 July 1836; Monument Lane (re-interred 1900), memorials 4 & 15

Canon **Denis Charles Henry Britt-Compton**; born 9 October 1912; Douglass & Allen Hall 1926~39; staff 1947-68; died 10 May 2002; buried elsewhere; memorial 3b (see page 21)

Canon **Edwin Hubert Burton**; born 12 August 1870; student 1883-85; staff 1898-1918; died 13 December 1925; Shrine Chapel; memorial 4 (see pages xiv & 10)

Mgr **Reginald Albert Claver Butcher**; born 9 September 1905; Allen Hall 1924-28; staff; crypt; memorial 3a (see page 12)

Fr **Robert Butler**; born 16 January 1836; student 1854-58; died 1902; Lady Chapel; memorial 4

Fr **Thomas Roussel Davids Byles**; born 26 February 1870; staff 1895-99; died 14 April 1912; body never found; memorial 2 (see page 51)

Maurice Edward Cauvin; born 23 July 1904; College & Talbot 1918-22; died 21 May 1968; graveyard; no memorial

Dom Maurice Chauncy; born 1513; died 2 July 1581; buried elsewhere; memorial 8a

Thomas Cleghorn; born circa 1740; staff 1795-1823; died 1823, crypt (re-interred), memorial 4

Fr **Herbert Henry John Collins**; born circa 1882; student 1894-1902; died 9 April 1917; buried elsewhere; memorial 16

Fr **William Crook**; born 21 December 1812; student 1838-41; died 27 March 1841; crypt (re-interred), memorial 4

Denis Michael Cronly Dillon; born 20 April 1868; St Hugh's & College 1879-88; died 4 December 1893; buried elsewhere; memorial 10b (see page 53)

Bishop **John Douglass**, date of birth not known; died 1812; crypt (re-interred 1908); memorial 4 (see page x)

Arthur Guy Ellis; dates of birth and death unknown; buried elsewhere; memorial 17b

James Elwood; date of birth unknown; dates at the College unknown; died 1866; crypt; memorial 4

Mgr **Patrick Fenton**; born 19 August 1837; student 1855-66; staff 1882-87; died 2 August 1918; Galilee Chapel; memorial 4 (see page 9)

Fr **Michael Gustav Garvey**; born 16 February 1925; Douglass & Allen Hall 1940-49; staff 1953-84; died 24 May 2002; crypt; memorial 5c (see pages 22, 118 & 133)

Fr **Andrew Giffard**; date of birth unknown; died 1714; Monument Lane (re-interred 1907); memorial 4

Bishop **Bonaventure Giffard**; born 1642; died 12 March 1734; Monument Lane (re-interred 1907); memorial 4

Bishop **Robert Gradwell**; born 1777; died 15 March 1833; Monument Lane (re-interred 1900); memorial 17a & memorial 4

Bishop **Thomas Griffiths**; born 2 June 1791; student 1805-15; staff 1816-34; died 19 August 1847; Griffiths Chantry; memorial 4 (see page 7)

Fr **Francis Dolores Healy**; born 17 September 1882; student 1892~1908; staff 1908-29; died 11 June 1933; crypt; memorial 4 (see page 19)

Canon **William Joseph Heffernan**; born 19 December 1889; College & Allen Hall 1903-16; staff 1917~24; died 25 January 1965; crypt; memorial 4

Fr **Peter Hillenmeyer**; date of birth unknown; staff 1859-60; died 1860; crypt; memorial 4

Bishop **William Johnston**; date of birth unknown; died 1909; Galilee Chapel (re-interred); memorial 4

Daniell Duncan Kennedy-Bell; born circa 1880; Allen Hall 1918-19; died 21 February 1919; graveyard; no memorial

Fr **Joseph Kimbell**; born circa 1778; staff 1795-1819; died 5 December 1835; Monument Lane (re-interred); memorial 4

John Haldane Walton-King; born circa 1907; staff 1930-76; died 13 May 1983; buried in parish graveyard; memorial 5b (see pages 20, 119, 128 & 133)

Fr **Bernard Vincent Lagrue**; born 13 June 1922; Allen Hall 1946-52; staff 1956-93; died 9 May 1995; buried elsewhere; memorial 5a (see page 117)

Constantine Lowe; born August 1829; student 1842-50; died 29 December 1850; crypt; memorials 4 & 20

Napoleon John Lowe; born 26 May 1828; student 1842-54; died 1854; crypt; memorials 4 & 20

Charles Lynch; born circa 1827; student 1840-41; died 7 January 1841; crypt (re-interred); memorial 4

Thomas MacDonnell; date of birth unknown; student 1879-80; died 1880; crypt; memorial 4

Canon **Edward J Mahoney**; born 2 May 1888; College & Allen Hall 1905-13; staff 1913~54; died 7 January 1954; crypt; memorials 4 & 18

Joseph Patrick McFaul; born January 1828; student 1845-49; died 18 March 1849; crypt, memorials 4 & 11a

Colin Joseph McNair; born 17 February 1888; St Hugh's & College 1899-1903; died 13 August 1906; buried elsewhere; memorial 13

Fr **Alexius Felix Mills**; born 29 August 1827; student 1844-55; died 3 January 1902; graveyard

Michael Morin; date of birth unknown; staff 1836-37; died 1837; crypt (re-interred), memorial 4

Fr **Joseph Murray**; born 7 December 1906; Douglass 1922-24; staff 1929~49; died 30 September 1989; graveyard; no memorial

Archbishop **Edward Myers**; born 8 September 1875; student 1893-97; staff 1903-32; died 13 September 1956; Galilee Chapel; memorial 4 (see page 11)

Henry Neal; born 1 April 1804; student 1818-27; died 11 July 1827; crypt (re-interred) memorial 4

Henry Edward O'Reilly; born circa 1884; student 1898-1900; died 12 Feb 1902; buried elsewhere; memorial 14

Canon **Clement Henry Parsons**; born 2 June 1892; student 1903-15; staff 1966-68; died 6 March 1980; crypt; no memorial (see page 50)

Bishop **James Laird Patterson**; born 16 November 1822; staff 1870-80; died 1 December 1902; Shrine Chapel; memorial 4 (see pages xiii & 9)

Bishop **Benjamin Petre**; born 1672; died 1758; Monument Lane (re-interred 1907); memorial 4

Fr **John Potier**; born 22 September 1758; staff 1792-1810; died 23 March 1823; buried in Standon Churchyard; memorial 7 (see page 5)

Bishop **William Poynter**; born 20 May 1762; staff 1795-1813; died 10 April 1827; Monument Lane (re-interred 1900), memorials 4 & 19 (see pages x & 6)

Dr **Frederick Rymer**; born 31 January 1825; student 1835-48; staff 1848~70; died 9 November 1910; Rood Screen; memorial 4 (see page 8)

Edward Scholfield; date of birth unknown; died circa 1862; Scholfield Chantry; no memorial

Fr **Thomas Patrick Sherlock**; born circa 1900; Allen Hall 1923-27; staff 1927-40; died 26 May 1945; obituary says buried in graveyard but no evidence of grave; no memorial (see page 20)

Mgr Canon **George Duncan Smith**; date of birth unknown; Allen Hall 1906-12; staff 1918-52; died November 1960; crypt; memorial 4

Dr **Victor Soenens**; date of birth unknown; staff 1868~92; died 28 April 1891; crypt; memorial 4

D'Arcy Clarence Clarkson Stanfield; date of birth unknown; St Hugh's & College 1903-06; died 22 January 1906; graveyard; no memorial

Field Stanfield; born 13 March 1844; student 1855-57; died 20 December 1905; buried elsewhere; memorial 8b

Edward Christopher Sweeney; born 1 May 1940; Allen Hall 1959-64; died 21 November 1964; graveyard; no memorial

Bishop **James Talbot**; born 1726; died 1790; Monument Lane; memorials 4 & 6 (see page viii)

Canon **William Paul Tilbury**; born 25 January 1784; student 1806-09; died 28 May 1863; buried elsewhere; memorial 12a

Charles H Trapp; born 1876; student 1892-97; died 12 July 1901; buried elsewhere; memorial 9

Fr **Francis Tuite**; born 1769; staff 1795-1810; died 4 March 1838; Monument Lane; memorial 4

David James Kedgerley Walters; born 24 February 1945; staff 1986-97; died 28 August 1997; graveyard

Eileen Walters; born 1922; died 1997, graveyard

Moss Walters; born 1917; died 1997, graveyard

Bishop **Bernard Nicholas Ward**; born 4 February 1957; student 1868-75; staff 1882~1916; died 21 January 1920; Shrine Chapel; memorial 4 (see pages xiii & 10)

Bishop **William Weathers**; born 12 November 1814; student 1828-38; staff 1838-68; died 4 March 1895; Rood Screen; memorial 4 (see page 8)

Philip Weld; born circa 1829; student 1840-46; died 16 April 1846; crypt; memorials 4 & 10a (see page 114)

Maurice White; born circa 1883; St Hugh's 1891-93; died 3 May 1893; crypt; memorial 4

Fr **Peter Worrall**; date of birth unknown; staff 1965-68; died 18 May 1968; crypt; no memorial

David Glen Wright; born 23 July 1927; St Hugh's & Challoner 1937-44; died 16 September 2002; graveyard

Appendix V

Places named after Edmundians

Allen Hall
Location: the south wing of the main College building
Eponym: Cardinal William Allen (see page vii)

Bickford Dining Room
Location: currently the study of the Head of the Sixth Form
Eponym: Mgr Francis Bickford (see page 11)

Bickford Dormitory
Location: currently English classrooms
Eponym: Mgr Francis Bickford (see page 11)

Bickford Gallery
Location: currently English classrooms
Eponym: Mgr Francis Bickford (see page 11)

Butler Hall
Location: formerly the area occupied by the Old Farmyard
Eponym: Bishop Christopher Butler (see pages 13, 104 & 128)

Douglass House
Location: the centre of the main College building from 1922
Eponym: Bishop John Douglass (see page x)

Garveys
Location: the girls' boarding area
Eponym: Fr Michael Garvey (see pages 22 & 118)
He first introduced girls to the College in 1974

Godfrey Wing
Location: the south wing of St Hugh's, opened in 1961
Eponym: Cardinal Godfrey
He laid the foundation stone

Gosselin Library
Location: currently the Poynter common room
Eponym: Mr Hellier R H Gosselin
A former High Sheriff of Hertfordshire & Mayor of Hertford, who donated his art & archaeology books to the College on his death in 1924

Griffiths Chantry
Location: The side chapel on the south side of the Antechapel
Eponym: Bishop Thomas Griffiths (see pages xii & 7)
He is buried there

Cardinal Hume Centre
Location: formerly the Allen Hall sacristy
Eponym: Cardinal Basil Hume (see pages 14, D & G)

King Room
Location: currently the Rhetoric study room
Eponym: Hal "Rex" King (see pages 20, 119 & 128)

Lindsay Pitch
Location: all-weather sports field at the back of the College
Eponym: Derek Lindsay (see pages 95 & 129)

Lloyd-Fenton Library
Location: currently the Receptionist's office
Eponyms: Fr William Lloyd and Mgr Patrick Fenton (see page 9)
Their combined collections of literature books, donated to the College, was set up in 1912

Maguire Library
Location: currently the infants' dining room
Eponym: Canon John Maguire
He was a former Vice-President, who on his death left his books to the College; the Maguire Library was previously housed in the room named Hospitium in the Ambulacrum

McEwen Wing
Location: the north wing of the College, opened in 2002
Eponym: Donald McEwen (see page 22)

Mivart Collection

Location: the ground floor of the south wing of the College, currently classrooms, formerly the Allen Hall common room, built in 1908
Eponym: St George Jackson Mivart
His collection of biological specimens was donated to the College in 1903

Myers Library

Location: the south east corner of the ground floor of Allen Hall
Eponym: Archbishop Edward Myers (see page 11)
Used to house theological books

Myers Room

Location: the south east corner of the ground floor of Allen Hall
Eponym: Archbishop Edward Myers (see page 11)
Used to house theological books

Rymer Library

Location: the Rhetoric & boarding common room, formerly the staff common room
Eponym: Dr Frederick Rymer (see page 8)
His collection of books was donated to the College in 1911

Schofield Chantry

Location: the end of Monument Lane
Eponym: Edward Scholfield
A gift in 1862 from Mrs Jane Scholfield in memory of her husband who is buried underneath this chapel

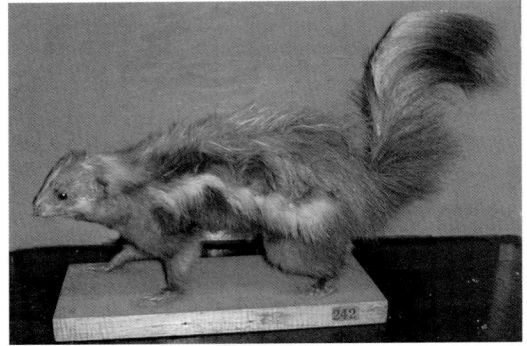

A furry remnant of the Mivart Collection

Southworth Room

Location: currently the priest-in-residence's study
Eponym: St John Southworth, who was martyred in 1640

Ward Library

Location: the College Library
Eponym: Mgr Bernard Ward (see page 10)
After 1897 when Mgr Ward paid for half of the library's books

Ward Wing

Location: the west wing of the College
Eponym: Mgr Bernard Ward (see page 10)
Named for a time after 1908, when a second floor was built on the wing

Willacy's

Location: the house between Old Hall and the squash courts
Eponym: Fr James Willacy (see page 52)

Index

This index includes those subjects about whom there are principal references or photographs in this book. It does not include people whose names only appear in the information in lists.

David Kay wishes personally to thank the following for supporting the production of this book

Jim Aram, Peter Blackman, Brian Boshell, Provost Michael Brockie, Michael Burgess, Luigi Camisa, Stuart Cavill, Mr & Mrs Chipperfield, Mary Code, Tony Conway, Michael Corey, David Dickson, Jeral D'Souza, Michael Elgood, Tim Fuller, Dr Adrian Gillham, Jeremy Gillham, Eugene Hassett, Garry Hlavaty, Terence Hypher, Basil Jackson, Brian Juniper, Brian Kelaart, Henryk Klocek, Margarita Lehrian, Peter Lightfoot, Peter Morgan, Ivor O'Mahony, Canon Peter Phillips, Bernard Precey, Ann Purcell, Stephen Quin, Alex Roberts, Mark Rodrigues, Lawrence Ross, John Rowe, Canon Desmond Sheehan, Ian Stevens, Fr George Talbot, Hugh Thomas, John Vaughan-Shaw, Major Tony Webster, John Whitney, John Whitworth, Mary Woodcock & Bill Wright